T0353341

Contemporary Identity and Access Management Architectures:

Emerging Research and Opportunities

Alex Chi Keung Ng
Federation University, Australia

A volume in the Advances in
Business Information Systems and
Analytics (ABISA) Book Series

Published in the United States of America by
  IGI Global
  Business Science Reference (an imprint of IGI Global)
  701 E. Chocolate Avenue
  Hershey PA, USA 17033
  Tel: 717-533-8845
  Fax: 717-533-8661
  E-mail: cust@igi-global.com
  Web site: http://www.igi-global.com

Library of Congress Cataloging-in-Publication Data

Names: Ng, Alex Chi Keung, 1957- author.
Title: Contemporary identity and access management architectures : emerging
  research and opportunities / by Alex Chi Keung Ng.
Description: Hershey, PA : Business Science Reference, [2018] | Includes
  bibliographical references.
Identifiers: LCCN 2017032399| ISBN 9781522548287 (hardcover) | ISBN
  9781522548294 (ebook)
Subjects: LCSH: Computer networks--Security measures. | Computer
  networks--Access control. | Computers--Access control. | Online identity
  theft--Prevention.
Classification: LCC TK5105.59 .N3484 2018 | DDC 005.8/3--dc23 LC record available at https://
lccn.loc.gov/2017032399

This book is published in the IGI Global book series Advances in Business Information Systems
and Analytics (ABISA) (ISSN: 2327-3275; eISSN: 2327-3283)

British Cataloguing in Publication Data
A Cataloguing in Publication record for this book is available from the British Library.

All work contributed to this book is new, previously-unpublished material.
The views expressed in this book are those of the authors, but not necessarily of the publisher.

For electronic access to this publication, please contact: eresources@igi-global.com.

Advances in Business Information Systems and Analytics (ABISA) Book Series

ISSN:2327-3275
EISSN:2327-3283

Editor-in-Chief: Madjid Tavana, La Salle University, USA

MISSION

The successful development and management of information systems and business analytics is crucial to the success of an organization. New technological developments and methods for data analysis have allowed organizations to not only improve their processes and allow for greater productivity, but have also provided businesses with a venue through which to cut costs, plan for the future, and maintain competitive advantage in the information age.

The **Advances in Business Information Systems and Analytics (ABISA) Book Series** aims to present diverse and timely research in the development, deployment, and management of business information systems and business analytics for continued organizational development and improved business value.

COVERAGE

- Strategic Information Systems
- Management Information Systems
- Business Models
- Legal information systems
- Data Governance
- Business Process Management
- Data Analytics
- Business Intelligence
- Information Logistics
- Data Management

IGI Global is currently accepting manuscripts for publication within this series. To submit a proposal for a volume in this series, please contact our Acquisition Editors at Acquisitions@igi-global.com or visit: http://www.igi-global.com/publish/.

The Advances in Business Information Systems and Analytics (ABISA) Book Series (ISSN 2327-3275) is published by IGI Global, 701 E. Chocolate Avenue, Hershey, PA 17033-1240, USA, www.igi-global.com. This series is composed of titles available for purchase individually; each title is edited to be contextually exclusive from any other title within the series. For pricing and ordering information please visit http://www.igi-global.com/book-series/advances-business-information-systems-analytics/37155. Postmaster: Send all address changes to above address. ©© 2018 IGI Global. All rights, including translation in other languages reserved by the publisher. No part of this series may be reproduced or used in any form or by any means – graphics, electronic, or mechanical, including photocopying, recording, taping, or information and retrieval systems – without written permission from the publisher, except for non commercial, educational use, including classroom teaching purposes. The views expressed in this series are those of the authors, but not necessarily of IGI Global.

Titles in this Series

For a list of additional titles in this series, please visit:
https://www.igi-global.com/book-series/advances-business-information-systems-analytics/37155

Cloud Computing Technologies for Green Enterprises
Kashif Munir (University of Hafr Al-Batin, Saudi Arabia)
Business Science Reference ● ©2018 ● 424pp ● H/C (ISBN: 9781522530381) ● US $215.00

Smart Technology Applications in Business Environments
Tomayess Issa (Curtin University, Australia) Piet Kommers (University of Twente, The
Netherlands) Theodora Issa (Curtin University, Australia) Pedro Isaías (Portuguese Open
University, Portugal) and Touma B. Issa (Murdoch University, Australia)
Business Science Reference ● ©2017 ● 429pp ● H/C (ISBN: 9781522524922) ● US $210.00

Advanced Fashion Technology and Operations Management
Alessandra Vecchi (London College of Fashion, University of London Arts, UK)
Business Science Reference ● ©2017 ● 443pp ● H/C (ISBN: 9781522518655) ● US $200.00

Maximizing Business Performance and Efficiency Through Intelligent Systems
Om Prakash Rishi (University of Kota, India) and Anukrati Sharma (University of Kota, India)
Business Science Reference ● ©2017 ● 269pp ● H/C (ISBN: 9781522522348) ● US $175.00

Maximizing Information System Availability Through Bayesian Belief Network...
Semir Ibrahimović (Bosna Bank International, Bosnia and Herzegovina) Lejla Turulja
(University of Sarajevo, Bosnia and Herzegovina) and Nijaz Bajgorić (University of Sarajevo,
Bosnia and Herzegovina)
Information Science Reference ● ©2017 ● 180pp ● H/C (ISBN: 9781522522683) ● US $140.00

Handbook of Research on Advanced Data Mining Techniques and Applications...
Shrawan Kumar Trivedi (BML Munjal University, India) Shubhamoy Dey (Indian Institute
of Management Indore, India) Anil Kumar (BML Munjal University, India) and Tapan
Kumar Panda (Jindal Global Business School, India)
Business Science Reference ● ©2017 ● 438pp ● H/C (ISBN: 9781522520313) ● US $260.00

For an enitre list of titles in this series, please visit:
https://www.igi-global.com/book-series/advances-business-information-systems-analytics/37155

701 East Chocolate Avenue, Hershey, PA 17033, USA
Tel: 717-533-8845 x100 ● Fax: 717-533-8661
E-Mail: cust@igi-global.com ● www.igi-global.com

Table of Contents

Foreword

It is a particular pleasure for me to be invited to write a foreword to this highly topical book, in that quite a few years ago I was Dr. Ng's research supervisor. In this carefully researched book he introduces and explains in detail what in recent years has been his major interest, Identity and Access Management (IAM).

IAM has become the new frontier for ensuring that providers and users of Internet services can enjoy all the benefits of global 'on-line' connectivity while safely avoiding the ever-present pitfalls of cybercrime, identity theft, phishing and their like. Identity theft has become a major aspect of cybercrime and is a serious worldwide problem because of the pivotal role of identity in many contemporary strategic applications - government services, financial services, banking, homeland security, the judicial system, health services, aviation and manufacturing. Consequently, IAM system design and implementation has become a critical activity for almost all providers of networked services.

In this book, Dr. Ng provides a comprehensive coverage of IAM, explaining its technicalities as well as covering what is available and what is emerging, carefully comparing and evaluating candidate offerings. There are currently many implementation options, and acronyms almost without number, for identity management frameworks and systems. This book identifies and explains these in useful detail and assists the reader in plotting a path to the most effective solution for their particular business or organisational needs. In the process, it identifies and explains the various competing and overlapping standardisation initiatives. Interoperability is always an issue for IAM frameworks and systems, since interoperability across different contexts is impossible without shared and clearly defined semantics. This is especially true for technical platforms, operating systems, database formats and communication protocols. This book addresses these issues directly, in a clear and practical manner, including a discussion of various biometrics based solutions.

Currently there is a variety of IAM products on offer. Dr. Ng carefully describes and explains their key features and distinguishing differences. He also provides a brief look at the future of IAM, emphasising the important point that traditional IAM techniques and services are designed for intra-organisational use, controlling access to data and systems behind a firewall. Now, as he points out, we are moving into an era of an "Internet of Things" (eventually an "Internet of Everything") where the addition of network "intelligence" facilitates convergence, orchestration and visibility across previously disparate systems. This will place much greater demands on IAM services in providing secure relationships across the Internet; bringing IAM out from behind the firewall so that any device or thing, permanent or transient, connected to the Internet has a properly managed identity.

Dr. Ng provides the reader with many useful references covering further and more detailed aspects of IAM that for reasons of limited space are not addressed in the text.

R. J. Offen
Macquarie University, Australia

Preface

Identity and Access Management has become one of the challenging areas in today's business information architecture. The importance and impacts of Identity and Access Management to the Internet Age has long been overlooked by the IT practitioners and researchers until recently being caught up by the upsurge of breaches in identity theft.

This is due to the proliferation of distributed mobile technologies, heavy usage of social media, continuous harnessing of information analytics, and the Cloud. Business-to-Customer, Business-to-Business and Government-to-Citizen evolved into situations that trust between user and application are required to be established on-the-spot since they are no longer a given perquisite.

Today, businesses are facing new challenges in implementing contemporary Identity and Access Management solutions due to difficulties in deciding when and what to get started. IT personnel are facing new ways of implementing Identity and Access Management solutions such as Identity Governance Administration (IGA) and Identity Management as a service (IDaaS) solutions. They need a comprehensive picture of their needs in Identity and Access Management in order to correctly plan, assess and deploy the right solutions for their organisation.

There are very limited literatures available to highlight the challenges faced by researchers and developers in offering an Identity and Access Management solution that can meet the present and future situations.

The author observed that most of the literatures available at present are either narrowly focused on specific Identity and Access Management environments (Unix / Windows), or covering too general on outdated technologies. There is lack of the information that captures, as many as possible, the critical elements required by contemporary Identity and Access Management solutions and architectures.

There are a vast number of Identity and Access Management solutions and architectures available commercially and as open source. Unfortunately, IT practitioners find it difficult to get hold of the critical information in order for them to make appropriate decisions.

The purpose of this book is to provide our readers succinct answers to the following questions:

- What is Identity and Access Management and what are the core technologies employed by different Identity and Access Management solutions and architectures?
- What is the role of Identity and Access Management in different contexts? For example: public and individual safety; internal and external business processes; and the influence of new technologies.
- How can we evaluate the applicability of different Identity and Access Management architectures and solutions?
- What are the state of the art Identity and Access Management architectures and solutions? How well do they perform?
- Who are the major players and contributors in Identity and Access Management technologies and solutions?
- What are the key challenges in Identity and Access Management that have not been addressed in the existing frameworks and solutions? What are the paths available to deal with those challenges?
- What are the potentials available for integrating different Identity and Access Management solutions?
- What are the challenges and the progress in the research of future Identity and Access Management architectures and solutions?

This book will provide answers to the above questions such that the readers can acquire the critical knowledge in selecting and implementing an appropriate Identity and Access Management solution for their organisations.

Recently, there are a multitude of Identity and Access Management solutions flocking the market, such as Okta, PingIdentity, Oracle Identity Management, Microsoft Identity Integration Server, IBM Security Identity Manager, Novell Identity Manager, Hitachi ID Management Suite, Intercede MyID etc. These commercial systems provide application and platform specific identity and access control functionality. However, there is little objective third party information available for practitioners to understand the capabilities exhibited by these commercial Identity and Access Management systems.

Therefore, one of the aims of this book is to review, assess and consolidate the research and development activities of a number of existing Identity and Access Management architectures in privately and publicly funded organisations. The author will discuss the advantages, limitations, and requirements of these architectures. Apart from that, this book will highlight those key challenges in Identity and Access Management that have not been addressed by these architectures and provide our readers some thoughts on how to deal with those challenges as well as the potential for integrating different identity management architectures and frameworks.

Furthermore, this book will discuss the pros and cons of some of the contemporary developments in Identity and Access Management, such as Social Login, Biometric Multi-modal Multi-factor Authentication, Federated Identity Management, and Cloud-based Identity & Access Management.

This book is targeting the academic readers, researchers as well as practitioners who are responsible for the implementation of Identity and Access Management solutions in business and government organisations.

Identity and Access Management researchers and practitioners shall find this book a useful resource. The author believes this book is first of its kind in Identity and Access Management that provides a holistic view on Identity and Access Management in regard to requirements, technologies, life cycle processes, evaluation methodologies of contemporary Identity and Access Management architectures, and overview of present and future commercial Identity and Access Management systems.

This book will fill the gap to enable Identity and Access Management practitioners in gaining an objective view of the contemporary Identity and Access Management architectures and the landscape of the technologies and processes required to drive the future direction in Identity and Access Management development. The contemporary information contained in this is book will be a valuable resource for university students, Identity and Access Management practitioners and researchers.

With the information contained in this book, our readers can achieve the goal of managing an organisation's identities, credentials, attributes, and assuring the identity of an user in an extensible manner set for Identity and Access Management, through different areas such as technology, processes and functionality (e.g. administration, management and maintenance, discovery, communication exchanges, correlation and binding, policy enforcement, authentication and assertions) that are required to work collaboratively.

Our readers will gain the following benefits from reading this book:

- Able to understand the concepts and technologies employed by contemporary Identity and Access Management architectures. Our readers shall be able to understand the roles, significance, advantages, limitations, and requirements of different Identity and Access Management technologies and architectures.
- Able to understand the vital concept of Identity and Access Management Life-Cycle. Our readers will understand the administration of the life cycle of digital identity entities; during which the digital representation of an identity is established, used and disposed of, when the digital identity is not required anymore.
- Able to elaborate the applications of processes and technologies in Identity and Access Management architectures by providing a taxonomy framework that captures and classifies the characteristics of different contemporary identity management architectures as well as compliance enforcement. Our readers can use the taxonomy framework in this book to benchmark other Identity and Access Management solutions.
- Able to evaluate the effectiveness of different Identity and Access Management architectures through business and bioinformatics applications life cycle and practices.

This book is structured in the following way:

- Chapter 1, "Identity and Access Management in the Internet Age," starts with a brief history of Identity and Access Management and then introduce our readers to some challenges to Identity and Access Management as exemplified by some scenarios such as social identity, biometrics and identity mobility.
- Chapter 2, "The Roles of Contemporary Identity and Access Management Standards," sets an anchor for our readers to grasp the technologies closely related to Identity and Access Management that are developed by different standards organisations.
  This chapter will discuss the following different generations of Identity and Access Management technologies:
  ◦ Security and Privacy technologies terms and definitions;
  ◦ First Generation: LDAP, Kerberos, Radius, X.509;
  ◦ Second Generation: Cross Domain Collaboration, SAML; and
  ◦ Third Generation: OpenID, OAuth.

This chapter also summarises the different views of identities and gives an overview of the state of art of both biometric multimodal and password/token based Identity and Access Management architectures and systems, highlights the key issues and argue why these issues are important for the successful enhancing the security of digital identities in the current Information Age.

- Chapter 3, "The Roles of Identity Management Life Cycle," will cover the importance of managing a person's identity life cycle, which includes the technologies used for provisioning and password resets, the processes and policies associated with different technologies, and the important events that happen around the management issues of a person's identity.

- Chapter 4, "The Goals and Requirements for Contemporary Identity and Access Management Systems," provides an assessment of the requirements for Identity and Access Management frameworks so as to give our readers some insights into the primary purposes and characteristics of Identity and Access Management solutions.

  The following requirements will be discussed in the chapter: user empowerment on awareness and control; minimal information disclosure for constrained use, non-repudiation, support for directional identity topologies, support for a universal identity bus, provision of defining strength of identity, decoupling the identity management layer from the application layer, usability issues concerning identity selection and disclosure, a consistent experience across contexts, and scalability.

  Furthermore, this chapter presents a taxonomy to our readers for classifying the different Identity and Access Management frameworks. This taxonomy can be used to study and benchmark the features and functionalities of different Identity and Access Management frameworks proposed by different organisations.

- Chapter 5, "A Survey of Contemporary Identity and Access Management Architectures," provides a summary of a number of organisations which are active in Identity and Access Management researches. We'll discuss the technological and application contributions from each organisation, their key deliverables and the active research areas.

  The following are the Identity and Access Management frameworks covered in this book:
  - Fast IDentity Online Alliance (FIDO);
  - Privacy and Identity Management for Europe (PRIME);

- ○ Privacy and Identity Management for Community Services (PICOS);
- ○ Secure Widespread Identities for Federated Telecommunications (SWIFT);
- ○ Telecommunication security & identity management (ITU-T Recommendations Y.2720, X.1250);
- ○ The Open Group Identity Management Architecture (Guide G072);
- ○ The OpenID Foundation Open Trust Frameworks for Open Government;
- ○ The Liberty Alliance Identity Federation, Governance, and Assurance Framework;
- ○ The National Institute of Standards and Technology (NIST) Ontology of Identity Credentials Framework; and
- ○ BioAPI.
- • Chapter 6, "An Introduction to Commercial Identity and Access Management Solutions," exhibits an objective third party evaluation on a number of commercially available Identity and Access Management solutions. The author is certain that our readers will find the information resourceful in helping them, as an Identity and Access Management practitioner, to make Identity and Access Management related decisions with high level of confidence.

  This chapter summarises the functionalities and capabilities exhibited by the following commercially available Identity and Access Management solutions:
  - ○ Microsoft Identity Manager and Microsoft Azure Active Directory;
  - ○ IBM Security Identity Manager and Cloud Identity Service;
  - ○ Okta;
  - ○ Centrify;
  - ○ Ping Identity;
  - ○ Oracle Identity and Access Management; and
  - ○ Salesforce.com.
- • Chapter 7, "The Role of Identity Theft in Identity and Access Management," discusses how personal identities can be stolen and exploited and proposes a Self-Learning Context Aware Identity Access and Management Framework (SCAIAM) for combating identity theft.
- • Chapter 8, "Challenges and Future Development in Identity and Access Management," is the concluding chapter of this book. This

chapter summarises the challenges and future development in relation to the following new technological trends: Internet of Everything (IoE), Identity Relationship Management, Transient Identities, and Autonomous Devices.

Lastly, the author would like to give credit to the following resources which have provided the author insights and enlightenments in accumulating useful knowledge in this Identity and Access Management research journey:

- **Book Title:** Identity and Access Management: Business Performance Through Connected Intelligence.
  Author: Ertem Osmanoglu
  Year: 2013
  Type: Paperback and Kindle eBook
  Pages: 618
  Publisher: Elsevier
  Comment: This guide is based on Ernst & Young's methodologies. It is written as a guide so that the readers can use it as an implementation guide providing a step-by-step instruction of how to plan, assess, design, and deploy Identity and Access Management solutions in business settings. Although this book seems lacking in information about the requirements and processes in evaluating the suitability of different Identity and Access Management architectures, it is a very good resource in the technologies used in Identity and Access Management.
- **Book Title:** Identity Management: A Primer
  Author: Gram Williamson, David Yip, Ilan Sharoni and Kent Spaulding
  Year: 2009
  Type: Paperback
  Pages: 220
  Publisher: MC Press
  Comment: This book provides good coverage on the issues and strategies for implementing Identity and Access Management best practices and solutions. It has a strong emphasis on some of the technical solutions such as Single Sign-On (SSO) and Role-Based Access Controls (RBAC) but seems lacking in a broader view of other technologies that are vital in the contemporary Identity and Access Management solutions.

- **Book Title:** Identity & Access Management: A Systems Engineering Approach
  Author: Peter Omondi Orondo
  Year: 2014
  Type: Paperback and Kindle
  Pages: 312
  Publisher: IAM Imprints
  Comment: This book is more recent than other similar books and provides good focuses on the risks of identity authorisation and the modelling of Identity and Access Management processes and financial issues.
- **Book Title:** Identity and Data Security for Web Development: Best Practices
  Authors: Jonathan LeBlanc, and Tim Messerschmidt
  Year: 2016
  Type: Paperback and Google Book
  Pages: 204
  Comment: This book provides contemporary information on identity and data security for Web developers. Although the authors seemed not interested in explaining the basic concepts of Identity and Access Management, they've discussed in detail about password encryption, hashing & salting techniques, SSO and identity security fundamental concepts. They've also discussed the OAuth 2 and OpenID implementations, and other contemporary concepts such as multi-factor authentication and other alternate method of identification.
- **Community Name:** Kantara Initiative
  Comment: Kantara Initiative is a non-profit, open professional association in the fields of identity assurance, privacy, policy and information systems assessment, and real world innovation for the digital identity transformation. Kantara Initiative provides great resources in the development of Identity Relationship Management (IRM), User Managed Access (UMA) and Identities of Things (IoT).

Acknowledgment

Unless the Lord builds the house, the builders labour in vain.

Unless the Lord watches over the city, the guards stand watch in vain.

(Psalm 127 verse 1 NIV)

First and foremost, as a Christian, I would like to give thanks and glory to Jesus Christ my Lord for giving me this opportunity to become the sole author of this book and enabled me to complete this project on time.

The Lord is my rock, and I dedicate this book to Him.

Secondly, I would like to thank my wife Linda Mi-Lin Mok for standing side-by-side with me throughout my research career and the authorship of this book. She has been my inspiration and motivation for continuing to improve my knowledge and advance my research career forward. I have the deepest feelings of praise for Linda, who also is my best friend and mate, for her enduring love, faithful prayers, persistent support, understanding, encouragement, tolerance and patience in so many ways throughout the duration of this research, without which I would never have completed this work. I am truly blessed for having Linda as my wife.

This book was produced with a great deal of help from a lot of people. I would like to thank the editorial staff of IGL Global for their high standard of editorial service offered to me. I have many years of pleasant publication experience with IGI Global since 2012. I am grateful to all the staff of IGL Global for their great effort in facilitating a smooth transition from manuscript to publication with clear and efficient direction throughout the development process of this book.

I would like to extend my sincerest thanks and appreciation to Dr. Paul Watters, Associate Professor in Cybersecurity of La Trobe University and Dr. Shiping Chen, Principal Research Scientist of CSIRO ICT Centre, for their joint effort in enabling me to complete two of my Identity and Access Management research papers published in the edited book, Inventive Approaches for Technology Integration and Information Resources Management, and Information Resources Management Journal. More importantly, I thank them for granting me the rights to use the materials in this book.

A/Prof Watters has given me a great deal of inspiration to the importance of cybersecurity and useful feedback in the impacts of identity crime. Dr. Chen has shown tremendous generosity in providing his research expertise in system performance evaluation which has helped me a lot in evaluating the features available from different Identity and Access Management platforms.

I also owe a great deal of inspiration to Professor Emeritus Ray Offen of Macquarie University and Dr. Paul Greenfield of CSIRO, who are my PhD. supervisors and mentors at Macquarie University and CSIRO. They have instilled my curiosity in research and provided me an environment that fostered my research interests in different areas. I am in debt to Prof. Offen for his generous financial, intellectual, and emotional support throughout my research journey.

Many thanks to the brothers and sisters in Jesus Christ, especially Dr. Stephen Wong, Mrs. Annie Wong, Dr. Thomas Lam, and Mrs. Yangtze Lam, who prayed for me regularly, shared my 'ups and downs' during my research and encouraged me to persevere. I would also like to dedicate this book to my godson, Joshua Lam, the son of Thomas and Yangtze. I hope this book can become an inspiration to Joshua in pursuing his personal life goals. To Rev. Frankie Law and Mrs. Cyla Law of the West Sydney Chinese Christian Church, I thank them for their regular prayer supports.

Last but not least, I would to thank the PICOS project for granting me the permission to use the PICOS High-Level View and PICOS 5-layers Architecture Model figures, Dr. Jan Camenisch for granting me the permission to use the figure for the Architecture of the components in PRIME, and the Legal Affairs Unit, ITU for granting me the permission to use Figure 2b (An example of a user-centric five-party identity management model) on page 6 of the Recommendation ITU-T X.1250.

Chapter 1

Identity and Access Management in the Internet Age:
The Challenges

ABSTRACT

This chapter presents a few scenarios to demonstrate the fact that identity management is employed in many aspects of our daily activities and gives a brief history of Identity and Access Management, showing our readers how the Internet has prompted identity problems. The author will discuss some of the challenges exemplified by some scenarios such as passwords, biometrics, social identity, and identity mobility.

INTRODUCTION

The Internet has evolved from merely a content delivery backbone to become the core engine in the intelligent connection of people, process, data and things (Internet of Everything, or IoE). The Internet has transformed information into actions that create new paradigms for military defence, and economic opportunity for businesses, individuals and countries.

Consumers, businesses and governments are benefiting from the online services transacted over the Internet. However, weak security practices and the lack of awareness of cybersecurity have created a growing risk of identity

DOI: 10.4018/978-1-5225-4828-7.ch001

theft and fraud. This chapter will provide a summary of the challenges that Identity and Access Management (IAM) system are facing in this Internet Age, and the inadequacy of the username/password security model that has its roots in the pre-Internet era.

A BRIEF HISTORY OF IDENTITY AND ACCESS MANAGEMENT

In the physical world, a person is a human social entity who has a name, lives in a physical address, with accessible home or mobile phones, and uses services provided by the government as well as financial institutions. When that person is starting to use applications on the Internet such as Facebook and Google+, that person starts to build up the digital identity profile with a variety of online organisations.

A typical online user may hold multiple accounts with different service providers such as Gmail, Hotmail, etc. This is a common scenario for a typical online user's digital profile may consists of multiple email addresses and multiple digital identities held with different application providers on the Internet. The person may use multiple mobile devices with multiple online accounts and a large number of online transaction histories held with different service providers.

Using passwords to identify the legitimacy of a person's access to protected resources has long been established. Watchword is a word or short phrase to be communicated, on challenge, to a sentinel or guard in the military. Ancient Roman military uses watchwords as a sign of recognition among members of the same Roman military tribune. The use of watchwords in military use evolved to include not just a word or phrase, but a challenge and a response pair. In the Second World War, paratroopers of the U.S. used the challenge and response style of identification (changed every 3 days).

Passwords have been used with computers since the early days of computing. In 1961, the Compatible Time-Sharing System (CTSS) at the Massachusetts Institute of Technology used user-id and password to establish personal access into the system so as to accommodate multiple users sharing the same Central Processing Unit (CPU) simultaneously using separate consoles. The goal is to set up multiple terminals that can be used by multiple persons but with each person having his own private set of system resources.

When a person wants to use the service of a particular provider, he or she is required to enter a valid password as a proof of identity to the service provider. This is to help keep the provider secure from unauthorised access. Most service providers require their users to follow basic rules when choosing their password to ensure that it cannot be easily compromised, for example:

- The password may need to be of a minimum length;
- The password may need to contain a specific number of or special characters;
- The password may need to be different from previous passwords that have been used before; and
- The password may need to be changed at a regular interval.

Contemporary IAM solutions have been developed by vendors such as Oracle, Microsoft, IBM, etc. These commercial identity management systems provide application and platform specific identity and access control functionality, by aggregating identity-related information from multiple data-sources. The primary goal of these enterprise identity management systems is to provide organisations with a unified view of a user's/resources identity in a heterogeneous enterprise IT environment.

According to Lasance (2013), the term 'Meta Directory' was first introduced by a company called Zoomit Corporation which was subsequently acquired by Microsoft in 1999. The managing director of Zoomit, Kim Cameron, became Microsoft's chief architect for identity and privacy.

The second acquisition that shaped the IAM market is IBM's acquisition of Metamerge and Access360 in 2002. Metamerge is a provider of directory integration software company based in Oslo, Norway. Access360 is another provider of identity management software based in Irvine, California. Metamerge was subsequently became Tivoli Directory Integrator (the adapter toolkit for Tivoli Identity Manager's provisioning connectors) and Access360 became Tivoli Identity Manager (TIM).

IAM has also been extended to the domain of telecommunications, as shown in the Cisco Identity-Based Networking Services (IBNS). IBNS authenticates entities, and determines access privileges based on policy, control network access policy to trusted network devices, and monitors network activities.

The IEEE 802.1X standard (Port-based Network Access Control) is another example of requiring authentication and authorisation process to allow or disallow devices attached to a LAN port with point-to-point connection characteristic.

On the other hand, cloud computing has revolutionised the way that organisations use computers to run applications and access services. Citrix OpenCloud Access is an example which provides Single Sign-on (SSO), provisioning, and access workflow management for a variety of cloud-based applications.

Recently, we have witnessed vendors are producing a number of new IAM products embracing the cloud and biometrics. The partnership between Fujitsu and ImageWare Systems Inc. in deploying a cloud-based, multi-modal biometric IAM product and model building on Fujitsu's Global Cloud Platform and utilises ImageWare's CloudID products and multimodal biometric engine is an example (ThirdFactor 2013). Another example is the establishment of organisations dealing with the usage of biometric in IAM such as the International Biometrics & Identification Association (IBIA), and the Security Identity Alliance in May 2013.

Nowadays, we can find identity management's footprints over the many aspects of our daily lives, such as:

- Public Safety (i.e., tracking of criminal identities);
- National Security (i.e., cyber security and cyber defence, tracking of terrorist activities and other criminal activities); and
- Online Transactions (i.e., all types of online financial activities, eGovernment activities, health care activities and social activities).

CHALLENGES OF IDENTITY AND ACCESS MANAGEMENT IN THE INTERNET AGE

Identity and Access Management is related to the administration and identification of individual entities in a system or environment (which can be a country, a network, an IT application, or an enterprise), and controlling their access to resources within that system, by associating user rights and obligations with the established identity. In order to achieve the goals of managing the identifiers, credentials, attributes, and assuring the identity of an entity in an extensible manner set for identity management, different areas such as technology, processes and functionality (e.g., administration, management and maintenance, discovery, communication exchanges, correlation and binding, policy enforcement, authentication and assertions) are required to work together.

IAM has been evolving in a loosely and disparate manner. There are many mission critical applications (such as defence or physical access control systems) that rely heavily on the biometrics industry to dictate the adoption of biometric access control with a disproportionate focus on technology issues. We observe that existing biometric IAM solutions and researches are confined to a limited number of pre-selected combinations of biometric modalities such as, face recognition, voice recognition, and/or hand geometry comparisons (Veeramachaneni et al., 2005) with add-on technologies such as Match-On-Card (Bringer et al., 2009).

On the other hand, many mission critical financial applications are still relying purely on digital security proof (such as user-id/password or chip-and-pin payment method). Making the situation even worse, multiple software vendors are supplying multiple IAM solutions with user credentials being stored and managed in multiple locations within an organisation, and users have to remember multiple user-ids and passwords. This creates redundant software/hardware investments, and hinder business growth due to degraded manageability of the business assets and processes (Beaver & Shaw, 2011).

There are four major functions required by an IAM solution: *Authentication and Authorisation* for the Access Management functions; and the *Credential Management and Repository Management* for the Identity Management functions.

A summary of the functions is depicted in Figure 1. We can see that the authentication function includes Credential Authentication, Password Service, SSO, and Session Management. The authorisation function includes Rule Based, Role Based, Attribute Based, and Social Based Protected Resource Authorisation. The credential management function includes User and Role Management, Credential Registration, Password Management, Provisioning, and Delegation. The repository management function includes Directory service, Meta Data, and Federation service.

Contemporary IAM solutions are required to provide services in the following manner:

- Strong and secured user authentication;
- Up to date authorisation check against private and individual control policies;
- Sufficient logging for non-repudiating;
- Timely de-provisioning, de-commissioning in user credential management; and
- Governance and compliance on a continuous manner.

Figure 1. Identity and access management functions

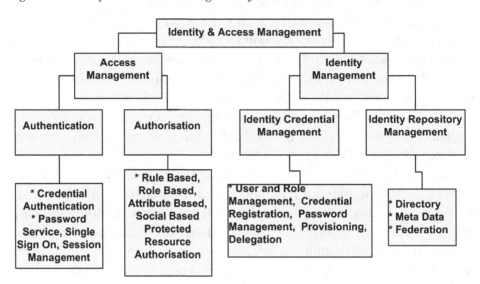

In today's information era, applications and information are everywhere. IAM practitioners are under immense pressure to manage the ever-evolving landscape. Today's business environments are highly distributed and with high demand in the use of mobile, cloud, and social technologies. Contemporary marketing strategies are harvesting customer online identities and related personal profile data to build and nurture relationships with users over time.

Traditional methods of deploying applications often rely heavily on privately joined desktops and VPN access control. Firms are relying on user names and passwords to provide access to online services for customers interacting from off sites. In traditional employee-centric IAM, privacy settings are usually determined at a corporate or geographic level. Only a few privilege users are allowed to setup and modify such policies. In this scenario, the IAM solution is only required to tie-in to the company's master data management solution to be able to present customer specific profile and preference information seamlessly to the customer.

However, contemporary mobile device application deployment methods are making use of App Stores and/or Cloud environments. Mobility adds to the identity complexity. People may access applications through multiple access points and each access point may use separate security policies and identity stores. This means the same IAM logic may need to be developed and deployed multiple times. In this customer centric scenario, consumers expect online services to provide granular user-centric preferences so they can manage how their online profile data are being treated by the service providers. We can see that this will be a challenging task for companies with millions of online customers.

At the moment, we assert that there is a lack of common access experience across mobile devices. It is logical to see that users are experiencing fragmented and repeated control access. There is also lacking of common user credentials across access points. The governance and auditing requirements differ between channels which also caused fragmentation issues.

Due to different service delivery models in private and public domains demand different requirements in managing identities, these two methods of application deployment post new challenges to IT security practitioners in identifying legitimate private internal and public external users accessing a huge number of diverse applications.

Customer identities in B2E environment are managed by enterprises, but becoming more distributed and influenced by the Cloud. B2C, B2B and G2C environments have driven IAM solutions into a state that trusts between users and applications are no longer a given.

With the help of the rules set by the providers, creating strong passwords may not be difficult. However, most people would agree that it is a painstaking effort in managing several passwords against a number of online service providers. The situation will only get worse with the number of service providers keep increasing each day.

Challenges With Password

The use of user-id and password has a long history dating from the first real-time multi-user operating system in the 1960s. Apart from writing down passwords in a secured manner, another simple strategy taken by many individuals and business entities is reusing the same password for multiple online accounts. According to a white paper issued by Swivel Secure (2014):

- One in five working Americans reuses the same username and password across their personal and business accounts;
- 63% of U.S. business owners reuse the same passwords to log in to different systems; and
- 73% of U.S. full-time workers admit to reusing the same batch of passwords online.

7

The obvious problem with writing down passwords and reusing the same password is that if it's compromised and someone gets hold of it, the rest of the person's identity is at risk.

Financial institutions usually have very secure online services. However, financial customers' online credentials are often the prime target of criminals using malware and phishing scams. Social media (Facebook, Twitter etc.) credentials are receiving much attention from hackers as they give access to many interconnected aspects of a person's life. Therefore, it is unwise to reuse our financial credentials to access a social media service.

Ideally each financial password should be secure and unique, but it must not have too many passwords that need to be written down. One suggestion is to use a common theme that leads to unique financial passwords which share a common link. The theme chosen must be kept personal.

Trapani (2006) has suggested the following simple themes for consideration:

- Choose a base password and then apply a rule that mashes in some form of the service name with it.

For example, we may use a base password with the first two consonants and the first two vowels of the service name. Say your base password is "asdf." Then the password for Yahoo would be asdfYHAO, and the password for eBay would be asdfBYEA.

- Use the same letters to start (say, a person's initials and a favourite number) plus the first 3 letters of a service name. In this case, the password for Amazon would be gmlt10AMA and for Hotmail gmlt10HOT.

Challenges of Biometrics

Password-only type access control systems are constantly under the attack of hackers. Therefore, there are advocates of alternatives to passwords, such as biometrics, two-factor authentication or SSO. Biometrics is using the unique physiological and/or behavioural properties exhibited by an individual to authenticate and verify the individual for access to protected resources or transactions. The next chapter will provide detail explanation about the application of biometrics in Identity and Access Management, in particular, the Multimodal Biometric Identity and Access Management.

Biometric identifiers are linked to persons themselves directly and in theory much difficult to be counterfeited, or lost. However, biometric identifiers could be sabotaged or taken-over. Bodhani (2013) illustrated with many examples such as face recognition with non-3D based cameras can easily be fooled with a single photo of the user's face. More recent technologies require the use of very high-resolution camera, or multiple cameras to recognise the face. Another example is the speed-of-typing recognition system making use of unreliable algorithms by assuming the user will always be using the same keyboard and type in the same manner. In reality, people may change in mood or sense of urgency that could affect the way they type and thus cause problems when authenticating.

One of the known challenges of biometrics is that measurements may often have to be collected in less than ideal conditions. Voice may have been colluded with the ambient background noise, signatures may be signed where someone is in an unnatural position, fingerprints may have been taken when the finger is misaligned or wet, and facial characteristics may have been checked with glasses or being affected by the colour of the background light.

Sources of potential error affect the false acceptance and false rejection rates. Biometrics systems are required to be tuned to an acceptable condition which may compromise the system to less precise.

Privacy is a new issue found in the application of biometrics because biometrics can turn existing surveillance systems into a powerful and much more invasive system. Currently, the police are relying on videos systems captured with facial-recognition technology to track down criminals. However, the people behind the controls can actively track anyone throughout his/her daily life.

Furthermore, once the face, iris or DNA profile of a person is captured, that file will be difficult to protect. At the moment, the responsibility of the custodian of a person's biometric profile is not yet clearly defined and agreed. Biometric identifiers are subject to theft. The consequence of that issue has not been quantified yet. We know that changing the password or replacing a stolen card is an easy task, but good luck in changing the biometric feature of a person.

Used properly, biometrics could help protect against them. But the potential for misuse is very obvious. Therefore, we must start developing rules to govern the use of these technologies now.

Challenges of Social Identities

Social login is a new trend of authentication using federated social sign-on. This is to allow users to use an existing social identity issued by a trusted third-party identity provider, such as Facebook, Google, LinkedIn, Microsoft, or Twitter, to access a third-party application without having to go through a new registration process. The identity provider authenticates the user and allows the third-party application to capture the user's identity attributes. Social login is increasing its popularity in recent years because users are complaining about the need for going through the registration process for different service providers in order to perform a particular service.

Social identities simplify the registration process and reduce the administration overhead from forgotten passwords. It is able to establish trust between the user, device, mobile network, Cloud and the service provider. Social identities can simplify the access to resources on different service providers with a SSO so that it eliminates the need for end users to remember multiple usernames and passwords when accessing various apps and systems.

Nowadays, social identities can provide ability to link and profile a person. The marketing companies make use of social logins for authenticating customers in low-risk, high-volume transactions, such as posting to bulletin boards or signing up with their email to a marketing email list.

However, there are challenges that we need to be aware about the use of social identities:

- Where and how to draw a line for information being shared and leveraged between different service providers;
- The need to protect from single point of failure thus increase the risk of identity theft, increased poor user experience, and high management cost; and
- The need to protect social identities for high-risk, high-reward transactions, such as a purchase or payment.

Challenges of Identity Mobility

Mobile Identity is composed of mainly three components: (1) the smart phone, (2) the phone number, and (3) the activity footprints and behaviour exhibited by the owner of the device. Smartphone has become the primary means for many people to access their daily social and financial services. According to a report by (Toi and Burns, 2014), more than 50 per cent of interactions with banks are conducted through smartphones.

Technologies nowadays allow service providers to track and accumulate history of activities demonstrated by the phone thus enable some sorts of reputational scoring and behaviour patterns recognition and prediction for a particular mobile number user. It is because each mobile device has its unique International Mobile Equipment Identity number (IMEI) and there are a multitude of attributes (such as Hardware model, O/S, Location Services, etc.) can be used for identification purposes.

For the purpose of tracking the physical location of a person, the phone number is more persistent than identifiers such as an email address. Furthermore, paying for owning multiple mobile phone services is more costly than multiple email addresses.

However, there are challenges to be faced by the server providers when considering using smartphones for their applications. First of all, smartphone has become one of the prime targets for cybercriminals to exploit at the points of weakness that exist in the smartphones which are connected to Internet.

A Mobile Digital Signature (MDS) is a digital signature generated either on a smartphone based on the IMEI or other user specified attributes or on the SIM card on the phone. MDS has the ability to safely, reliably and securely "sign" or commit to financial services using the smartphone through the use of a combination of actions, such as swiping a secret pattern on the screen, signing with fingerprint, or entering a passcode.

However, the major concern is about when the mobile phone is lost, stolen or changed to a new one. Furthermore, a person may keep multiple digital profiles which will evolve and change throughout their lifetime; unlike legal identity, which is mostly fixed. The challenge for IAM is how to keep track of the changes in identities for a particular person whose digital profiles are under constant changes due to change in lifestyle, physical, social environments or age.

The other challenge is inter-operational issue. People may access applications through multiple access points but each access point uses separate security policies and identity stores. The service provider may be required to redevelop and redeploy the same business logic multiple times to suit smartphones from different hardware manufacturers. This also leads to the fragmented situation of auditing and control issues across multiple applications and service channels. Users may also encounter different access experience across different devices and there are lacking in the use of common credentials across different access points.

CONCLUSION

The goal of this chapter is to provide our readers succinct background information about the following:

1. What is Identity and Access Management? and
2. What are the challenges that current Identity and Access Management systems are facing?

In the next chapter, we'll discuss the roles of different contemporary identity management standards. More specifically, we'll look into IAM technologies used in different generations, such as:

- Security and Privacy technologies;
- First Generation technologies: LDAP, Kerberos, Radius, X.509;
- Second Generation technologies: Cross Domain Collaboration, SAML; and
- Third Generation technologies: OpenID, OAuth.

The information provided in the next chapter will be a useful resource for IAM practitioners gaining an objective view of the development of contemporary IAM architectures.

REFERENCES

Beaver, K., & Shaw, J. (2011). *Identity & Access Management For Dummies, Quest Software Edition*. Hoboken, NJ: Wiley Publishing, Inc.

Bodhani, A. (2013). Biometric authentication is reality not fiction. *E & T Magazine*.

Bringer, J., Chabanne, H., Kevenaar, T. A., & Kindarji, B. (2009). *Extending match-on-card to local biometric identification. Biometric ID Management and Multimodal Communication*. Springer.

Lasance, M. (2013). *Identity Management Then and Now: The SAP MaXware story*. Available: https://identityspace.wordpress.com/2013/03/14/identity-management-then-and-now-the-sap-maxware-story/

Swivel-Secure. (2014). *Passwords: The Weak Link in Digital Security.* Author.

Thirdfactor. (2013). *Contract brings multi-modal biometrics to cloud platform.* Available: http://www.thirdfactor.com/2013/03/27/contract-brings-multi-modal-biometrics-to-cloud-platform

Toi, G. D., & Burns, M. (2014). *Customer loyalty in retail banking: Global.* Bain & Company.

Trapani, G. (2006). *Geek to Live: Choose (and remember) great passwords.* Available: http://lifehacker.com/184773/geek-to-live--choose-and-remember-great-passwords

Veeramachaneni, K., Osadciw, L. A., & Varshney, P. K. (2005). An adaptive multimodal biometric management algorithm. *Systems, Man, and Cybernetics, Part C: Applications and Reviews. IEEE Transactions on, 35,* 344–356.

KEY TERMS AND DEFINITIONS

Match-on-Card Technology: Combining biometric authentications with smart cards, enabling users to not only carry their biometric with them but also match it on the card. This achieves greater privacy for the cardholder and the ability to authenticate without connection to a backend biometric database.

Chapter 2

The Roles of Contemporary Identity and Access Management Standards:
(R)evolution of IAM Technologies

ABSTRACT

This chapter covers some of the core concept and technological background of IAM with topics such as, definitions of Identity, Identity Management, and different generations of IAM technologies. However, please take note that this chapter will not be providing in depth explanations of each topic because it is beyond the scope of this book.

INTRODUCTION

We all agree that nowadays we are living in a hyperconnected world. We are facing a complex and extensive web of digital relationships between people, devices and things that are required to be working in secure and manageable manner. In the chapter, we provide our readers the backgrounds how an Identity and Access Management solution are built to scale and understand how billions of users, devices, services, and things are managed and protected through the relationships between them.

DOI: 10.4018/978-1-5225-4828-7.ch002

Firstly, we'll provide a summary of the different views on identities, identity management, as well as an introduction to both biometric multimodal and password/token based IAM architectures and systems.

Secondly, we'll discuss the roles of different contemporary identity management technology standards. More specifically, we'll look into IAM technologies used in different generations:

- First Generation technologies: LDAP,Kerberos, Radius, and X.509,
- Second Generation technologies: Cross Domain Collaboration and SAML
- Third Generation technologies: OpenID and OAuth authentication
- Identity Management in the Cloud: System for Cross-domain Identity Management (SCIM)

We'll also discuss how different technologies are employed in the effective management of identities such as: Face Recognition Across Facial Expressions and Body Gestures, Audio and Video Motion Analysis for Detection of Spontaneous Emotions, and Biometrics beyond the Visible Spectrum.

Lastly, we'll also discuss some of the key issues and argue why these issues are important for the successful enhancing the security of digital identities in the current Information Age.

Different Views of Identity and Access Management

There are many different views and definitions about Identity and Access Management. The concept of self-identity is exhibited by the qualities, beliefs, and expressions of a person or group, which is the interest in psychology, sociology, anthropology and philosophy. This kind of self-identity is related to the self-image and self-esteem of a particular individual.

In this book, we put our interest in the meaning of personal identity in regard to the dealing of personal identity with the unique digital or biometrical characteristics of a person under the necessary and sufficient conditions in proving that a person at one time and a person at another time can be verified to be the same person, persisting over time.

Hird and Harrop (2010) define identity as a subset of attributes, where "the variety of attributes is limited by a framework with defined boundary conditions (the context) in which the entity exists and interacts."

Fearon (1999) defines personal identity with regarding identities as social categories:

Personal identity is a set of attributes, beliefs, desires, or principles of action that a person thinks distinguish her in socially relevant ways and that (a) the person takes a special pride in; (b) the person takes no special pride in, but which so orient her behavior that she would be at a loss about how to act and what to do without them; or (c) the person feels she could not change even if she wanted to.

The Liberty Alliance Project (Wason et al., 2005) defines a *network identity* for an individual user on the Internet interacting with different services with tailored personal preferences for what the user wants and how it displayed as being "the overall global set of these attributes constituting the various accounts".

The National Institute of Standards and Technology (NIST) (MacGregor et al., 2006) explains identity has two types of properties:

- *Intrinsic properties link our past, present, and future,*
- *While extrinsic properties, since they must be observed, are necessarily retrospective.*

In IT terms, for example, we rely on intrinsic properties to design authentication systems (because the systems must authenticate people in the future) and extrinsic properties, often as recorded in logs and audit trails, to establish trustworthiness and accountability.

Cameron (2005) defines a *digital identity* as "a set of claims made by one digital subject about itself or another digital subject". A digital subject is "a person or thing represented or existing in the digital realm which is being described or dealt with". Personal identification information (PII) include, but are not limited to: (a) *Name*, such as full name, maiden name, mother's maiden name, or alias; (b) *Personal identification number*, such as social security number (SSN), passport number, driver's license number, taxpayer identification number, or financial account or credit card number; (c) *Address information*, such as street address or email address; (d) *Personal characteristics*, including photographic image (especially of face or other distinguishing characteristic), fingerprints, handwriting, or other biometric image or template data (e.g., retina scans, voice signature, facial geometry; McCallister et al., 2009).

Jaquet-Chielle et al. (2006) proposed the concept of a virtual person acting as a mask of a subject. The same subject may have several masks; the same mask may hide several subjects. A virtual person is usually defined by what it knows, and/or what it has, and/or what it is, and/or what it does. It can also be defined by its *attribute(s)*, and/or its *role(s)*, and/or its *ability(-ies)*, and/ or its *acquisition(s)*. Sometimes, a virtual person can also be defined by its *preference(s)*, and/or its *habit(s)*. Therefore, we assert that a well-defined taxonomy for describing the identity of a person is important in the research of IAM and defence against identity theft.

We treat personal identity as the set of unique characteristics by which an object or person is recognised or known. For the purpose of an Identity and Access Management system, we consider that personal identity requires a set of information about a person or entity that is sufficient to identify that entity by the system in a particular context (ITU-T, 2009b).

The concept of identity management also takes different forms. Different standards organisations started their work in identity management with different perspectives. The International Organization for Standardization Joint ISO/IEC Technical Committee JTC 1/SC 27 (ISO/IEC, 2009), with an emphasis on biometric authentication, sees identity management as "a set of processes, policies and technologies that enable authoritative sources to accurately identify entities as well as helping individual entities to facilitate and control the use of identity information in their respective relations".

On the other hand, ITU-T SG17 works in the protection of telecommunications infrastructures and services. ITU-T X.1250 (ITU-T, 2009a) defines identity management as:

A set of functions and capabilities (e.g., administration, management and maintenance, discovery, communication exchanges, correlation and binding, policy enforcement, authentication and assertions) used for:

- *Assurance of identity information (e.g., identifiers, credentials, attributes);*
- *Assurance of the identity of an entity (e.g., users/subscribers, groups, user devices, organisations, network and service providers, network elements and objects, and virtual objects); and*
- *Supporting business and security applications.*

For the purpose of this book, we treat Identity and Access Management encompasses all the resources (both human and technologies) and processes required for the administration and identification of individual entities in a system or environment (which can be a country, a network, an IT application, or an enterprise), and controlling their access to resources within that system, by associating user rights and obligations with the established identity.

In order to achieve the goals of managing the identifiers, credentials, attributes, and assuring the identity of an entity in an extensible manner set for Identity and Access Management, different areas such as technology, processes and functionality (e.g., administration, management and maintenance, discovery, communication exchanges, correlation and binding, policy enforcement, authentication and assertions) are required to work together.

Biometrics

Biometrics is an authentication and verification mechanism that relies on the automated identification or verification of the unique physiological and/or behavioural properties exhibited by an individual.

The National Science & Technology Council (NSTC) Subcommittee on Biometrics (2006) defines the term "biometrics" is derived from the Greek words "bio" (life) and "metrics" (to measure).

Nadort (2007) explains that the term "biometrics" has two meanings:

1. The automatic recognition of individuals based on biological and behavioural traits; and
2. In biology, agriculture, medicine, public health, demography, actuarial science, and fields related to these, "biometrics," "biometry," and "biostatistics" refer almost synonymously to statistical and mathematical methods for analysing data in the biological sciences.

However, the two meanings of "biometrics" overlap both in subject matter: human biological characteristics. They define biometrics as the automated recognition of individuals based on their behavioural and biological characteristics.

In this book, we treat biometrics as a term referring to the identification of living organisms by their characteristics or traits. Biometrics is unique to individual human being. The delicate lattice of branching blood vessels snaking up across our palms is unique to each of us, just like the striations in our irises or the swirls of skin on our fingertips.

Furthermore, we'll refer biometrics in the context of security in computer science as a form of identification and access control used to identify individuals or groups that are under the sphere of identification and access control for a particular system or application.

The Biometrics Identity Management Agency (BIMA) explains that biometrics is "measurable, physiological and/or behavioural characteristics which can be used to verify the identity of an individual" (Kaucher, 2013).

According to the International Biometrics & Identification Association (IBIA; Pato & Millett, 2010) *identifiers* are the distinctive, measurable characteristics exhibited by individuals. Biometric identifiers are often categorised as *physiological* versus *behavioural* characteristics.

Physiologically, biometric identification is made possible by technology and algorithmic developments that enable precise measurement coupled with increasing computational power that captures the physiological and behavioural biometric measurements of a person to be transformed into mathematical representations that can be rapidly compared (Zeng & Watters, 2007).

There are technologies that identify people by their vein configurations or fingerprints using electronic or optical sensors that turn patterns once only defined as whorls and arches into mathematical representations called *biometric templates*. Other physical attributes that can be measured and converted into mathematical representations include: faces, fingerprints, hands, iris patterns, retinal patterns, vein patterns, voice patterns, and DNA.

Exploratory work has been done to establish whether physical characteristics such as earlobes and body odour may also be effectively measured, mathematically represented, and rapidly compared for use in electronic identity authentication.

Behaviourally, templates reflecting individual characteristics are exhibited in writing - the speed, angle of the pen and pressure exerted, as well as the physical appearance of the signature. Moreover, the way a person interacts with a keyboard can also be studied, measured, and committed to mathematical representation in keystroke dynamics. The unique ways in which a person moves when walking can be, and is observed, measured and expressed mathematically in a technique known as *gait recognition*; which is one of the biometric technologies most suited to personal identification at a distance.

Biometric system performance is measured by typical metrics such as: false rejection rate, false acceptance rate, crossover rate, verification time and failure to enrol rate. A short explanation of these metrics is provided in the following:

- *False Rejection Rate (FRR)*, also known as *Type I error* or *False Non-Match Rate (FNMR)*, measures the percentage of times an individual who should be positively accepted is rejected. That is, counting the number of times that the "genuine good guys" are being rejected by a system. The lower the FRR the better.

- *False Acceptance Rate (FAR)*, also known as *Type II error* or *False Match Rate (FMR)*, measures the percentage of times an individual who should be rejected is positively matched by the biometric system. That is, counting the number of times that the "bad guys" able get pass the system. This is an indicator of security breach. Hence, the lower the FAR the better.

- Crossover Rate, also known as the Equal Error Rate (EER), is the point on a graph where the lines representing the FAR and FRR intersect. A lower crossover rate indicates a system with a good level of sensitivity and generally means the system will perform well.

- *Verification Time* is the average time taken for the actual matching process to occur.

- *Failure to Enrol Rate (FTER)* is a measure of the rate of failed enrolment incidents. Factors such as quality of the equipment used, the enrolment procedures, the surrounding environment and quality a person's biometric will affect the FTER.

- *Maximum Template Capacity* is the maximum number of sets of data which can be stored in the system.

- *Receiver Operating Characteristic or Relative Operating Characteristic (ROC)*, is a diagram characterisation of the trade-off between the FAR and the FRR. In general, the matching algorithm performs a decision based on a threshold which determines how close to a template the input needs to be for it to be considered a match. The lower the threshold value, the fewer false non-matches but more false accepts.

- *Failure to Capture Rate (FTCR)* is the probability that the system fails to detect a biometric input when presented correctly.

Multimodal Biometric Identity and Access Management

Emerging biometric technologies are gaining ground with more and more organisations are willing to implement biometrical IAM solutions. There are systems of keystroke rhythm authentication which match the keystroke speed and cadence (dwell time vs. flight-time) for each user to grant access to Internet banking.

However, each biometric technology has its own limitation. For example, fingerprint and keystroke rhythm authentication may be affected by broken or damaged hands in changing the speed of keystroke entry.

NCR Corporation has developed a form of voice recognition to be used at the ATM level. First, the consumer records a voice pattern within the NCR system by responding to a series of questions. Next, the consumer would type their phone number into the ATM. The software system would call the user to confirm identification. The system seeks to leverage the wide acceptance of cell phone usage in the marketplace.

It was argued that voice recognition is not a preferred method of biometrics due to the extremely high error rate as compared to other biometrics methods (Rodier, 2008). A major disadvantage of voice authentication is that background noise can interfere with authentication.

More sophisticated voice authentication systems use text independent voice recognition. This is defined as a system that recognises the user not based upon specific phrases. However, text independent voice recognition systems are exponentially more difficult to successfully manage (Jain et al., 2008).

3D facial recognition is gaining wider acceptance than other form of biometric technologies especially at the travel level and for border security. Facial recognition is less intrusive because distant cameras can take a picture and verify identity while the subject is moving within the operational range of distance and speed.

Multimodal biometrics and analytics is the new form of emerging biometrics applications. Pato and Millett (2010) explained that biometric modality "is the combination of a biometric trait, sensor type, and algorithms for extracting and processing the digital representations of the trait. When any two of these three constituents differ from one system to the next, the systems are said to have different modalities."

When two or more biometric technologies are combined to provide enhanced security, the system is called a multimodal biometric system which provides higher level of assurance of a proper match in verification and identification systems. The multimodal biometric systems offer substantial improvement in the matching accuracy of a system depending upon the information being combined and the fusion methodology adopted (AlMahafzah et al., 2012):

- **Multi Sensor:** Multiple sensors can be used to collect the same biometric;

- **Multimodal:** Multiple biometric modalities can be collected from the same individual, e.g. fingerprint and face, which requires different sensors;
- **Multi Sample:** Multiple readings of the same biometric are collected during the enrolment and/or recognition phases, e.g. a number of fingerprint readings are taken from the same finger;
- **Multiple Algorithms:** Multiple algorithms for feature extraction and matching are used on the same biometric sample; and
- **Multi-Instance:** Use the same type of raw biometric sample and processing on multiple instances of similar body parts, (such as two fingers, or two irises).

Broadly speaking, information fusion process can be divided into three parts: *pre-mapping fusion, midst-mapping fusion, and post-mapping fusion* (or late fusion). In pre-mapping fusion, information can be combined at sensor level or feature level. On the other hand, multimodal biometric identification systems can be broadly categorised into 4 types based on the information extracted from the sensor:

- **Sensor-Level:** The consolidation of evidence presented by multiple sources of raw data before they are subjected to feature extraction. Sensor-level fusion can be organised in three classes: (1) single sensor-multiple instances, (2) intra-class multiple sensors, and (3) inter-class multiple sensors. Sensor level fusion can benefit multi-sample systems which capture multiple snapshots of the same biometric.
- **Score-Level:** The match scores output by multiple biometric matchers are consolidated into a match score (a scalar). It is commonly used to match scores that are available with sufficient information to distinguish between a genuine and a false claim.
- **Decision-Level:** Fusion is carried out at the abstract or decision level when only final decisions are available, this is the only available fusion strategy (e.g. AND, OR, Majority Voting, Weighted Majority Voting, Bayesian Decision Fusion). It is the most abstract level and consolidates multiple accept/reject decisions from multiple sensors into one decision. This approach takes advantage of the tailored processing performed by each biometric sensor. It also requires the least communication bandwidth and, thus, supports scalability in terms of the number and types of biometric sensors.

- **Feature-Level:** The feature sets originating from multiple biometric algorithms are consolidated into a single feature set by applying feature normalisation, transformation, and reduction schemes. Feature-level fusion can be organised in two categories: intra-class and inter-class. Intra-class is again classified into four subcategories: (a) Same sensor-same features, (b) Same sensor-different features, (c) Different sensors-same features, and (d) Different sensors-different features. Feature-level fusion has the benefit of detecting correlated feature values generated by different biometric algorithms and, in the process, identifying a salient set of features to improve recognition accuracy.

Feature and score level fusion have been shown to enhance accuracy to a greater degree than decision-level fusion. However, as the sensors become more dissimilar, feature- and score-level fusion become more complex to implement.

According to Veeramachaneni et al. (2005), ad hoc techniques in multimodal authentication have been demonstrated to be effective but not always optimum in terms of accuracy. For example, the BioID system (Frischholz & Dieckmann, 2000) chooses from different fusion strategies to vary the system security levels. The fusion options, however, contain only a few rules, typically the "and" and "or" rules, which severely restricting the rule search.

Multimodal systems help overcome limitations of single biometric solutions, such as when a user does not have a quality biometric sample to present to the system and to reduce the probability for the system to be tricked fraudulently. Call centres in various industries are implementing the type of technology incorporating speech detection with analytics. Call centres are not only positively identifies the person on the call, but the system will also judge the emotion of the caller base on factors such as: pitch, rhythm, tonality and cadence.

Other emerging methods are Face Recognition across Facial Expressions and Body Gestures, Audio and Video Motion Analysis for Detection of Spontaneous Emotions, and Biometrics beyond the Visible Spectrum.

Table 1 summarises the common biometric vectors used in human authentication.

Table 1. Some common biometric vectors

Biometric Vectors	Explanations
Brainwaves EEG (Electroencephalogram)	**Pros:** The patterns of our brainwaves are highly individual **Cons:** the equipment is bulky and takes long period to collect EEG data with electrodes or magnetic resonance imaging
Ear pinnae	**Pros:** the ridges of cartilage and skin that surround our ears have distinctive shapes that can be used to identify a person **Cons:** Techniques in capturing ear prints is immature
Heartbeat Electro-cardiography (ECG)	**Pros:** Simpler algorithms and capturing method (e.g. Fingertip sensor) than EEG **Cons:** False Positive Rate will require a combination with other form of identification method to augment unique matching
Retina Scan	**Pros:** High accuracy **Cons:** discomfort to people require gazing at light source
Iris	**Pros:** Iris not change much over age as fingerprint does; no need for bright light source as Retina Scan **Cons:** Can be fooled by contact lens
DNA (Deoxyribonucleic acid)	**Pros:** Unique to each person, simple sampling technique as forensic fingerprinting **Cons:** DNA may infringe the privacy of a person's genetic, ethnic and health information
Vascular or Palm Vein Pattern	**Pros:** Require active blood stream thus very difficult to forge, highly accurate, less intrusive than DNA **Cons:** Vendors holding secret their liveness detection methods
Hand Shape (Hand Geometry)	**Pros:** Robust in identifying people for border security **Cons:** Possible to fool with casts of hands using the appropriate materials
Face Recognition	**Pros:** Traditional for short and long range recognition **Cons:** high error rate for 2D recognition, moving to 3D still need time
Signature	**Pros:** Widely used in in the field of document examination **Cons:** Too many external factors under which signatures are written may affect the condition of the signature
Fingerprint	**Pros:** One of most familiar and widely acceptable methods, relatively cheap to implement **Cons:** Gelatine can be used to make false fingertips. Fingerprints can be distorted with age or wounds
Speech or Voice Recognition	**Pros:** Most widely used for both human and machine detection **Cons:** Not secure
Teeth	**Pros:** Dental records are one of the most reliable means of identifying a person **Cons:** Keep record update to reflect regular dental work makes it not practical
Lip Movement or Voice Activity Detection (VAD)	**Pros:** Cheap to implement and simple to capture **Cons:** may require work in conjunction with voice recognition to improve accuracy

CRYPTOGRAPHY AND IDENTITY MANAGEMENT

Cryptography is a security mechanism for protecting information from third party unauthorised disclosure. Secrecy of the message is protected by transforming the information into a form that is unreadable to humans and machines that are not specially taught to know the way to reversing the transformation back to the original information content. The transformation process performed on the original data is referred to as "encryption". The process of reversing the transformation, to restore the original data, is referred to as "decryption". A key is a randomly-generated number factored into the operation of the transformation process to make the result dependent on the key. The key helps make the transformed information more difficult to break and personalise the algorithm so that the same algorithm used on the same content can produce different outputs for each different key values.

In data communications, cryptography is necessary when communicating over the Internet, which is an untrusted medium. In relation to IAM, there are five primary functions of cryptography:

- **Privacy/Confidentiality:** Ensuring that only the intended recipients are able to read the message but no other one can.
- **Authentication:** Ensuring the person's identity is correct, belongs to the right person and legitimate.
- **Integrity:** Assuring the receiver that the received message has not been altered in any way from the original.
- **Non-Repudiation:** A mechanism to prove that the sender really sent this message.
- **Key Exchange:** The method by which crypto keys are shared between sender and receiver.

There are three board types of cryptographic algorithms based on the number of keys that are employed for encryption and decryption:

- **Symmetric Key Cryptography or Secret Key Cryptography (SKC):** Use single secret key for both encryption and decryption. The secret key is required to be protected and distributed between the sender and receiver prior use. This SKC is primarily used for privacy and confidentiality of the information.

Data Encryption Standard (DES) is one of the most well-known SKC algorithms designed by IBM in the 1970s. DES employs a 56-bit private key to operate on 64-bit blocks data with a complex set of rules and transformations that were designed specifically to yield fast hardware implementations. Triple-DES (3DES) is a variant of DES using three 56-bit keys and makes three encryption/decryption passes over the block of data.

- **Public Key Cryptography (PKC):** Using one key for encryption and another for decryption; also known as asymmetric encryption. PKC is primarily used for authentication, non-repudiation, and key exchange. PKC uses a key pair that consists of a private key and a public key; both keys are used for encrypting and decrypting messages. The private key kept secret to the owner only. The public key, on the other hand, is made known to anyone who needs to use it. The message sender encrypts the message using the receiver's public key. The receiver then decrypts the message with his private key.

Public key encryption is generally computationally expensive and requires much longer key material than a symmetric key algorithm to provide equivalent security. Hence it is used sparingly, preferably only for cryptographic operations that need its unique properties. Symmetric key encryption is more widely used for bulk data encryption/decryption, because it demands less of the CPU.

The Rivest-Shamir-Adleman (RSA) algorithm is the most common PKC implementation, named for the three MIT mathematicians who developed the algorithm. Today, RSA is widely used for key exchange, digital signatures, or encryption of small blocks of data. RSA uses a variable size encryption block and a variable size key. RSA key-pair is derived from a very large number, n, that is the product of two prime numbers chosen according to special rules; these primes may be 100 or more digits in length each, yielding an n with roughly twice as many digits as the prime factors. The public key information includes n and a derivative of one of the factors of n; an attacker cannot determine the prime factors of n (and, therefore, the private key) from this information alone and that is what makes the RSA algorithm so secure.

Identity Based Cryptography (IBC) is one of the types of public key cryptography, which was initially proposed by Shamir (1984) to reduce the need for certificate authorities to distribute public key certificate. IBC use users' identifier information such as phone number, email, IP addresses, or domain name as a public key using RSA algorithm to allow users to perform verification from digital signatures. IBC allow any two users to communicate securely, and verification of signatures each other without exchanging any type of keys.

A key pair can be used to authenticate the identity of a message sender using the X.509 digital identity signature using his own private key. The receiver then decrypts the digital signature using the sender's public key.

Public and symmetric key encryption methods are often combined. One example of their combination is the Internet Key Exchange (IKE) protocol of the IP Security Protocol (IPSec). IPSec provides security services for traffic at the network layer, or IP layer through use of both cryptographic and protocol security mechanisms. IPSec supports data confidentiality, data integrity, data origin authentication, and access control. IPSec may be used to protect packets between two hosts, between a host and a security gateway, or between two security gateways.

- **Hashing:** Refers to the process of using mathematical functions to perform one way irreversible transformation of the information, providing a digital fingerprint. Hashing is used primarily for message integrity. Hashing functions, also called message digests and one-way encryption, are algorithms that, in essence, use no key. Hash algorithms are typically used to provide a digital fingerprint of a message's contents, often used to ensure that the message has not been altered by an intruder. Message Digest (MD) algorithms use a series of byte-oriented algorithms that produce a 128-bit hash value from an arbitrary-length message.

MD2, MD4, MD5, SHA, and SHA-256 are examples of hashing algorithms. MD2 is suitable for systems with limited memory, such as smart cards. MD4 is designed specifically for fast processing in software. MD5 has been implemented in a large number of products. Secure Hash Algorithm (SHA) SHA-1 produces a 160-bit hash value. SHA-2 comprises five algorithms in the SHS: SHA-1 plus SHA-224, SHA-256, SHA-384, and SHA-512 which can produce hash values that are 224, 256, 384, or 512 bits in length, respectively. SHA-2 recommends use of SHA-1, SHA-224, and SHA-256 for messages less than 264 bits in length, and employs a 512 bit block size; SHA-384 and SHA-512 are recommended for messages less than 2128 bits in length, and employs a 1,024 bit block size.

SHA-3 is the current Secured Hashing Standard from NIST is an alternative to SHA-2 using a family of hash algorithms based on sponge functions. The NIST version can support hash output sizes of 256 and 512 bits.

Password/Token-Based Identity and Access Management

Password and token based Identity and Access Management refers to the systems and processes that require the users to use password with or without the incorporation of a token to perform the authentication and authorisation activities. The token is required to provide unique identification of the holder of that token to identify themselves to the IAM system to gain access to applications and system resources according to the access right assigned to each of the particular user is allowed to access to while preventing he/she from accessing the system resources he/she is forbade.

A security token is a physical device used to prove a person's identity electronically in addition to or in place of a password to prove that the user is who he/she claims to be. The physical door key is one of the examples of a security token to control the access through the door.

There are different kinds of security tokens. The security token can be a USB key with bootstrap secret passcode; a dedicated random number generator; a smart card; a Radio-frequency identification device (RFID); or even a mobile phone.

The following Figure 1 shows two generations of security tokens used by a bank, the older generation has one button only. Pushing the button will generate a one-time password (OTP) based on a pre-installed cryptographic algorithm. The new generation token has a few more buttons. Different buttons are required in different operations and a device password is required each time when the device is activated.

The token usually requires a serial number to pair with a seed file synchronised with the server at the set up time. Other type of OTP token may use a hash chain algorithm to generate a series of OTP based on a synchronised secret shared key between the device and the server. The vulnerability of first generation OTP token setup is that attackers could steal details of which serial numbers correspond to which seed files or keys.

Figure 1. Two generations of security token

The Google Authenticator mobile app is an example of using the mobile phone as the token that uses time synchronisation (which involves the token and the server both generating new OTPs based on a numeric version of the current time) to increase the security level of access a person's Google account. After a person has entered the Google user name and password on the usual login screen, a second screen prompts for the onetime security code, to be generated by the mobile app, which valid for 60 seconds only.

FIRST GENERATION ACCESS CONTROL TECHNOLOGIES

LDAP, Kerberos, Radius, and X.509

A directory is required to authenticate the name of an entity. The directory is able to provide specific functions for searching, browsing, and updating. The directory contains descriptive, attribute-based information about the entities listed in the database and is able to offer sophisticated data mining capabilities.

In the 1980s, telecommunication companies such as, the International Telecommunication Union (ITU), developed the X.500 Directory Access Protocol (DAP) specifications to introduce the concept of directory services to information technology and computer networking basing on the Open Systems Interconnection (OSI) protocol stack. Lightweight Directory Access Protocol (LDAP) is one of the well-known alternatives to DAP in 1990s. LDAP has influenced the design of many Internet protocols, such as the XML Enabled Directory (XED), and the Service Location Protocol (SLP). Microsoft has incorporated LDAP as part of its Active Directory services.

An LDAP directory is replicated among many servers called Directory System Agent (DSA), which are synchronised periodically. A DSA receives a request (such as, Bind, Search, Modify, Add and Delete) from a client will take responsibility for the request and pass it to other DSAs to receive the result of the request and provide a single coordinated response back to the client. The default port used on TCP and UDP is 389, or on port 636 for LDAPS.

LDAP authentication ranges from anonymous authentication, which gives the least access to information; to administrator authentication, which gives complete access to the information on the DSA as well as the ability to add and remove data. The core unique identifier of each request is the Distinguished

Name (DN), which consists of the user-id plus other information that identifies the user uniquely on the network.

The Kerberos protocol was developed by MIT in the 1990s with specific aim to provide reliable authentication over open networks. In 2007, MIT established the Kerberos Consortium to foster continued development. The Kerberos technology is widely adopted in many UNIX and Linux operating systems. Microsoft Windows 2000 and later operating systems use Kerberos as the default authentication method for setting changing user passwords.

Kerberos uses the term Ticket to describe the token that a client presents to an Application Server to demonstrate the authenticity of its identity. Tickets are issued by the Authentication Server and are encrypted using the secret key of the service they are intended for. Each ticket has an expiration period (for example 10 hours). This is to control the authentication server not able to reuse any already issued ticket to limit any abuse over time.

The core control centre in Kerberos is the Key Distribution Centre (KDC), which consists of the Authentication Server (AS), Ticket Granting Server (TGS) and a Database.

Figure 2 shows the Client performs Request and receives Response with the Application Server (AP-REQ & AP-REP), the Ticket Granting Server (TGS-REQ / TGS-REP) and the Authentication Server (AS-REQ / AS-REP).

Remote Authentication Dial-In User Service (RADIUS) was originally developed by Livingston Enterprises for their PortMaster series of network

Figure 2. A simple Kerberos schematic

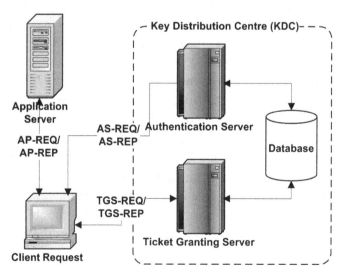

access servers in early 1990s, which was subsequently bought over by Lucent Technologies in 1997. RADIUS is used for remote access servers to communicate with a central server to authenticate dial-in users and authorise their access to the requested system or service.

RADIUS is used extensively to manage access to the Internet or internal networks, using different access mechanisms such as modems, DSL, optical access points, VPNs and network ports. RADIUS messages are sent as User Datagram Protocol (UDP) messages. In general, UDP port 1812 is used for RADIUS authentication messages and port 1813 is used for RADIUS accounting messages.

A RADIUS server is able to provide *Authentication, Authorisation* and *Accounting* services. The RADIUS accounting service keeps track of the session start and end information, indicating the amount of resources (such as time, packets, bytes, and so on) used during the session. Therefore, Internet service provider (ISP) might use RADIUS access control and accounting software to perform special security and billing.

The RADIUS authentication mechanism is as follows:

1. Users establish a PPP connection with a network access server.
2. The user and the access server exchange authentication information using CHAP (Challenge Handshake Authentication Protocol) or EAP (Extensible Authentication Protocol).
3. The access server prepares an "Authentication Packet" and sends to the RADIUS server with the password being encrypted.
4. The RADIUS server validates the user against the accounting database for appropriate access rights and then returns either an "Authentication Acknowledgment" or an "Authentication Reject" message to the access server.

X.509 is one of the vital standards that support the Public Key Infrastructure (PKI) used in secured web and email transport. X.509 v3 certificate standard is defined in RFC 5280 (IETF, 2008).

Applications in web browsers use X.509 certificates enable Transport Layer Security (TLS) protocol to provide private and authenticated traffic. Software vendors used X.509 certificate to sign their software coding with proprietary code-signing schemes, such as Microsoft Authenticode.

Before we touch further on X.509, we like to provide a little bit of the Public Key Infrastructure (PKI). PKI solves the problem of releasing secret keys to other parties over the Internet. PKI uses a set of key pair (one public key and one private key) which are mathematically related.

The way how PKI works is that the owner of a key pair sends the public key to the correspondents and asks them to use that public key to encrypt all the messages before sending to the owner of the key. The owner then uses the private key to decrypt the message.

To ensure that the public key we use to encrypt the message really belongs to the owner, PKI incorporates a Certification Authority (CA) to issue signed (encrypted) binary certificates that affirm the identity of the certificate subject and bind that identity to the public key contained in the certificate. Comodo, Symantec and GoDaddy are some of the most widely trusted CAs. However, one point that we need to be aware of is that if one CA is compromised, the security of the entire PKI would be affected.

We provide a layout of a X.509 certificate in following Table 2. It contains the user's name and public key, as well as other information about the user. X.509 certificate enables the CA to give a certificate's receiver a means of trusting not only the public key of the certificate's subject, but also other information about the certificate's subject. There are other information can be included in the certificate such as, email address, an authorisation to sign documents of a given value. An X.509 certificate has a Validity Period which sets when the certificate will expire and no longer be valid. A CA can issue a Certificate Revocation List (CRL) for the users to validate a certificate received.

Table 2. An X.509 certificate format

X.509 Version
Serial Number
Signature Algorithm Identifier
Issuer Name
Validity Period
Subject Name
Public Key Information
Issuer Unique ID
Subject Unique ID
Extensions

To further protect the authenticity, confidentiality, and integrity of a message being sent, people would perform the followings before sending the whole package across:

- Encrypting the message digest with the sender's private key, (produce a unique hash for non-repudiation purpose);
- Encrypting the message with a symmetric key (the symmetric key needs to be sent to the receiver for decryption purpose); and
- Encrypting the symmetric key with receiver's public key.

There is an SSL utility called DigiCert which verifies the authenticity of a secure website that the web browser visits and provides an X.509 SSL certificate. DigiCert is located in Lehi, Utah, and has provided full line of 2048-Bit SSL Certificates with strong encryption and authentication, tools, and platforms for optimal SSL certificate management. DigiCert offers a full line of SSL Certificate products (https://www.digicert.com):

- **Wildcard SSL:** Using one certificate to secure all servers and subdomains in a domain.
- **Single Certificate:** Secure a single server with a single name.
- **Multi-Domain Certificate:** Using one certificate to secure up to 250 server connected in a SAN.
- **Extended Validation Certificate:** Controlling the activation of the green bar in newer versions of browsers.
- **Extended Validation Multi-Domain Certificate:** Using one certificate to secure up to 25 server names with EV security.

SECOND GENERATION ACCESS CONTROL TECHNOLOGIES

Cross Domain Federation and SAML

The need for efficient access to distributed resources is becoming increasingly important for mobile end users. The ability to manage identity effectively is a paramount concern. Federated identity is a set of mechanisms through which companies can share identity information between secure networks. The Cross Domain Federation of Identity is established with a set of technologies, standards and use-cases which serve to support the federation of identity information across different security domains. The goal is to enable users of one domain to securely access data or systems of another domain seamlessly.

The notion of identity federation is broad. There are different approaches to Cross Domain Identity Federation: User-Controlled or User-Centric scenarios, as well as Enterprise-Controlled or Business-to-Business scenarios. OpenID and CardSpace are examples of User-Centric federation model since they put the user in control of his/her identity as well as deciding whether or not to extend an identity to other participating domains.

Identity federation relies heavily on the use of open industry standards and/ or openly published specifications, covering aspects such as cross-domain web-based SSO, cross-domain user account provisioning, cross-domain entitlement management and cross-domain user attribute exchange.

Security Tokens (such as, Simple Web Tokens, JSON Web Tokens, and SAML assertions) are heavily used in the Cross Domain Federation. WS-Security defines the mechanisms for providing security-token-based integrity and confidentiality on Web Service. On the other hand, WS-Security Extensions (WS-Trust, WS-Policy, WS-Federation) is a collection of Web Service specifications for layering authentication, authorisation and policy across multiple security domains. WS-Federation defines a framework for federation by allowing users to develop Profiles to specify the details for implementation.

The author treats the Security Assertion Mark-up Language (SAML) as the second generation of IAM technologies in the sense that SAML is able to eliminate the need for application-specific sign-on credentials with the use of XML-based signed X.509 digital certificate to achieve SSO. SAML SSO uses existing IAM technologies such as Active Directory, LDAP, and single-use, expiring, X.509 digital certificates to exchange authentication and authorisation credentials between an identity provider (IdP) and a service provider (SP) that have an established trust relationship.

SAML was defined by the OASIS Security Services Technical Committee in 2002 and version 2.0 was approved as an OASIS Standard in 2005. Approved errata for SAML V2.0 was last introduced in 2012 (Lockhart & Campbell, 2008).

According to the SAML 2.0 specification (Lockhart and Campbell, 2008), SAML is an XML based messaging protocol detailing whether particular users are authenticated, what kind of rights, roles and access they have and how they can use the resources based on those rights and roles. SAML works with HTTP, SMTP, FTP and SOAP, among other protocols and technologies.

There are three roles defined in the SAML specification: the Principal (typically a user), the Identity Provider (IdP), and the Service Provider (SP).

SAML describes trust assertions for user identities and authorisations. It defines how to transfer the security level (authorisation and authentication), along with XML encryption and PKI. XML Key Management Specification (XKMS) can be used to manage XML encryption keys used by SAML.

The three main components of the SAML specification are:

- **Assertions:** There are three kinds of SAML assertions. *Authentication assertions* are those in which the user has proven his identity. *Attribute assertions* contain specific information about the user, such as his spending limits. *Authorisation decision* assertions identify what the user can do, for example, whether he can buy an item.
- **Protocol:** SAML can specify the way that SAML asks for and gets assertion, for example, using SOAP over HTTP.
- **Binding**: This details exactly how SAML message exchanges are mapped into SOAP exchanges.

Each assertion involves at least two parties: (a) the Asserting party (such as SAML authorities) which asserts that a particular object (i.e., a user) has been authenticated and has given associated attributes. (b) the Relying party (the system, or administrative domain) which relies on the information supplied to it by the asserting party. It is up to the relying party as to whether it will trust the assertions provided to it.

The assertions are exchanged among sites and services using the protocol and binding. Those assertions are the core information required to authenticate the user among different sites.

The following Figure 3 is an example of steps that are involved when a person is authenticated at a SP and then wants to go to a partner SP.

1. The user has authenticated himself with SP1 and wants to visit SP2. He clicks on a link to go to SP2.
2. Instead of being sent straight to SP2, the user is sent to the SAML service for SP1.
3. The SAML service of SP1 appends a partner ID and a special handle to SP2's URL in the user's request message and sends the request to the SAML service of SP2.
4. The user is allowed to access SP2, fully authenticated. The user can perform transactions on SP2 just as if he had logged directly into SP2.

Figure 3. A sample SAML authentication flow

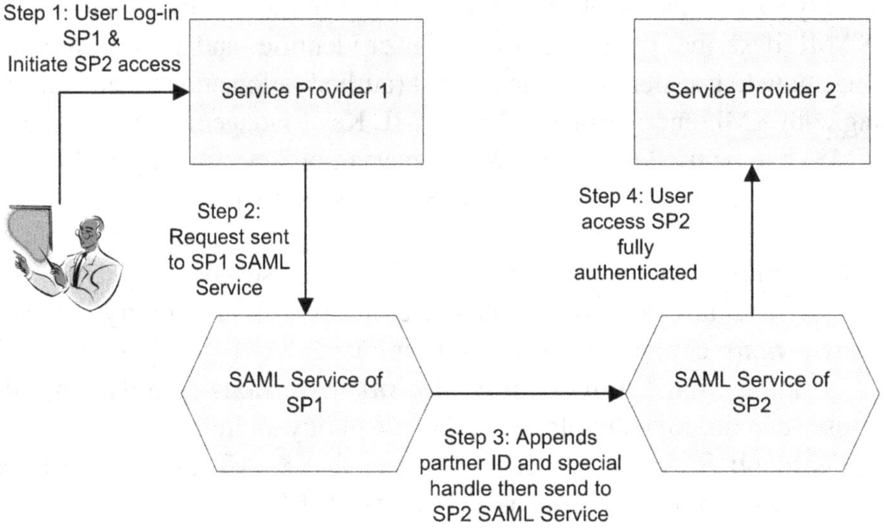

The following is a sample AuthenticationQuery SAML request message:

```
< ?xml version="1.0" encoding="UTF-8"?>
< Request
RequestID="String"
MajorVersion="0" MinorVersion="0" >
< AuthenticationQuery>
<saml:Subject>
< saml:NameIdentifier Name="admin" SecurityDomain="UserID"/>
< saml:NameIdentifier Name="admin" SecurityDomain="Password"/>
< /saml:Subject>
< /AuthenticationQuery>
</Request>
```

There are many companion protocols working alongside with SAML. In here, we like to touch on the XML Key Management (XKMS) protocol. XKMS is a protocol for distributing and registering public keys, for use in conjunction with the proposed standard for XML Signature. The XKMS specification comprises two parts, the XML Key Information Service Specification (X-KISS) and the XML Key Registration Service Specification (X-KRSS).

X-KISS defines how a Trust service can resolve public key information contained in XML-SIGelements. The X-KISS protocol allows a client of such a service to delegate part or all of the tasks required to process <ds:KeyInfo> elements to an underlying service implementation.. A key objective of the protocol design is to minimise the complexity of application implementations by allowing them to become clients and thereby to be shielded from the complexity and syntax of the underlying PKI used to establish trust relationships. The underlying PKI may be based upon a different specification such as PKI for X.509 certificates (PKIX), Simple Public Key Infrastructure (SPKI), and Pretty Good Privacy (PGP).

Another one is the XML Access Control Language (XACL) or XML Access Control Markup Language (XACML), which is an XML-based language to specify security policies to be enforced on specific accesses to XML documents. XACL enables the initiator not only to securely browse XML documents but also to securely update each document element. Similar to existing policy languages, XACL is used to specify an object-subject-action-condition oriented policy in the context of a particular XML document. The notion of subject comprises identity, group, and role.

The XACL provisional authorisation process works in the following stages: (1) the user makes an access request to a SP. The SP informs the user that his request will be authorised provided he/she (and the system) takes certain actions or that the request is denied but the system must still take certain actions. (2) The XACL processor conducts certain provisional actions such as: auditing, digital signature verification, encryption, and XSL transformations in addition to write, create and delete actions. (3) The SP performs the required transaction based on the results of the provisional actions and the result is returned to the XACL processer. (4) The XACL processor returns the resulting message based on the provisional actions taken.

These provisional actions enable us to specify policies such as the following:

- Whether a user is authorised to access confidential information, but the access must be logged.
- Whether a user is authorised to read sensitive information, but must sign a terms and conditions statement first.
- If unauthorised access is detected, a warning message must be sent to an administrator.

In the existing access control mechanisms, these provisional actions are required to be pre-programmed within the applications. However, in the XACL provisional system, they can be processed by in the policy enforcement plug-in modules instead.

Third Generation Access Control Technologies: OpenID and OAuth

We now come to our coverage of the third generation access control technologies. The author treats OpenID and OAuth are two of the candidates in this category because they work hand-in-hand and are defined at more recent stage of the Internet age. These two standards have embraced the concepts of decentralised and federated identity management practices rather than the centralised approach.

A person can choose to use an OpenID or become an OpenID Provider. Open ID supports the notion of *SelfIssued OpenID Provider*, which allows the establishment of a personal, self-hosted OpenID Provider to operate and issues self-signed ID Tokens. There is no need for any registration or approval by any governing organisation.

OpenID is founded in 2005 by an open source community, now called the OpenID Foundation. The current specification is OpenID 2.0 (OpenID, 2007). The OpenID 2.0 Connect Core specification defines the core OpenID Connect functionality of OpenID. OpenID's authentication is built on top of OAuth 2.0 with the use of claims to communicate information about the user.

Today, OpenID is widely supported by large organisations such as Google, Yahoo, AOL, and Flickr. Many sites such as Google and Yahoo have already given their users an OpenID.

The core of OpenID is the *ID Token*. It is a JavaScript Object Notation (JSON) Web Token (JWT) containing Claims about the Authentication event. Nesting of ID Token is allowed, which means it may contain other Claims. JWT encodes the Claim as a JSON object contained in a JSON Web Signature (JWS) structure or as the plaintext of a JSON Web Encryption (JWE) structure enabling the Claims to be digitally signed.

Another core OpenID entity is the *OpenID Provider (OP)*. An example of OP is an OAuth 2.0 Authorisation Server which provides the functions of Authenticating the EndUser and providing Claims to a Relying Party about the Authentication event and the EndUser.

The third core OpenID entity is the *Relying Party (RP)*, which is an OAuth 2.0 Client application requiring EndUser Authentication and Claims from an OP.

OpenID also defines an entity called the *UserInfo Endpoint*, which is a secured resource, when presented with an *Access Token* by a SP, returns authorised information about the EndUser represented by the corresponding *Authorisation Grant*.

With OpenID, a person only needs to remember one Open ID username and one password. The OpenID Connect protocol implements authentication as an extension to the OAuth 2.0 authorisation process. It involves the following steps as depicted in Figure 2.4:

1. When a person (the EndUser) enters the OpenID into a website's log-on screen (the RP), the RP sends a request to the OP and browser will divert the person to the appropriate OP for authentication purpose.
2. The EndUser logs in with the OpenID username and password and that OP will authenticate the EndUser and obtain authorisations.
3. The OP will inform the result of the authentication back to the RP with an ID Token and usually an Access Token.
4. The RP can send a request with the Access Token to the UserInfo Endpoint to obtain the EndUser's profile.
5. The UserInfo Endpoint returns Claims about the EndUser to the RP.

One point that needs our attention is that OpenID implements SSO which posts the typical problem of single point of attack. If the OpenID credential of a person is being hacked or phished, the hackers can test websites with which they think that person might have an account and log in as that person.

Open Authorisation (OAuth) is a standard for token-based authentication and authorisation over the Internet. OAuth (http://oauth.net/about/) was conceived in 2007 as an authentication method for the Twitter OpenID implementation. OAuth 2.0 Authorisation Framework contains the following prime components: Bearer Token Usage; JSON Web Token (JWT) Section 2; OpenID Connect Discovery 1.0 and OpenID Connect Dynamic Client.

OAuth and OpenID work hand-in-hand. OAuth tackles the issue of allowing the users to grant access to their private resources on one site (which is the SP), to another site (called Consumer), while OpenID is offering the solution for a single identity to sign into different sites.

The current version OAuth 2.0 (IETF, 2012) provides a framework for OpenID applications to obtain and use identity information about the authentication of an EndUser. The OpenID client (the RP) requests an OpenID Connect with an OpenID Scope Value in the Authorisation Request to the OAuth 2.0 Authentication Server (the OP). The OAuth 2.0 specification assumes that the RP has already obtained configuration information about the OpenID Provider, including its Authorisation Endpoint and Token Endpoint

Figure 4. OpenID connect flow

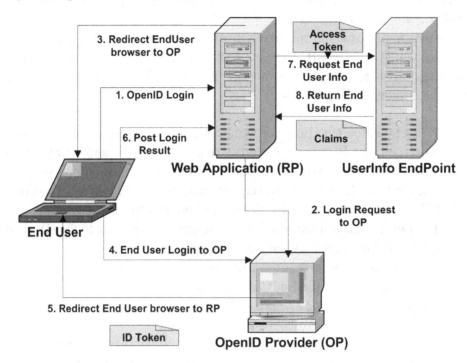

locations. This information is normally obtained via Discovery. Likewise, OAuth 2.0 assumes that the RP has already obtained sufficient credentials and provided information needed to use the OpenID Provider via Dynamic Registration, as described in RFC6749.

According to WiKiPedia (https://en.wikipedia.org/wiki/XACML), OAuth 2.0 is considered to be an authorisation standard. It differs from XACML. OAuth 2.0 is about delegating access control by allowing the users to delegate what an RP service can do; eliminating the needs of providing user credentials among servers; and a policy language with which to express a wide range of access control policies including policies that can use consents handled / defined via OAuth.

On the other hand, XACML does not handle user approval or delegated access or password management. XACML simply provides an access control architecture with the notion of a PDP and a PEP. However, XACML and OAuth can be combined together to deliver a more comprehensive approach to user authorisation.

The OAuth Web site (https://oauth.net/articles/authentication/) stipulates that there are some common risks that need to be considered when using an OAuth-based authentication system:

- OAuth does not define a specific format or structure for the access token itself, it is required for other protocols like OpenID Connect's ID Token to provide a secondary token alongside the access token that communicates the authentication information directly to the client.
- Refresh tokens and assertions may be used to get access tokens without the user being present, and in some cases access grants can occur without the user having to authenticate at all.
- Threat occurs when a client that uses the implicit flow (where the token is passed directly as a parameter in the URL hash) and don't properly use the OAuth state parameter to stop accepting access tokens from sources other than the return call from the token endpoint.
- Most OAuth APIs do not provide any mechanism of audience restriction for the returned information. The system must be designed to communicate the authentication information to a client along with an identifier that the client can recognize and validate, allowing the client to differentiate between an authentication for itself versus an authentication for another application.
- An attacker is able to intercept one of the calls from the client. The attacker could alter the content of the returned user information without the client being aware of the situation. This can be mitigated by getting the authentication information directly from the identity provider during the authentication protocol process (such as alongside the OAuth token) and by protecting the authentication information with a verifiable signature.

Identity and Access Management in the Cloud: System for Cross-Domain Identity Management (SCIM)

The System for Cross-domain Identity Management (SCIM) was originally designed by a working group organised under the Open Web Foundation. It was subsequently transferred to the IETF in 2011, and the current standard, SCIM 2.0 was released as IETF RFC 7643 & 7644 in 2015. SCIM was developed in 2011 using modern protocols like REST and JSON to provide a straightforward approach to manage user identities. SCIM is an HTTP-based application-level protocol for provisioning and managing identity information specified using the SCIM schema. SCIM builds on prior standards such as SPML, vCards, and LDAP in an attempt to be easier for Cloud service providers to adapt.

SCIM uses JSON to define resources and attributes schemas. The schema contains a list of one or more URIs that indicates the attributes contained within a resource. SCIM defines resources such as "id", "externalId", and SCIM resource URIs to enable SCIM to identify and locate resources (Hunt et al., 2015).

IANA has created the "System for Cross-domain Identity Management (SCIM) Schema URIs" registry to manage entries within the "urn:ietf:params:scim" namespace. SCIM schemas and SCIM messages is specified using URIs to identify a specific schema for use with other relevant parties.

SCIM requires the use of Transport Layer Security (TLS) and/or other standard HTTP schemas to handle authentication and authorisation. The different HTTP schemas suggested in the RFC are: TLS Client Authentication, HTTP Origin-Bound Authentication (HOBA), Bearer tokens, Proof-of-possession (PoP) token, HTTP cookies over TLS that contain an authentication state, and even the relatively static and basic authentication methods.

SCIM protocol messages are fixed and defined by the SCIM specifications. The message must contain a URI whose namespace prefix begin with "urn:ietf:params:scim:api:" SCIM is intended for use for cross domain collaborations with varied schemas and implementations. The following Table 3 shows SCIM uses different HTTP Methods to perform different SCIM actions.

SCIM defines a set of query parameters for retrieval, filtering, sorting, and paginating resources. Below is an example of requesting the lastName for all Users start with the letter "J":

Table 3. SCIM usage with HTTP methods

HTTP Method	SCIM Usage
GET	Retrieves one or more complete or partial resources.
POST	Depending on the endpoint, creates new resources, creates a search request, or MAY be used to bulk-modify resources.
PUT	Modifies a resource by replacing existing attributes with a specified set of replacement attributes (replace). PUT MUST NOT be used to create new resources.
PATCH	Modifies a resource with a set of client-specified changes (partial update).
DELETE	Deletes a resource.

```
GET /Users?filter=lastName sw "J"
Host: test.com
Accept: application/scim+json
Authorisation: Bearer iakdj03s93hd8
```

The SCIM standard has grown in popularity with more and more Cloud service providers embracing the technology. Companies including Salesforce. com, Cisco and Google, leading identity management providers Ping Identity, SailPoint, Technology Nexus, and UnboundID Corp., are among those supporters of SCIM implementations. Microsoft Azure Active Directory also supports the automatic provisioning of users and groups to any application or identity store with the SCIM 2.0 protocol.

SCIM 2.0 is released as RFC7642, RFC7643 and RFC7644 under IETF in September 2015, which consists of the following:

• RFC7643 - SCIM: Core Schema

RFC7643 contains a platform-neutral schema and extension model for representing users and groups.

• RFC7644 - SCIM: Protocol

This core specification explains how SCIM supports application-level, REST protocol for provisioning and managing identity data on the web.

• RFC7642 - SCIM: Definitions, Overview, Concepts, and Requirements

This document lists the user scenarios and use cases of SCIM.

Many SaaS providers support proprietary interfaces as well as mechanisms like SCIM to allow standardised communication between identity data stores. This enables organisations to leverage commercial solutions with built-in support for both inbound and outbound SCIM provisioning for a SCIM client application to connect to the user directory of the IdP and monitors it for changes. The changes shall be pushed to the target directories or to SP SCIM endpoints when users are added, modified or deleted. The SaaS providers function as a SCIM server to receive requests for user management and then modify the target directory as required.

Figure 5 explains that SCIM 2.0 is built on an object model where a "Resource" is the common denominator and all SCIM objects are derived

Figure 5. SCIM object model (2016)

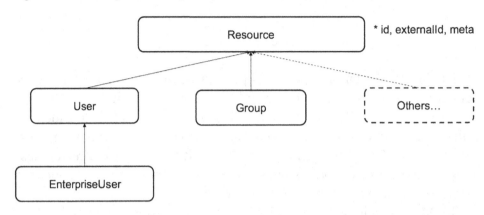

from it. It has "id", "externalId" and "meta" as attribute and RFC7643 defines "User", "Group" and "EnterpriseUser" that extends the common attributes.

SCIM provides a REST API with a set of operations to perform the following operations on resources:

- Create = POST https://example.com/v/resource
- Read = GET https://example.com/v/resource/id
- Replace = PUT https://example.com/v/resource/id
- Delete = DELETE https://example.com/v/resource/id
- Update = PATCH https://example.com/v/resource/id
- Search = GET https://example.com/v/resource?filter={attribute}{op} {value}&sortBy={attributeName}&sortOrder={ascending|descending}
- Bulk = POST https://example.com/v/Bulk

SCIM 2.0 provides three end points to discover supported features and specific attribute details:

- GET /ServiceProviderConfigs

An endpoint used to specify compliance, authentication schemes, and data models.

- GET /ResourceTypes

An endpoint used to discover the types of resources available.

- GET /Schemas

An endpoint with the purpose to introspect resources and attribute extensions.

The create resource operation is performed by sending an HTTP POST request to the resource's respective end point. An example is showed in the following:

```
POST /v2/Users  HTTP/1.1
Accept: application/json
Authorization: Bearer hxc2346793hd8
Host: sample.org
Content-Length: ...
Content-Type: application/json

{
  "schemas":["urn:ietf:params:scim:schemas:core:2.0:User"],
  "externalId":"angschenpwatters",
  "userName":" angschenpwatters ",
  "name":{
    "familyName":"NgChenWatters",
    "givenName":"AlexShipingPaul"
  }
}
```

The SP replies with a response containing the created Resource and HTTP code 201 to indicate that the Resource has been created successfully. The "id" and "meta" data elements have been added by the SP to complete the profile of the User resource. A location header is included to specify where the resource can be found in subsequent requests. An example is given in the following:

```
HTTP/1.1 201 Created
Content-Type: application/scim+json
Location:https://sample.org/v2/Users/1234c256-7f89-345a-
929d-123456704646
ETag: W/"e123ee45f6789b1"

{
  "schemas":["urn:ietf:params:scim:schemas:core:2.0:User"],
```

```
  "id":"1234c256-8f90-453a-919d-1234567046345",
  "externalId":" angschenpwatters ",
  "meta":{
    "resourceType":"User",
    "created":"2016-12-01T09:32:55.567Z",
    "lastModified":"2016-12-01T09:32:55.567Z",
    "location":
"https://sample.org/v2/Users/1234c256-7f89-345a-
929d-123456704646",
    "version":"W\/\" e123ee45f6789b1\""
  },
  "name":{
    "familyName":"NgChenWatters ",
    "givenName":" AlexShipingPaul"
  },
  "userName":" NgChenWatters "
}
```

The following example shows the HTTP GET request is sent to the desired resource end point to fetch the content:

```
GET /v2/Users/1234c256-7f89-345a-929d-123456704646
Host: sample.org
Accept: application/scim+json
Authorization: Bearer hxc2346793hd8
```

The response to a GET contains the Resource. The "etag" header can be used to prevent concurrent modifications of Resources. SCIM supports fetching sets of Resources by querying the Resource end point without the id of a specific Resource. SCIM supports typical filtering operations such as equals, contains, starts with and more. Sorting is also supported in SCIM 2.0. The following shows an example of the response to a GET request with a list of 3 matching resources:

```
{
  "schemas":["urn:ietf:params:scim:api:messages:2.0:ListRespon
se"],
  "totalResults":3,
  "Resources":[
    {
      "id":"c4a56dd7-23a0-8dec-a9dc-ce456e789f10",
      "title":"Director",
      "userName":"ang"
    },
    {
```

```
      "id":"tgvetgh56-334g-d4g4-bfn5-sdf44e54g5f99",
      "title":"Director",
      "userName":"schen"
   }
   {
      "id":"tfgtj6h78-67ug-dnm5-we45-sjli8454g7659",
      "title":"Director",
      "userName":"pwatters"
   }
  ]
}
```

RECENT DEVELOPMENT IN BIOMETRIC TECHNOLOGIES

Face Recognition Across Facial Expressions has gained much market success with many countries' boarder security authorities have implemented many boarder control system using this technology. Traditional facial recognition systems using techniques such as feature based recognition, face geometry based recognition, classifier design and model based methods.

A typical facial recognition system contains a set of EigenFaces (Turk and Pentland, 1991), which are generated by performing Principal Component Analysis (PCA) on a large set of facial images. The EigenFaces is a set of "standardised face ingredients" known as the face space. A new face image is calculated with a set of weights based on the input image and the EigenFaces by projecting the image on each of the EigenFaces. The weights are checked to see if the image is sufficiently close to the face space and try to determine the weight pattern as either a known or unknown person.

Historically, face recognition is facing challenges from different kinds of variations such as facial expressions, poses, non-uniform light illuminations and occlusions (such as: clothing, make up, hair colour or hair style). These approaches use two complementary steps: facial expression recognition and face recognition to improve face recognition across facial expression variation.

The Mutual Information (MI; Riaz et al., 2008) technique is frequently used in the first step to determine the most expressive regions responsible for facial expression appearance. Such a process helps not only improve the facial expression classification accuracy but also reduce the features vector size. In the second step, traditional PCA and EigenFaces for each facial expression class are applied. A face recognition is performed by projecting the face onto the corresponding facial expression EigenFaces.

Body Gesture-based identification system captures and analyses human body gestures and gaits to recognise a particular person. There are a variety of equipment used to capture the human body gestures, such as accelerometer (an electromechanical device used to measure the acceleration forces of a person), video camera recorder, and Microsoft Kinect (a gaming device tracking a person's body gesture with an advanced infrared camera, sensors, and a microphone). The device can capture the patterns at a distance while a person is walking or performing poses in different scenarios. The benefits can be easy to operate and non-intrusive while performing user authentication. However, extra equipment may be required to perform user login, which means it may not be portable and not suitable for daily personal use as yet. Some suggest that the hand operational features, which include parallel, closed, opened, and circular hand movements is able to achieve reach a 90% accuracy rate with a single gesture (Sae-Bae et al., 2012).

Audio and video motion analysis for detection of spontaneous emotions is one of the emerging research advances in the field of "affective computing" with emphasis on teaching the computers to express and recognise affect with the ability to detect and track a person's affective state. This offers the potential to allow a computer system to initiate dialogue with a person based on the perceived emotion of the user so that the system can offer relevant information when a user needs help, such as at a public transport kiosk.

The development is still at its infancy stage as it requires lengthy training process such as the Adult Attachment Interview (AAI) technique, which is a semi-structured interview requiring the participants to describe their early relationships with their parents, and revisit a variety of emotional episodes so as to characterise an individual's current state of mind. The technique of Support Vector Data Description (SVDD) is also employed to fit a boundary with minimal volume around the data space basing on the assumption that the outliers distribute evenly in the feature space. This assumption is to ensure that the error minimisation is corresponding to the minimal volume of the data.

Moreno-Moreno et al. (2009) have described a number of techniques employed in the area of biometrics beyond visible spectrum; which include X-ray (0.01nm to 10nm), Infrared ($0.7\mu m$ to $100\mu m$), Millimetre Waves (1mm to 10mm), and Submillimeter Waves ($100\mu m$ to 1mm). Images captured by Infrared are called the thermograms (or thermographs), which contain patterns of the heat radiated from the body's surface. Images captured beyond the visible spectrum present the benefit that they are less affected by ambient factors such as lighting conditions and occlusions. Another benefit is that they are more robust to spoofing than other biometric traits using images within the visible spectrum.

There are two types of imaging systems. Passive Imaging is collected by receiving natural radiation which has been emitted and reflected from the image. The result is a map of brightness temperature. On the other hand, Active Imaging requires a radiation to be transmitted to the scene and then collect the radiation after reflection form the image, The result is a map of reflectivity of the radiation.

The Infrared imaging is classified into two types of technique, the Reflected Infrared (0.7-2.4 µm) and Thermal Infrared (beyond 2.4 µm). The Reflected IR captures the solar radiation reflected from the object which means it does not capture the information about the thermal properties of the materials of the object. On the other hand, the Thermal Infrared is concerned with the thermal radiation emitted by the objects.

Research (Wang & Leedham, 2006) shows that face and hand vein pattern captured using Near Infrared (NIR 0.7 to 1µm), Medium Wave IR (MWIR 3 to 5µm) and Long Wave IR (LWIR 8 - 14 µm) are to some extent, environmental illumination static. Images captured by NIR systems are body condition invariant and can provide good quality vein patterns near the skin surface.

CONTEMPORARY ISSUES AFFECTING THE SECURITY TECHNOLOGY DEVELOPMENT OF DIGITAL IDENTITIES

Despite the insecurity problem of using password, it remains the simplest and cheapest solution to the IAM problem domain. Over the year we have witnessed numerous improvements been put in the password and token based identity management and authentication systems. All the improvements have help one way or the other, but have also opened up newer form of attacks and insecurities, such as the two-factor authentication scheme may be defeated by using the man-in-the-mobile technique; and the IAM system could be spoofed into false recovery mode to open up unauthorised access.

Nowadays, many governments give top priority to countering the threat from terrorism at home and overseas. However, finding a universal cure to the problem proves to be difficult as potential suspects changing their identities and their digital identities constantly.

What it really comes down to is to what extend can we define who we are, whether we are the contents of our brains, the words utter from our mouths, the text and emojos we keyed in our phones, the gestures we pose, the shapes, textures and rhythms of our bodies, or the tools and devices we create and use.

Perhaps an approach which uses aspects of all of these will best cover all our needs is requiring a dedicated identity hardware for each person. The cost cannot be prohibitively high, so that governments can issue one to every citizen to cover all their identity needs. One point we need to be aware of: we are stepping into civil rights privacy issue – a very sensitive issue for most democracy countries.

CONCLUSION

This chapter has discussed the technologies and standards used at different generations of IAM solutions such as LDAP, Kerberos, Radius, X.509, Cross Domain Collaboration, SAML, OpenID, and OAuth. The next chapter will present to our readers about the importance of managing a person's identity life cycle, which covers the entire process of IAM over time.

REFERENCES

Biometrics History. (2006). Available: http://www.biometrics.gov/documents/biohistory.pdf

OverviewS. C. I. M. (2016). Available: http://www.simplecloud.info/

Almahafzah, H., Imran, M., & Sheshadri, H. (2012). *Multibiometric: Feature Level Fusion Using FKP Multi-Instance biometric*. arXiv preprint arXiv:1210.0818

Cameron, K. (2005). *The Laws of Identity*. Microsoft Corporation.

Fearon, J. D. (1999). *What is Identity (as we now use the word)?* (Unpublished manuscript). Stanford University.

Frischholz, R. W., & Dieckmann, U. (2000). BioID: A multimodal biometric identification system. *Computer*, *33*, 64–68.

Hird, M. R., & Harrop, M. (2010). *X.idmdef* (Final version for approval). International Telecommunication Union.

Hunt, P., Grizzle, K., Wahlstroem, E., & Mortimore, C. (2015). *System for cross-domain identity management: core schema.* Internet Engineering Task Force. doi:10.17487/RFC7644

IETF. (2008). RFC 5280: internet x.509 public key infrastructure certificate and certificate revocation list profile.

IETF. (2012). RFC6749: The OAuth 2.0 Authorization Framework.

ISO/IEC. (2009). 24760 (working draft) information technology -- security techniques -- a framework for identity management.

ITU-T. (2009a). Recommendation ITU-T X.1250: Baseline capabilities for enhanced global identity management and interoperability. International Telecommunication Union.

ITU-T. (2009b). Recommendation ITU-T Y.2720: NGN identity management framework. International Telecommunication Union.

Jain, A. K., Flynn, P. J., & Ross, A. A. (2008). *Handbook of biometrics.* Springer. doi:10.1007/978-0-387-71041-9

Jaquet-Chielle, D., Benoist, E. & Anrig, B. (2006). *Identity in a networked world use cases and scenarios.* Future of Identity in the Information Society.

Kaucher, C. 2013. *Biometrics 101.* Available: http://www.dfba.mil/References/Tutorial/default.aspx

Lockhart, H., & Campbell, B. (2008). Security assertion markup language (SAML) V2.0 technical overview. *OASIS.*

Macgregor, W., Dutcher, W., & Khan, J. (2006). *An Ontology of Identity Credentials Part 1: Background and Formulation. October: Draft Special Publication 800-103.* National Institute of Information and Technology.

Mccallister, E., Grance, T., & Scarfone, K. (2009). *Guide to Protecting the Confidentiality of Personally Identifiable Information (PII) (Draft).* National Institute of Standards and Technology.

Moreno-Moreno, M., Fierrez, J., & Ortega-Garcia, J. (2009). *Biometrics beyond the visible spectrum: imaging technologies and applications. Biometric ID management and multimodal communication.* Springer.

Nadort, A. (2007). *The Hand Vein Pattern Used as a Biometric Feature. Master of Science programme Physics of Life.* Free University.

OPENID. (2007). *OpenID Authentication 2.0 - Final*. Available: http://openid. net/specs/openid-authentication-2_0.html#toc

Pato, J. N., & Millett, L. I. (2010). *Biometric recognition: Challenges and opportunities*. National Academies Press.

Riaz, Z., Mayer, C., Wimmer, M., & Radig, B. (2008). Model based face recognition across facial expressions. *BUJICT Journal*, *1*, 17–24.

Sae-Bae, N., Ahmed, K., Isbister, K., & Memon, N. (2012). Biometric-rich gestures: a novel approach to authentication on multi-touch devices. *30th ACM Conference on Human Factors in Computing Systems (CHI '12)*, 977 - 986. doi:10.1145/2207676.2208543

Turk, M., & Pentland, A. (1991). Eigenfaces for recognition. *Journal of Cognitive Neuroscience*, *3*(1), 71–86. doi:10.1162/jocn.1991.3.1.71 PMID:23964806

Veeramachaneni, K., Osadciw, L. A., & Varshney, P. K. (2005). An adaptive multimodal biometric management algorithm. *Systems, Man, and Cybernetics, Part C: Applications and Reviews. IEEE Transactions on*, *35*, 344–356.

Wang, L., & Leedham, G. (2006). Near- and far- infrared imaging for vein pattern biometrics. *2006 IEEE International Conference on Video and Signal Based Surveillance*. doi:10.1109/AVSS.2006.80

Wason, T., Cantor, S., Hodges, J., Kemp, J., & Thompson, P. (2005). *Liberty ID-FF Architecture Overview: Version: 1.2-errata-v1.0*. Liberty Alliance Project.

Chapter 3
The Role of Identity Management Life Cycle

ABSTRACT

The life cycle management of a person's identity includes the technologies used for provisioning and password resets, the processes and policies associated with different technologies, and the important events that happen around the management issues of a person's identity. This chapter will discuss the entire process in managing the life cycle of identities using scenarios in illustrating how life cycle management is being used in handling the different activities in IAM.

INTRODUCTION

A person's Identity Life Cycle Management (ILM) requires a complete security policies, processes, and technologies in managing a person's identity over a long period of time. It utilises different processes and policies associated with different technologies used for provisioning, audit, governance, synchronisation across different platforms, and ongoing management of user credentials, entitlements and password establishments.

The life cycle of a person's identity encompasses the entire lifespan of a person's need to access critical data, applications and other resources so as for the person to effectively perform tasks and accomplish some kind of business objectives in a particular system.

DOI: 10.4018/978-1-5225-4828-7.ch003

Design questions for ILM may consist of the following:

- Who decides what access a user needs;
- How easy should it be for a user to reset a password;
- How to implement different levels of authentication for highly sensitive information; and
- When and how do we disable a person's identity.

There are policy issues to be considered apart from the processing issues in dealing with the management of the life cycle of identities. Rules and policies shall be appropriately set up so as to ensure a person has the necessary access facility and rights at different times and locations while logging, monitoring and restricting access to enforce appropriate security and protect the organisation from intrusions and frauds. ILM addresses the need for decommissioning, or removing, access when a person leaves the organisation or changes roles within the organisation.

ILM policies need to address the tasks associated with provisioning access to information resources. Personal identities for people such as new customers, employees, or business partners are highly visible and frequently repeated tasks like password resets, moves and changes must be securely and efficiently dealt with to safeguard commercial transactions done over the Internet from using stolen people's identity.

Chapters 1 and 2 have discussed different techniques and technologies which are employed in overcoming the challenges of managing and sharing digital identities. For example, identity federation allows trusted parties to share digital IDs in support of SSO to gain access to more than one network system. The federated model relies on SAML to achieve interoperability across different vendor platforms that provide authentication and authorisation services.

In this chapter, the readers shall learn about the importance of managing a person's identity life cycle, which covers the entire process of identity management over time. This chapter will include different scenarios to illustrate how the life cycle management is used to manage the different activities of IAM.

A BRIEF HISTORY OF IDENTITY LIFE CYCLE MANAGEMENT

The topic of personal Identity life cycle did not gain much attention in the research community until 2006 when Quinn et al. (MacGregor et al., 2006) formed a set of models or "planes" representing different projections of the Identity Credential Ontology (ICO).

The ICO uses the following planes to describe various functionalities in IAM:

- The *Actor Plane* is used to describe the most significant actors and relationships in the domain of identity credential systems.
- The *Issuance Plane* is used to describe the relationships between the Issuing Authority and other parties that are relevant to identity credential issuance, but it does not describe a specific workflow or sequencing.
- The *Maintenance Plane* is used to describe relationships of the Issuing Authority with other parties after issuance of an identity credential. The Issuing Authority interacts with the Credential in order to perform updates, including termination, renewal, suspension, resumption, and modification.
- The second last plane is the *Transaction Plane* which describes the use of an identity credential in a transaction between the Subject and a Relying Party. The Subject presents the identity credential to the Relying Party, and typically receives a receipt from the Relying Party containing information from the identity credential, during the transaction.
- The last plane is the *Life Events Plane* which illustrates events in the life of a Subject that might cause primary identity credentials, secondary identity credentials, or other identity documents to be produced.

This model has captured different aspects ranging from the actors, actions and events involved in the working of identity credentials. However, this multidimensional model incurs difficulties in automating this model for real-world applications.

According to Currie (2013) the term Identity Life Cycle Manager (ILM) was used as one of its products in 2007 offering the ability to manage smart cards and provide credential management features to both Windows Server and third party certification authorities. ILM's predecessor was a Canadian company called Zoomit, which released the product named VIA in 1996. VIA was a meta-directory service which provides directory integration services to combine metadata from a variety of directory sources into a unified view of identity objects, known as the Metaverse.

In early 2010, Microsoft re-branded its product under the name Forefront Identity Manager (FIM). FIM superseded the Microsoft Identity Life Cycle Manager with the addition of a new portal that supports codeless provisioning, user self-service, group management and a workflow engine.

Recently, Microsoft offered Microsoft Identity Manager (MIM) 2016 superseding FIM 2010 R2 adding new features such as Privileged Identity Manager and support in Certificate Management for REST API access. MIM adds a multi-forest topology for virtual smartcard and certificate life cycle management as well as hybrid cloud Microsoft Azure multi-factor authentication.

A GENERIC IDENTITY LIFE CYCLE MANAGEMENT FRAMEWORK

This section will present a generic Identity Life Cycle Management Framework with the help of a taxonomy; which is a particular classification arranged in a hierarchical structure.

A minimal identity life cycle consists of 3 phases: *identity account setup*, *maintenance*, and *culling*.

Account setup consists of assigning users the appropriate access rights to system resources. *Account maintenance* consists of keeping user identity information up-to-date and to adjust levels of access to resources according to each individual's functional needs. *Account culling* consists of deactivating an account and the associated access rights when the user is no longer associated with the organisation.

However, this 3-phase life cycle is inadequate in describing the complex situation of existing ILM needs. The author provides a summary of some definitions and concepts from other works in the following (Seltsikas & Heijden, 2010; AGIMO, 2009):

- **Government Agency (GA):** A branch of government, which provide online services to citizens;

- **Identity Stores (IS):** The database where verified identities are captured for use by the government and other trusted commercial parties. The stores should support government to share identity stores in a distributed architecture;
- **Identity Registration System:** Online systems of the government services where identities are managed and maintained. They should be shared by more than one different service;
- **Identity credentials (or Evidence of Identity) (IC):** Credentials are the evidence that an individual supplies to demonstrate rightful "ownership" of the identity. Examples of credentials include pin codes, passports, proof of address, bank statement, etc.;
- **Evidence of Relationship (EoR):** Evidence (e.g., in the form of shared knowledge/secrets, or documentary) used to substantiate that the presenting party has an existing relationship with the relying party.

From the identity management process perspective, the followings are the core identity management processes. They involve the administration of the life cycle of digital identity entities, during which the digital representation of an identity is established, used and disposed of, when the digital identity is not required anymore:

1. **Enrolment:** Capturing of user identity data (what type of biometric and non-biometric information to be captured and how), validating (data quality, data integrity check), privacy protection, and secured storage of the information captured.
2. **Credentialing:** The issuing of evidence or testimonials by an authoritative source concerning a person's right to credit, confidence, or authority in a particular environment.

Issues to be addressed are: the types of credentials (such as, badging, ID Card or biometric); uniqueness of the identity; the condition of granting special privileged status; how to deal with stolen credentials (i.e., 1-to-N against registration database or matching against watch-lists).

3. **Identification:** Qualifying a person's identity by asking, "Who is the person?" The process may include background check, or trusted credentials.
4. **Authentication/Verification:** Confirming or denying a person's claimed identity by questioning "Is this person whom he/she claims to be?"

This is an important precursor for access control (at physical, logical and transactional levels). Authentication can be achieved by applying authorisation and role-based rules.

5. **Intelligence:** The process of maintaining and linking white/black list databases to uncover identities that could pose a threat. This requires data-sharing amongst trusted third parties (federal, state, local, and international), data-mining of multimodal biometric information and technology platform, link analysis on data resided in different standards, data formats and communication protocols or interfaces.

6. **Detection:** Fraud surveillance, on demand real-time ID detection against watch-lists, on demand mobile identification and screening.

This chapter is going to present a seven-phase life cycle for identity management called Personal Identity Management Cycle (PIMC) as illustrated in following Figure 1. This life cycle is based on our observation of a diverse number of requirements specified by a number of major commercial stakeholders and standards bodies

This seven-phase life cycle for identity management describes the seven stages that an identity would go through, which includes *Creation, Change,*

Figure 1. Personal identity management cycle (PIMC)

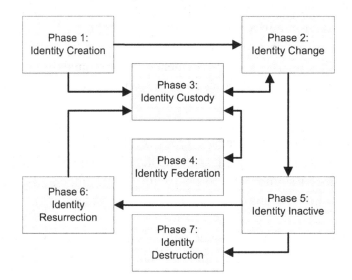

Capture & Custody, Provisioning or Federation, Inactivity, Resurrection and *Destruction*. The seven phases of PIMC is described in the following:

1. **Identity Creation:** A new identity for an entity is created in this stage. This phase is entered in scenarios such as when a new customer is enrolled in the system. This creation phase is the responsibility of the Identity Stores (IS) that are responsible for the registration of new identities. The IS acts as the authoritative source of authenticating a person's asserted identity provided to any business entities. The author stresses the need for business entities to verify the authenticity of any captured personal identities through an authoritative organisation before a service request from a customer is granted. The author also suggests that activating this phase should only be accomplished by authorised roles when verified with a set of registered secret preconditions for each role, to act as one of the security measures against hacking.

2. **Identity Change:** This phase is related to the update of attributes against a particular existing identity. It includes activities such as change in residential address, marital status, etc. Any changes will incur a time-stamp and it is logical for the identity management framework to have mechanisms in relation to the accessing and manipulation of identity information, such as access control and event logging, in providing a complete chronological sequence of events that have occurred.

3. **Identity Custody:** This phase is concerned with the capturing, secured storage and access control of personal identity information. It had happen that internal and external parties compromised such sensitive information (Hall, 2007). Therefore, it is important to pay careful considerations for an identity management framework to safeguard aspects of what/when/how/why situations, through to capturing and protecting sensitive personal identities from unauthorised malicious access.

4. **Identity Provisioning/Federation:** According to ITU-T (2009), federation is the establishing a relationship between two or more entities, or an association comprising any number of service providers and identity providers. This phase involves all activities concerning the provisioning of identities across multiple domains and architectures, to achieve the purpose of unified personal identity theft detection, and appropriate response in a timely, secured, auditable and controlled manner. All request and response of personal identity activities are to be monitored in a secured, traceable and ordered manner.

5. **Identity Inactive:** This is the phase when an identity is put into inactive mode, due to events such as an entity has been flagged inactive due to some conditions or actions (i.e., death of a person, claimed missing, or being classified as inactive by authorities of a particular government office). Key considerations for the identity management framework in this phase are the mechanisms in monitoring and preventing unauthorised actions in changing an identity's status.

6. **Identity Resurrection:** This phase enables a particular identity to be "resurrected" to become active again from the "Inactive" situation. Specific mechanisms should be put in place to safeguard from unauthorised resurrection taken place.

7. **Identity Destruction:** "Lest we forget" is the motto for all ILM to keep logging of all event traces and should be remembered permanently. This means even after an identity is "deleted permanently" and goes into this phase. This will only mean that particular identity cannot be "Resurrected" again. The particular identity will not be culled or recycled for other purpose.

USAGE SCENARIOS FOR THE GENERIC IDENTITY LIFE CYCLE MANAGEMENT FRAMEWORK

Typically, transactions undertaken over the Internet by individuals or businesses fall into the following categories: (a) enquiries; (b) new business establishment information provision; (c) provision of new, remove or change of standing instructions; (d) declarations; (e) statements; (f) financial transactions and (g) termination of business relation.

The nature and extent of threats associated with these Internet transactions vary according to the sensitivity of the information to be exchanged, the value of the transaction and/or the legal issues associated with the transaction.

Jaquet-Chielle et al. (2006) used a set of scenarios to explore anonymity services in the Internet, web-based shopping system, the use of pseudonyms in various pseudonym domains, model for identities for the Information Society, issues related to money laundering and the financing of terrorism and concept of Identity in the Digital Social Environments.

In order to determine the degree of confidence that can be placed in assertions that a user or identity is who and/or what they purport to be; the

Australian Government NeAF e-Authentication framework (AGIMO, 2009) makes use of a combination of the followings:

- Something the user knows (e.g., password, secret questions and answers);
- Something the user has (e.g., security token);
- Something the user is (e.g., biometric); or
- A combination of the above.

The following sections will apply some of the above scenarios to walkthrough how PIMC tackles the kind of situations based on specific requirements in each phase.

Scenario 1: Establish New Business

The first scenario illustrates the processes involved in the typical *Creation, Change* and *Custody* requirements for an asserted identity.

The key process is the *Obtain Identity Information* whereby customers require filling out forms (paper or online) with personal information and is required to provide the required *Identity Credential*.

In accordance with compliance policies and government regulations, the business organisation runs a series of background checks, including a credit check on each applicant as well as a search against an online database of individuals with a history of failing to fulfil business obligations.

The signature collection procedure for opening new accounts poses challenge to the way businesses are transacted electronically over the Internet. The Electronic Transactions Act allows a person to satisfy a legal requirement for a manual signature by using an electronic communication. The method used must identify the person and indicate their approval of the information communicated. The Act does not ordain a particular electronic signature technology to be used, providing flexibility for people and businesses to determine the signature technology that is as reliable as appropriate to their particular needs such as a digitised version of a written signature, a PIN to biometric technology.

There are many electronic signature software available, such as DocuSign, Wondershare eSign+, Adobe Sign (Formerly EchoSign), HelloSign, and AuthentiSign, which help the users enter a secure website where they can upload, electronically sign and send their documents for signing to parties involved.

In this scenario, we have a person wants to perform online stock-exchange activities with an online stock-broker provided by a commercial bank. The person is going to create a new person identity which will undergo a few phase changes.

The assumption taken for this scenario is that the person's identity does not exist in a trusted *Identity Store (IS)*. This means the particular person's identity will need to be created and stored in a secure manner in a particular IS. The *Creation* phase is entered where relevant personal identity information of the particular person is captured in the *Obtain Identity Information* process and a request is sent to the IS.

The content contained in the *Create Identity Request* shall be encrypted and are tagged with a new unique Universal Personal Identity (UPID) code. A set of rigorous identity checking and verification rules will be required to verify the captured identity information is correct and belongs to the rightful owner. The Guidance note 11/02 issued by AUSTRAC (2011) is a good reference.

The following constraints and conditions are set for the *Creation* phase: each person must be uniquely identified either by a UPID or a set of key properties such as name, date and place of birth etc. known as the profile for a particular person.

However, as shown in Figure 2, a person is allowed to have multiple profiles which detail its membership with different organisations or societies in different times.

Figure 2. Multiple profiles (memberships) for a person

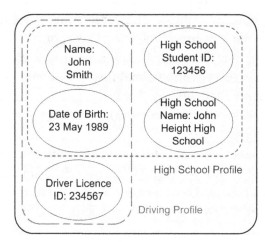

After an identity is created in the IS, the particular piece of identity information will go from *Creation* to *Custody* or *Update* phases depending on if any subsequent action is required to modify the identity.

There are requirements how to ensure a secured and fail-proofed execution in *Updating Identity Information, Destroying Identity, and Archiving Identity Information*. The author suggests timestamp, before-look and after-look checksums are to be employed to provide an audit trail of all relevant actions taken for a particular identity entity.

For the typical distributed IS architecture, the issue of using a standard "*Secured In Transit Identity*" format will be required which specifies what and how different personal and private information are encoded in the In-Transit Data for presenting from different distributed parties such as the Stock Exchange Company to the Government IS. The format complies with the ISO27001 certification for storing and transmitting data.

The format shall also consider the result of any request received from the IS such as "Verify Identity", "Record Signature", "Create and maintain identity information stores", "Synchronize identity information stores", "Split and merge stores to reflect organizational changes", and "Apply information access control for update and read-access".

Figure 3 depicts the workflow of Scenario 1 involving the three main processes: Obtain Identity Information, Background Check, and Create New Identity.

Scenario 2: Provisioning of New, Remove, or Change of Standing Instructions

The second scenario "Provisioning of new, remove, or change of standing instructions" illustrates typical events and considerations happen in the Federation Phase of identities. According to (CA, 2007), Identity Federation can be conducted in different styles.

The first identity federation style is *Based On Account Linking*, where a company a.com maintains user identities for a group of persons under its custody. When a person who is transacting with another company_b.com requires access to company_a.com, an identifier for the person is passed from company_b.com to company_a.com in a secure manner. This identifier allows company_a.com to determine who the user is and what access to allow for that user.

Figure 3. Workflow of Scenario 1: establish new business

Scenario 1: Establish New Business

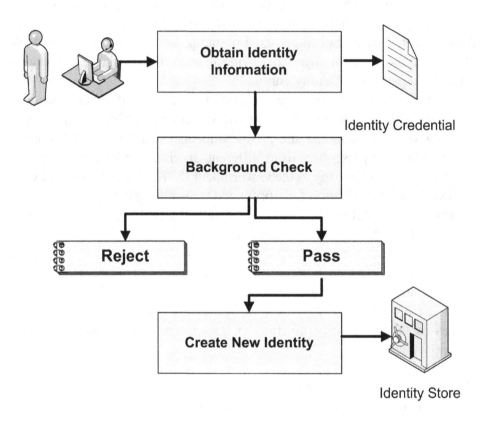

The second style of identity federation is *Based On Roles*, where in this use case a company company_w.com buys parts from a partner company_p.com. An employee of company_w.com authenticates at the portal of company_w.com and information at company_p.com. Note that company_p.com does not maintain user identities for all employees of company_w.com. However, company_p.com controls access to sensitive portions of its web site by maintaining a limited number of role identities for company_w.com users.

When an employee of company_w.com accesses company_p.com, user attributes are federated from company_w.com to company_p.com in a secure manner. These attributes define the role of the user and determine what role profile identity is used to control access at company_p.com. Attributes, such as user name, are passed from company_w.com to company_p.com to personalise the interface for the individual user.

The third identity federation style is *With No Local User Account*. In this use case, a company company_b.com does not maintain any identities or roles for users of company_w.com. The company company_b.com simply allows all users of company_w.com to access company_b.com as long as they have been authenticated at company_w.com. Additional attributes, such as user name, are passed from company_w.com to company_b.com to personalise the interface for the individual user.

Figure 4 is a schematic diagram showing the three different styles of federation involved in the provisioning of new, remove or change of standing instructions scenario.

Scenario 3: Termination of Business Relationship

The third scenario "Termination of Business Relationship" illustrates the typical *Inactive, Destruction*, and *Resurrection* Phases in the PIMC. The *Resurrection* phase proposed in here differs from other similar researches. Although the term resurrection is commonly found in religious arena, it is rarely used in scientific researches. We use this term to reflect the case that there are needs to allow an inactive identity to be resurrected.

One example is that we need to allow a person who is under protection or a secret agent who is to be in deep cover to change its identity as such could make a certain identity inactive. After the secret agent has completed its assignment and is required to resume a "normal" identity, the resurrection process is thus required otherwise would make the Identity Store's design more complicated and lose track of the exact sequent of events.

Figure 5 shows the workflow involved in Scenario 3 for a trustee B works on behalf of a deceased person A in terminating business relationship with a bank C.

An identity can be made "*Inactive*" based on a set of conditions. In this scenario, we take a person A has been declared deceased and the trustee of that particular deceased person B performs activities to inform a bank C to terminate the business relationship. The processes involved are as follows:

- In this situation, B is required to provide the IC of A and itself together with the EoRs to bank C to request the termination.
- Bank C is required to verify the credentials and the evidence of A & B by making identity verification request to the GA.

Figure 4. Scenario 2: three federation styles

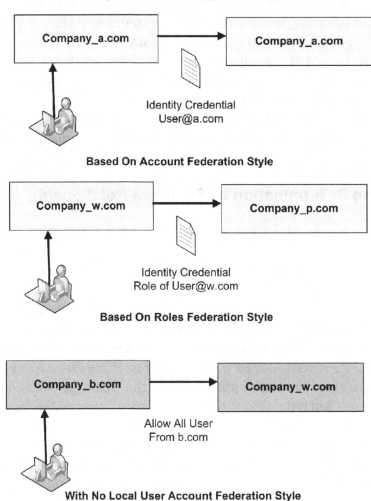

Scenario 2: Provisioning of New, Remove or Change of Standing Instructions

The GA, which is responsible to change to status of an identity into *"Inactive"* state, will solicit necessary official evidence before updating a particular identity to become inactive.

- The required evidence shall follow the legislative requirement such as the Death Certificate. All legal evidence should be digitised or properly linked to the appropriate authority to ensure data integrity.

Figure 5. Workflow of Scenario 3: termination of business relationship

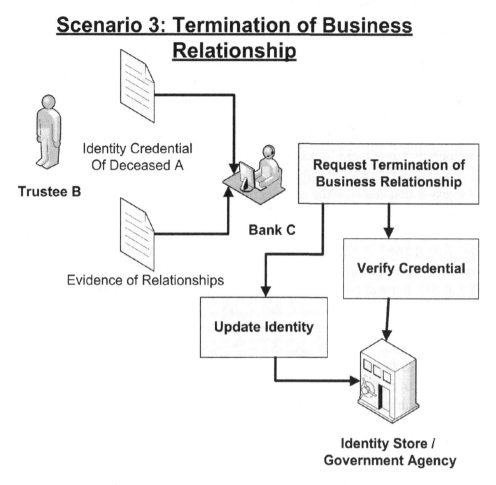

Once an identity has entered into "*Inactive*" state, it is logical that no further business activities are allowed unless it is conducted by the appointed trustee to transfer or terminate the business. This model uses the "*Destruction*" phase to differentiate the "*Inactive*" phase to further classify situations that certain identities were made "*Inactive*" not due to the death of a person but for some other reasons. The difference between "*Inactive*" and "*Destruction*" phases is that an identity in "*Destruction*" phase cannot be resurrected. This model uses this feature to reflect real-life situation that some missing persons which had been claimed dead were in actual fact alive using a different identity.

DIFFERENT VIEWS OF IDENTITY
LIFE CYCLE MANAGEMENT

Different organisations have proposed different views on the processes involved in the management a typical life cycle of identities. We use this proposed PIMC to discuss the features provided by a number of identity management life cycle frameworks available in the market.

Firstly, the author found not all Identity and Access Management frameworks has Identity Life Cycle Management component defined. Secondly, it was observed that most Identity and Access Management frameworks do not have a life cycle that cater for the resurrection of identities.

PICOS architecture (Crane, 2010) defined the Identity Life Cycle Management component to interact with the main components to support the life cycle of a member, namely the Registration, Partial Identity Management, Privilege Management, Delegation and Revocation components. The Identity Management functionalities of PICOS consist of Registration, Creation, Modification, Delegation, and Revocation. An identity is typically only valid for a period of time (i.e. has a start/end date) and its existence may be dependent on context. Only PICOS has the design to change an identity from Suspended to Terminated state but did it does not have the option of allowing the change from the opposite.

The possible states of an identity in PICOS are the following:

- **Not Established:** The identity of an entity is unrecognised in a given context.
- **Established:** The identity of an entity is recognized in the context but the entity is not yet able to interact with other entities.
- **Activated:** The identity of an entity is recognized in the context and the entity is able to interact with other entities in the context.
- **Suspended**: The identity of an entity is recognized in the context. However, the entity is no longer able to interact with other entities.
- **Terminated:** An entity is no longer recognized in a context.
- **Archived:** An entity is no longer recognized in a context but records may be required to remain available.

ITU-T Y.2720 NGN identity management framework (ITU-T, 2009) stipulated a four stage life cycle consists of *Proofing, Enrolment, Issuance,* and *Revocation*. The life cycle is concerned with the process in subscribing an identity or credential associated with a particular entity. Proofing includes verifying attributes and claims associated with an identity. Successful completion of the enrolment process results in the granting of a means (e.g., a credential) by which the entity can be authenticated in the future. Identity revocation is the process of rescinding an identity and the associated credentials.

The Australian Government has launched the National e-Authentication Framework (NeAF) (AGIMO, 2009) which covers two aspects of authentication: (a) electronic authentication of the identity of individuals and businesses; and (b) authentication of government websites.

NeAF proposed an Identity and Access Management Life Cycle, which consists of activities such as (a) *Identity Checking*, (b) *e-authentication credential Registration*, (b) *Enrolment of online service*, (d) *Issue of Identity Credential*, (e) *De-registration of Identity Credential*, and (f) *Transacting with e-Applications*. NeAF applies the concept of assurance levels by assessing through a comprehensive risk assessment process to determine the severity of the impact of getting e-Authentication wrong.

Microsoft's Microsoft Forefront Identity Manager (FIM) 2010 established a four-phase life-cycle for identity management: *(1) New User, (2) Account Change, (3) Password Management, and (4) Retire User.* FIM combines identity data across multiple directories and systems in conjunction with role-based group certificate management process, user account provisioning and identity integration.

There are life cycles proposed by other organisations such as FIDIS (Backhouse and Dyer, 2007) incorporated the operation aspect as the life cycle of an identity using *Input, Storage, Access, Maintenance,* and *Deletion* to represent the different states of an identity entity. Apart from that, the Open Group's proposal of the life cycle of an identity in an organisation, from *Initial Enrolment (or registration)*, through *Maintenance* of changes during *Operational* life, to eventual *Removal* and *Destruction* of identity information and associated rights, permissions, and authorities (Slone, 2004).

Finally, it was observed that different frameworks hold different views on controlling the entire identity life cycle. The life cycles are mostly base on operational views of identity. The common stages are *creation/enrolment, maintenance* and *deletion*. It was also observed that all the current framework do not treat identities in federation stage as part of their framework in life cycle management and do not cater for special situation to resurrect retired identities. Although the need for resurrecting retired identities may not be frequent, we see that it is important to have that stage to properly describe the management life cycle of identity.

A summary of some identity management life cycles are provided in Table 1.

CONCLUSION

This chapter has outlined a generic life cycle management model called Personal Identity Management Cycle (PIMC) in capturing essential events and conditions for a person's identity and has discussed a brief history of identity life cycle management and some of the life cycle management features provided by a few IAM frameworks.

Due to the increasing challenges in the chances of cyber attacker gaining full administrative access to a system, there are calls for the need to include some kinds of privileged Identity Management controls in the life cycle of an identity. The purpose is to manage administrative access by providing temporary, task-based access to sensitive resources with the sole objective of giving users only as much permission as necessary and as short as possible for the period of access.

However, the author considers that this requirement should be tackled at the access control function rather than grouping this into the life cycle management issue. The next chapter will discuss different views of the goals and requirements for contemporary IAM systems.

Table 1. Summary of different identity management life cycles

Our Proposed PIMC	Microsoft	PICOS	ITU-T Y.2720	FIDIS	NeAF
Creation	New User	Not Established	Proofing	Input	Issue
Change	Account Change	Established	Enrolment	Storage	eAuthentication
Custody	Password Management	Activated	Insurance	Access	Id Checking
Federation		Suspended		Maintenance	Transacting
Inactive	Retire User	Terminated	Revocation	Deletion	Deregistration
Resurrection					
Destruction		Archived (optional)			

REFERENCES

AGIMO. (2009). *National e-authentication framework*. The Australian Government Information Management Office.

AUSTRAC. (2011). *Verification of identity: The use and disclosure of personal information by reporting entities and credit reporting agencies for the purposes of verifying an individual's identity – natural persons (e-verification)*. ATRAA Centre.

Backhouse, J., & Dyer, B. (2007). *D4.7: Review and classification for a FIDIS identity management model*. Future of Identity in the Information Society.

CA. (2007). *Identity federation: Concepts, use cases and industry standards*. Computer Associate.

Crane, S. (2010). *D4.2 platform architecture and design 2*. Privacy and Identity Management for Community Services.

Currie, R. (2013). *History of Microsoft forefront identity manager 2010*. Available from: http://www.fimspecialist.com/fim-fundamentals/history-of-microsoft-forefront-identity-manager-2010/

Electronic Transactions Act. (2000). Australian NSW State Government.

Hall, J. (2007, May 12). Custodian pleads guilty in identity theft case. *The Californian*.

ITU-T. (2009). Recommendation ITU-T Y.2720: NGN identity management framework. International Telecommunication Union.

Jaquet-Chielle, D., Benoist, E., & Anrig, B. (2006). *Identity in a networked world use cases and scenarios*. Future of Identity in the Information Society.

Macgregor, W., Dutcher, W., & Khan, J. (2006). An ontology of identity credentials. Gaithersburg, MD: National Institute of Standards and Technology.

Seltsikas, P., & Heijden, H. V. D. (2010). A taxonomy of government approaches towards online identity management. *43rd Hawaii International Conference on System Sciences*.

Slone, S. (2004). *Identity management*. The Open Group.

Chapter 4

The Goals and Requirements for Contemporary Identity and Access Management Solutions

ABSTRACT

INTRODUCTION

In order for an organisation to determine the effectiveness of its IAM solution, the first thing to do is to assess the extent to which its deployed IAM system fulfils the functional, technological and process requirements.

The author has identified a set of requirements that are related to user empowerment on awareness and control, minimal information disclosure for constrained use, non-repudiation, support for directional identity topologies, support for a universal identity bus, provision of defining strength of identity, decoupling the identity management layer from the application layer, usability issues concerning identity selection and disclosure, a consistent experience across contexts, and scalability.

The above requirements will be discussed in this chapter and illustrations will be used where appropriate. The author also presents a taxonomy to help classifying the different IAM frameworks. This taxonomy will act as a tool to study a number of IAM frameworks proposed by different organisations in chapter 5 of this book.

DOI: 10.4018/978-1-5225-4828-7.ch004

CHALLENGES OF CONTEMPORARY IDENTITY AND ACCESS MANAGEMENT FRAMEWORKS

Chapter 1 has discussed the different challenges that contemporary IAM solutions are currently facing. This chapter will recap some of the issues which are related to the design of contemporary IAM systems.

Identity today has increased in complexity and challenges are in place in every aspect that is related to identity management: *Identity Capture, Uniqueness, Universality, Interoperability, Secure Storage, Secure Communication, Scalability, Flexibility, Business & Work Flow, Interface, Privacy, User Acceptance, Overall TCO, Assurance, Distributed Deployment, System Integrity, Performance, Advocacy*, etc., just to name a few.

Contemporary trend is that Business-to-Employee (B2E) identities are still managed by enterprise, but more distributed and influenced by the Cloud. Business-to-Customer (B2C), Business-to-Business (B2B), Government-to-Citizen (G2C), Government-to-Government (G2G) and Peer-to-Peer (P2P) identity management evolved into a state that trust between user and application are no longer a given relationship.

Furthermore, mobility adds to the identity complexity. People access applications through multiple access points simultaneously with each access point using different security policies and identity stores. This leads to the scenario that the same identity management policy may need to be developed and deployed multiple times. At the moment, there is lack of common access experience across devices which lead to fragmented user experience and control access. There is also lack of common user credentials across different access points. The governance and auditing requirements differ between channels which also caused fragmentation issues.

The concept of eGoverment has been proposed by different countries. The Digital Agenda for Europe is one of the examples in setting a goal that 50% of EU citizens to use eGovernment by 2015 (EU_Commission, 2014). However, there is still lacking in a unified eGovernment that can be relied as the sole online verifier. The basic fact is that not all governments have the same capabilities and not all countries are agreeable on a common model.

The concept of global e-iD is more than technologies alone can provide the solution because it requires negotiations amongst different countries on conditions and terms how a country may accept and process the e-iDs issued by another country and vice versa. It is difficult to find an open and flexible solution acceptable to all countries as the perceived risk of government monitoring online behaviour can inhibit adoption. Furthermore, private sector has the required skills and expertise and the flexibility to form non-government alliances to provide choices for consumers. Another practical problem is that there are more than 200 million individuals in the world have dual citizenship (The Economist, 2012).

According to empirical studies (Zimmerman, 2012; Pooe & Labuschagne, 2011), one of the major challenges facing the enterprise is adopting biometric technology by modernising legacy systems using updated standards. Technology transitions can become one of the key enablers for evolutionary acquisition of interoperable biometric and biographical data as well as any associated requirements, policy, and national laws.

Other challenges in biometric identity management may also include issues such as technologies immaturity and compatibility, user acceptance, workflow interruptions, scalability concerns, data security issues, integration issues and architectural complexity issue. Many people are concerned with the security and privacy issues (Down & Sands, 2004; Prabhakar et al., 2003) on protecting the biometric digital information of the users from being accessed, stolen or tampered with by unauthorised parties. High concern is placed on the misuse of a biometric information because once compromised, the effect could continue to be an issue for the life of the person involved.

From the control perspective, the challenge of physical and logical controls over access to biometric data in regard to the location of biometric storage, the underlying digital representation of the biometric is controlled as standing data during transmission, the security of the computers hosting the application and databases; and audit trails for tracing system user activities all post a certain level of challenge to the adoption of the biometric technologies.

In summary, although biometric identification is one of the promising approaches in dealing with the management of personal identities across wide boundaries, in any large scenario some portion of the general population, it is likely to be physiologically unable to use one or more of the biometric identification techniques due to different empirical inhibiting factors as indicated by (Scott & Johnston, 2010, Pooe & Labuschagne, 2011):

- **Technology:** This is due to comprising legacy systems and technology immaturity. Technology challenges are related to the collection, correlation, retention and retrieval requirements. For two disparate biometric IAM systems able to work with one another, the basis of trust is most important. The challenge of immutable linking to trusted third-party biometric devices needs to be addressed in a cost and time effective manner so as to achieve a defined level of certainty or trust, who (or which entity) is making the assertion(s). Furthermore, the extensibility issues for biometric devices, form-factors and communications being able to work with anything and anywhere that needs identity pose another level of challenges;

- **Cultural:** Human and organisational cultures have deep structural effect on the decision. Biometrics is still perceived as imperfect, unsafe or unfamiliar to end users. Some people have a concern for the physical effects of the technology upon them. This accounts for the greater acceptance of newer iris recognition technology over the older retinal scan technology;

- **Governance:** Which is due to legislative limitation, lack of available standards on the use of biometrics, and human cultural habits;

- **Lack of Centralised Shared Biometric Database Available for Positive Identification:** The demand for assertion of attributes from authoritative sources is deem necessary because all parties working together in an open system require the attributes of the entity to be asserted from their authoritative source, thus minimising/eliminating the liability problem; and

- **Cost:** The cost of implementing an IAM solution as compare to a viable return on the investment is required so as to justify for a reasonable and sustainable solution. There are overheads incurred to workflow changes with the introduction of new or enhanced biometric security measures that would impact on ROI.

REQUIREMENTS FOR IDENTITY AND ACCESS MANAGEMENT FRAMEWORKS

The need for an IAM solution may be driven by a risks management and compliance initiative, an operational effectiveness or efficiency initiative, a business enablement initiative or possibly a combination of all three considerations. In order to understand the primary purposes and characteristics of some of the IAM frameworks that are available in the market, we need to understand some of the requirements for a contemporary Identity and Access Management framework.

Microsoft (Cameron, 2005) have stated the "seven laws" of identity that should underlie the requirements for an identity management system:

- End user controls on the use and revelation of personal identity information;
- Disclosure of the least amount of identifying information;
- Disclosure of identifying information limited to justifiable parties only;
- Public entities should use omni-directional identifiers, while private entities should use unidirectional identifiers;
- Support for multiple identity technologies run by multiple identity providers;
- Support for human-machine communication mechanisms; and
- A guarantee of a simple, consistent experience, while enabling separation of contexts through multiple operators and technologies.

On the other hand, Akram and Hoffmann (2008) have proposed ten requirements for an identity management framework using the HYDRA middleware architecture. The requirements are related to user empowerment on awareness and control; minimal information disclosure for constrained use, non-repudiation, support for directional identity topologies, support for a universal identity bus, provision of defining strength of identity, decoupling the identity management layer from the application layer, usability issues concerning identity selection and disclosure, a consistent experience across contexts, and scalability.

Apart from that, a position paper on the W3C Web site (OneName, 2001) provides seven requirements for establishing a Web based global identity management framework, which includes portability and interoperability, extensibility, negotiated privacy and security, accountability, a distributed registration authority, a distributed certification authority, and an independent governing authority. These requirements stipulated a universally portable and interoperable architecture that support unlimited identity-related attributes; with adequate mechanisms for privacy and accountability; and that it must be overseen by an independent governing authority.

Furthermore, based on the NGN architectures (ITU-T, 2010) and reference models, the ITU-T Y.2720 identity management framework (ITU-T, 2009) specified the following eight functions and capabilities requirements: an identity lifecycle management, operation, administration, maintenance and provisioning (OAM&P) functions, signalling and control functions, federated identity functions, user and subscriber functions, performance, reliability, and scalability, security, and legal and regulatory rules.

Moreover, The Open Group issued a white paper on identity management (Slone, 2004) which proposed a six "actors" model to describe the functions and capabilities requirements of an identity management framework, consisting of:

- An *Identity Policy Authority* to define identity;
- An *Identity Manager* to accept identification information, conformance with the terms of Identity Policies to request that an identity is issued to the Identity Owner;
- An *Identity Issuer* who issues identities at the request of one or more Identity Managers;
- An *Identity Issue Auditor* who establishes the technical and operational rules for all Identity Issuers within its domain;
- An *Identity Owner* who is the individual making use of an electronic identity to achieve some task or purpose; and
- A *Relying Party* who is the recipient of an identity.

In addition, the Liberty Alliance Project's open standard for Identity Federation Framework (Wason et al., 2005; Tiffany & Kemp, 2005) is used in Web HTTP/SOAP XML based scenarios to promote a federated identity management approach, which focuses on maintaining trust relationships between business and the federation of isolated accounts of users among well-defined trust circles. This framework highlights openness (OS, programming language, and network infrastructure) as one of the core requirements, along with other functional requirements in identity federation, authentication, use of pseudonyms, support for anonymity, and global logout.

This Identity Federation Framework has been widely accepted by research and government organisations. Some examples are the role- and relationship-based identity management system proposed by Anwar and Greer (2008) for the e-learning domain uses public roles to assigned guarantor privileges and facilitate usage control over disclosed information. Another example is Maler (2005) who proposed a federated identity management system using widely deployed solutions of Security Assertion Markup Language and the Liberty Alliance framework.

Moreover, the National Institute of Standards and Technology (NIST) has advocated the Identity Credential System Models (MacGregor et al., 2006) which uses a set of "planes" (which consists: Actor plane, Maintenance plane,

Transaction plane, Issuer plane and Life Events plane) to describe the events and relationships of different projections of the identity credential ontology.

Traditional authentication and verification solutions use a combination of passwords (knowledge-based security) and/or ID cards (token-based security) to restrict access to a variety of systems. However, these two modes of authentication are vulnerable to attacks and security can be breached by carefully architected schemes.

In the consideration of the requirements for IAM solutions employing biometric technologies, we are well aware that biometrics technology augments the traditional authentication methods with specific requirements in the Collection, Correlation, Retention, and Retrieval of biometrics information.

In the context of applying biometric technologies in identity management, Jain et al. (2004) asserted that any human physiological and/or behavioural characteristic can be used as a biometric characteristic as long as it satisfies the following characteristics: universality; distinctiveness; permanence; and collectability.

On top of that, they also asserted that a practical biometric system must consider issues such as: performance (i.e., recognition accuracy and speed, as well as the operational and environmental factors that affect the accuracy and speed); acceptability (i.e. the extent to which people are willing to accept the use of a particular biometric identifier); and circumvention (how easily the system can be fooled using fraudulent methods).

Apart from that, Jain and Kumar (2010) stressed the selection of appropriate biometric technology for person identification depends on the application requirements. These requirements are typically specified in terms of identification accuracy, throughput, user acceptance, system security, robustness, and return on investment.

Although the requirements, functions and roles for identity management frameworks specified by different organisations are diverse, some common and core aspects can be identified. We have consolidated the following set of core requirements for all identity management frameworks, as depicted at the bottom part of Figure 1:

- Biometric enrolment;
- Authentication;
- Verification and Audit;
- Multimodal biometric collection;
- Correlation, Retention, and Retrieval;

Figure 1. Requirements for identity and access management frameworks

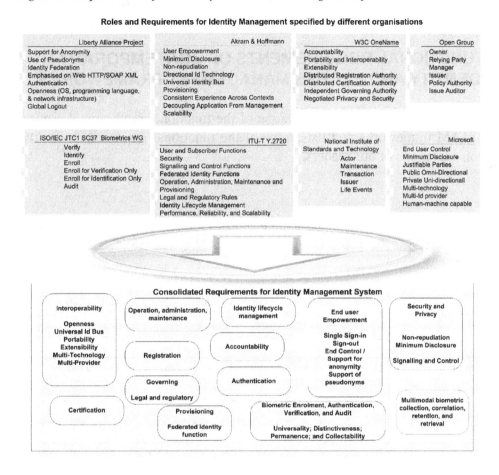

- Interoperability;
- Certification;
- Operation Administration and Maintenance;
- Registration;
- Governing;
- Identity Lifecycle Management;
- Accountability;
- Authentication;
- Provisioning;
- End user empowerment; and
- Security and Privacy.

A brief explanation of the consolidated requirements is provided in Table 1.

FUNCTIONAL REQUIREMENTS OF CONTEMPORARY IDENTITY AND ACCESS MANAGEMENT FRAMEWORKS

This section puts our focus on some of the functional requirement aspects of IAM frameworks and lists some of the functional requirements for the considerations of our readers.

Table 1. Consolidated requirements for identity and access management frameworks

Requirement	Description
Interoperability	Interoperability is one of the key requirements for contemporary identity management. We have seen the requirements for openness, portability, extensibility, universal ID bus, multi-technology and multi-provider specified by different organisations. These are all closely related to the requirement of interoperability. We agree with (Slone, 2004) that Multi-OS interoperability for identity management does not require convergence toward a common authentication or authorization protocol, but requires convergence toward a common form of identity, such as Universally Unique Identifier (UUID) pair.
Operation, Administration, and Maintenance	Includes functionality such as registration, accountability, certification, assurance and governing, which are vital in shaping how the identity management framework would behave.
Identity Lifecycle Management	Specifies how the identity entities are to be created, changed, stored, and deleted from the system. A detailed discussion of the identity management lifecycle is discussed in the next section.
End User Empowerment	Specifies how well a framework would empower end users to manage and control critical attributes of their identities in a system.
Security, Privacy and Trust	Focuses on how an identity management framework deals with protecting the management issues of identities in terms aspects such as authentication, non-repudiation, access control, and signalling of alerts.
Provisioning	Federation and provisioning are closely related to the requirement of interoperability. Issues in automated provisioning, de-provisioning, and re-provisioning of identities are to be considered.
Governance	This requirement fosters the standardisations of governance and auditing practices so that differ channels could work according to an agreed set of legislative rules on the use of biometrics, and human cultural habits because some people may have a concern for the physical effects of the technology upon them.
Multimodal Biometric Collection, Correlation, Retention, and Retrieval	The choice of two or more biometric characteristics will improve the accuracies. Furthermore, the use of a centralised shared biometric database available for positive identification will reduce the cost of implementing biometric identification solution. Other application requirements include: identification accuracy, throughput, user acceptance, system security, robustness, and return on investment
Biometric Authentication and Verification Applicability	Human physiological and/or behavioural characteristic can be used as a biometric characteristic for authentication and verification must satisfy the following characteristics: universality; distinctiveness; permanence; and collectability

According to Vienne (2014), there are 4 major functional areas required by an IAM framework:

- *Authentication* and *Authorisation* for the Access Management functions; and
- *Credential* and *Repository Management* for the Identity Management functions.

For the *Identity Management* function, the following functions and activities are highlighted:

- **Creation of Identity:** Establishing a new digital identity record, including associated identifiers and credentials.
- **Modification/Update of Identity**: The subsequent updating of digital identity records after to reflect changes in attributes and associated digital credentials.
- **Cross Boundary Support:** Able to support identity data from foreign platforms and organisations as well as the support for non-English characters in data attributes.
- **Person-to-Person, Person-to-System and System-to-System Identity Support:** The ability to support identities for persons and non-persons such as service accounts and devices. It is also vital for a system being able to associate non-person identities to a responsible entity regardless of it being a person or an entity.
- **Collusion of Identity:** The system should be able to identify any identities that are related and being able to merge the identities in cases where multiple identities are created for a single person as well as the ability to split the identities that are wrongly merged.
- **Delegation of Management Tasks:** The system is able to distribute the management activities to outside of the central IAM team, through a well-designed granular multi- level identity administration permission scheme.
- **Delegation of Authority:** The system is able to allow users to assign a delegate while away from the office

For the *Provisioning* function, the following features are required:

- **Synchronisation of Credentials:** The system should be able to synchronise identities to and from other data stores.

- **Automatic Provisioning and De-Provisioning:** The ability to provide credentials based on pre-set event conditions, i.e. uses events such as approved requests to determine when access should be granted or removed and automatically performs an update on the target system.

- **Support for Enterprise Service Bus (ESB) Provisioning:** The system should be able to leverage an ESB to provision identity credentials to distributed heterogeneous target systems.

- **Platform-specific Provisioning Connectors:** The system should be able to provide out-of-the-box (OOTB) software components to interface with a software package or platform to provision identities.

- **Logging of Provisioning Activities:** The ability to monitor and keep log of all the provisioning and de-provisioning activities with real-time alert message send to the IAM administrators about any suspicious activities.

- **Reconciliation of Identities:** The ability in automatically identifying any "orphan" identities that do not access any target systems.

For the *Password Management* functions, the following features are identified:

- **Password Policies:** The need to establish flexible yet cohesive, non-self-conflicting policies to enforce rules related to password complexity, expiry and, length.

The system should be able to define rules in computing a password complexity score based on meeting different complexity and length requirements. The system should require passwords to comply with a certain level of complexity requirements such as: the mandatory usage of special characters "@", "#" and perform dictionary check to prevent the use of some common words. The system should also prevent a user from including his or her personal information in a password.

Furthermore, the system should allow multiple usernames and multiple password or biometric credentials to be associated with the same identity.

- **Self-Service Password Management:** The ability to allow users to manage their passwords and to reset a forgotten password without the intervention of a system administrator.

- **Administrative Password Management:** The ability to enable system administration staff to manage on-behalf of an end-user under strictly monitored and bounded capability.

For the *Access Management* function, the following features are required:

- **Access Request Management:** The ability to provide a consistent and auditable process for the handling of access request to multiple locations and platforms.
- **Access Reconciliation:** The ability to present audit trails of "who has access to what" data to the appropriate stakeholders on a configurable frequency for review and compliance check against the established access control policies.
- **Delegated Group Administration:** The ability to allow authorised end-users to perform group creation, deletion and maintenance tasks outside of the central IAM team.
- **Public and Private Groups Administration:** The ability to add filters and rules in making some groups to become publically visible while limiting the visibility of others to privileged populations.
- **Static and Dynamic Groups Administration:** The ability to define group membership by working on individual members or based on a set of rules.
- **Nested Groups:** The ability to support groups to be members of other groups.

For the *Role* management function, the following features are proposed:

- **Role Management Delegation:** The ability to end-users to perform role management tasks outside of the central IAM team.
- **Role Mining:** The provision of tools for end-users to analyse IAM data ("who has access to what") to review patterns across users with similar access.
- **Role Compliance Check:** The ability to verify changes to roles to be approved prior to being implemented in production environment.
- **Root Roles:** The ability to assign roles based on a set of membership rules which are relying on attributes from an authoritative source system.
- **Roles Upon Request:** The ability to assign roles based on the request received from the access request system.

- **Nested Roles:** The ability to define a role to contain other roles.

For the *Auditing*, *Logging*, and *Reporting* functions, the following features are highlighted for consideration:

- **Audit and Logging:** The ability to monitor and log all activities happened within the system and operations performed. The audit trail should be available to the technical people for analysis, event tracing, and debugging purposes.
- **Compliance and Operations Reporting:** The ability to generate reports that can be drilled down upon request to be reviewed regularly meeting the requirements of regulatory compliance and operations management purposes.
- **Ad-hoc Reporting:** The ability to generate ad-hoc reports with ease through a user-friendly reporting interface.

The requirements listed in the above are for an understanding of the nature and scope of managing personal identity assets and the operations of those assets need to be acquired. The nature of the IAM architecture representing the applications and resources must align with the business operations of the organisation. Knowledge of the processes and technology platforms that underpin business operations are essential as organisations migrate towards heterogeneous IT environments and distributing processes comprising a mix of ad hoc cloud services and mobile devices.

A TAXONOMY OF IDENTITY AND ACCESS MANAGEMENT FRAMEWORK

After discussing the process and technology requirements for IAM frameworks, this section presents a taxonomy for classifying the different IAM frameworks. As a control measure, an IAM system often forms part of security architecture to minimise risks to the identity assets. The taxonomy provides a framework for risk assessment in specifying the assets and processes to be protected, their value and vulnerabilities, acquire threat intelligence, and ascertain incident probabilities and the likely impact on those assets in the event of an attack.

Another purpose of this taxonomy is to be used for studying the different IAM frameworks proposed by different organisations, to better understand the contributions of each IAM solution. With the help of this classification, the critical areas in IAM can be identified for those require further effort. In addition, it will be useful in future work to relate this taxonomy to other taxonomies that deal with identity fraud vectors once an identity has been compromised (Stabek & Watters, 2010).

Meints and Zwingelberg (2009) noted that identity management system development has evolved from identity management for account management, implementing authentication, authorisation, and accounting, to profiling of user data by an organisation for personalised services or the analysis of customer behaviour. More recent developments have focused on hybrid type identity management for user-controlled context-dependent roles and pseudonym management. Identity management therefore represents a convergence of technologies and business processes.

This chapter puts emphasis on the *technology* and *process* aspects of different IAM frameworks.

In Figure 2, the technology aspect is further enhanced into the following sub-classes: *interoperability, security and privacy, trust, and federation.*

Federation of identity covers mainly the technologies, as well as standards and processes which enables interoperability of identity information across multiple security domains. The author has assessed the interoperability aspect of different IAM frameworks for the abilities of these frameworks to interoperate across a trusted network of businesses, partners and services regardless of the platform, programming language or application with which they're interacting.

The author then studied the technologies and standards the framework used, the degree of openness to accommodate other different frameworks, the portability aspect of how easy for the framework to be adopted and work with other frameworks in different domains and the mechanisms they used to cater for future extension.

The technology aspect of security and privacy for identity management covers *the non-repudiation, access control, and signalling and control* aspects. The access control aspect is further broken down into *authentication and verification, enrolment, retention and retrieval* sub-classes. The authentication & verification aspect is further elaborated with *password, token-based and biometric* sub-classes.

On the other hand, as showed in Figure 3, the process aspect can be classified into the following areas: *Identity lifecycle management, actors and roles required in the framework, the operation, administration and maintenance processes in handling registration, certification, authentication, governing and accountability* issues in the identity management framework.

Figure 2. A technology taxonomy of identity and access management framework

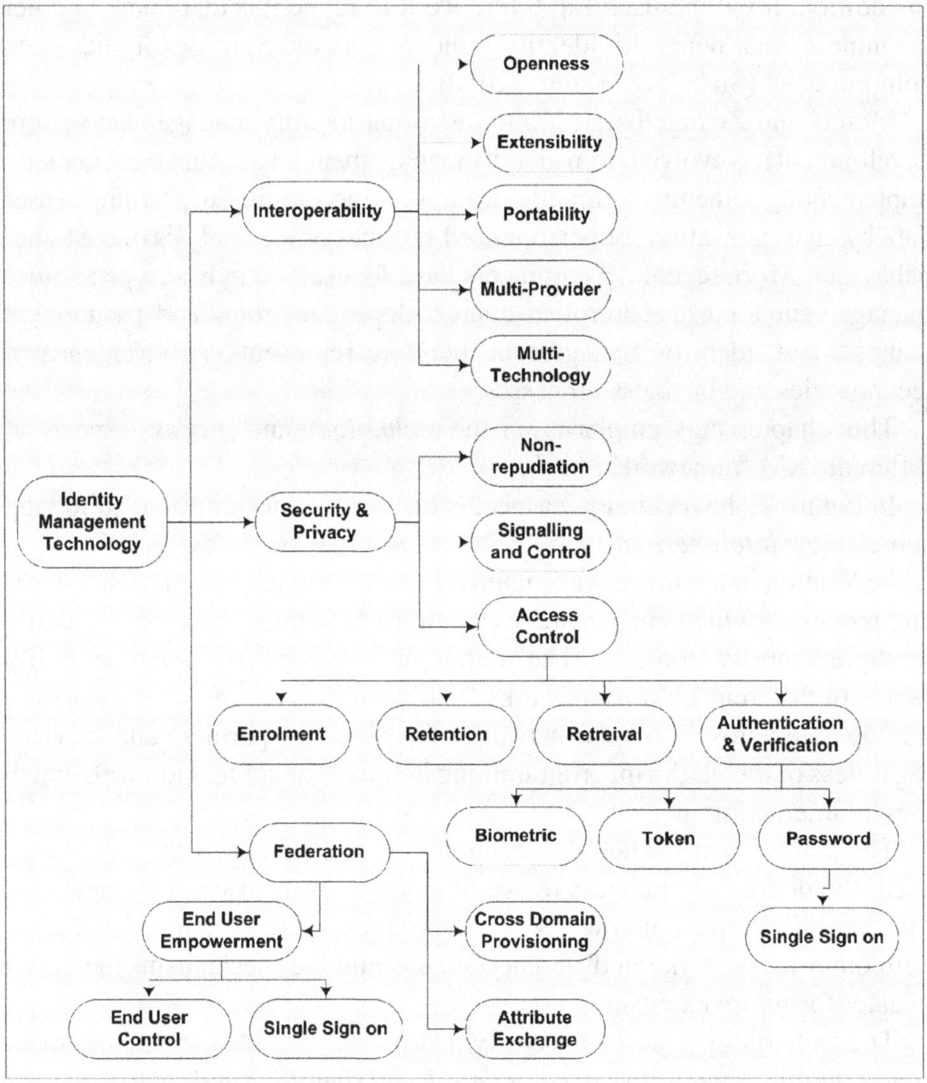

CONCLUSION

After getting a list of technological and process requirements for IAM frameworks, the IAM system owners need provide evidence to demonstrate compliance with privacy, social accessibility and corporate governance policies, as well as forming part of the organisation's security architecture and

Figure 3. A process taxonomy for identity and access management framework

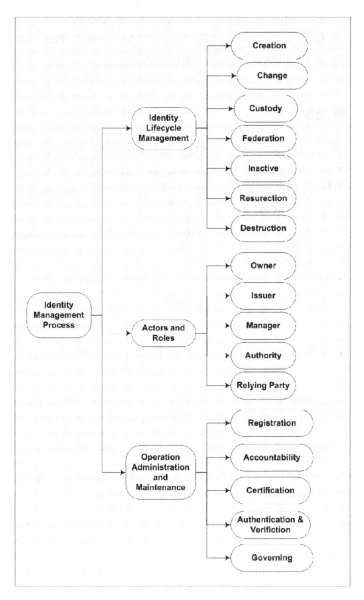

the controls that are aligned with the agreed security controls. By studying the process aspects of different IAM frameworks, the readers can be better prepared for the challenges required to integrate the different frameworks.

Finally, with the help of the taxonomy, it is necessary to gain an understanding of the data that are required to perform periodic audit reviews, security investigations and information for compliance purposes and substantiate claims of improved effectiveness of the IAM framework.

The next chapter will discuss the technical and process architectures of a number of the contemporary IAM frameworks.

REFERENCES

Akram, H., & Hoffmann, M. (2008). *Requirements Analysis for Identity Management in Ambient Environments: The HYDRA Approach.* The 2nd International Workshop on Combining Context with Trust, Security, and Privacy, Trondheim, Norway.

Anwar, M., & Greer, J. (2008). *Role- and relationship-based identity management for private yet accountable e-learning.* Joint iTrust and PST Conferences on Privacy, Trust management and Security, Trondheim, Norway.

Cameron, K. (2005). *Microsoft's Vision for an Identity Metasystem.* Microsoft Corporation.

Commission, E. U. (2014). *The EU explained: Digital agenda for Europe.* Author.

Down, M. P., & Sands, R. J. (2004). Biometrics: an overview of the technology, challenges and control considerations. *Information Systems Control Journal, 4.*

In praise of a second (or third) passport. (2012). *The Economist.*

ITU-T. (2009). *Recommendation ITU-T Y.2720: NGN identity management framework.* International Telecommunication Union.

ITU-T. (2010). *Recommendation ITU-T Y.2012: Functional requirements and architecture of next generation networks.* International Telecommunication Union.

Jain, A. K., & Kumar, A. (2010). *Biometrics of next generation: An overview.* Second Generation Biometrics.

Jain, A. K., Ross, A., & Prabhakar, S. (2004). An introduction to biometric recognition. *IEEE Transactions on Circuits and Systems for Video Technology, 14*(1), 4–20. doi:10.1109/TCSVT.2003.818349

Macgregor, W., Dutcher, W., & Khan, J. (2006). *An Ontology of Identity Credentials Part 1: Background and Formulation. October: Draft Special Publication 800-103*. National Institute of Information and Technology.

Maler, E. (2005). *Federated Identity Management An Overview of Concepts and Standards*. Sun Microsystems, Inc.

Meints, M., & Zwingelberg, H. (2009). *D3.17: Identity Management Systems – recent developments*. Future of Identity in the Information Society.

Onename. (2001). *Requirements for a Global Identity Management Service.* Available: http://www.w3.org/2001/03/WSWS-popa/paper57

Pooe, A., & Labuschagne, L. (2011). Factors impacting on the adoption of biometric technology by South African banks: An empirical investigation. *Southern African Business Review*, 15.

Prabhakar, S., Pankanti, S., & Jain, A. K. (2003). Biometric recognition: Security and privacy concerns. *Security & Privacy, IEEE, 1*(2), 33–42. doi:10.1109/MSECP.2003.1193209

Scott, K., & Johnston, C. R. (2010). Factors affecting the adoption of consumer oriented information technology biometrics solutions by the credit union industry. *Journal of Technology Research, 17*, 13.

Slone, S. (2004). *Identity management*. The Open Group.

Tiffany, E., & Kemp, J. (2005). *Liberty ID-FF 1.2 Static Conformance Requirements version 1.0*. Liberty Alliance Project.

Vienne, D. (2014). *RFP#721-1420 Identity and Access Management Software*. University of Texas at Austin.

Wason, T., Cantor, S., Hodges, J., Kemp, J., & Thompson, P. (2005). *Liberty ID-FF Architecture Overview: Version: 1.2-errata-v1.0*. Liberty Alliance Project.

Zimmerman, W. (2012). *Electronic Biometric Transmission Specification (DoD EBTS) Version 3.0 Transition and Adoption Guidance. Version* (1.0 ed.). Department of Defense.

Chapter 5

A Survey of Contemporary Identity and Access Management Architectures

ABSTRACT

This chapter provides a summary of a number of organisations which are active in IAM researches. The technological and application contributions from each of the IAM contributing organisations, their key deliverables and the active research areas are discussed with the sole purpose in enlightening the knowledge base of the readers.

INTRODUCTION

This chapter is one of the core contributions to the IAM industry offered by the author. The author has spent great effort in studying the technical architectures of a number of contemporary IAM solutions. This chapter will discuss the technological and application contributions for each of the organisations, their key deliverables and the active areas. The author has identified over 20 public and private institutions in different countries which are active contributors in the area of Identity and Access Management. In particular, we'll look into some initiatives that have been established with the primary goal of eliminating passwords. Some of the examples are Microsoft's Cardspace, the Higgins project, the Liberty Alliance, NSTIC, the FIDO Alliance and various Identity 2.0 proposals.

DOI: 10.4018/978-1-5225-4828-7.ch005

FIDIS, PICOS, PrimeLife, and SWIFT

(Glässer and Vajihollahi, 2010) assert that identity management has a crucial role in many strategic applications, including investigation contexts, government services, business intelligence and homeland security. Reviewing current identity management frameworks poses many challenges including establishing proper associations between different identity frameworks and architectures which targets different application aspects and functionalities.

Organisations such as the Future of Identity in the Information Society (FIDIS), Privacy and Identity Management for Community Services (PICOS), Privacy and Identity Management for Europe (PRIME), Privacy and Identity Management in Europe for Life (PrimeLife), and Secure Widespread Identities for Federated Telecommunications (SWIFT) are publicly funded by the European Union's Framework Programme.

FIDIS' work is structured into 7 research activities, which include research into interoperability of identities and identity management systems from the technical, policy, legal and socio-cultural perspectives. FIDIS had contributed significant understanding of the concepts and developments in identity managements from different perspectives in eHealth, eGovernment, and technology. Before FIDIS research activity ended in 2010, FIDIS had proposed a high-level framework for identity management (Backhouse & Dyer, 2007) as showed in Figure 1 which highlights the considerations for Approach, Mechanisms, Obfuscating, and Disclosing aspects for Identification, Identity and Information Management functionalities.

PICOS has set the objective to develop and build a platform for providing the trust, privacy and identity management aspects of community services on the Internet and in mobile communication networks. It has gone through the community analysis phase, context and requirement analysis phase, and development and evaluation phase. PICOS has gone through the assessment and completion phase (PICOS, 2011a). PICOS has developed the *Partial Identity* and *Pseudonyms* (PICOS, 2011b) concept to enable users to create multiple Partial Identities represented by a dedicated identity profile, which contains selected personal information about the user, associated with this identity. This helps user members to manage their real-life roles and contexts within a certain community, and assists in hiding and revealing relations between personal information in different communities.

Figure 1. FIDIS framework for identity management (Backhouse & Dyer, 2007)

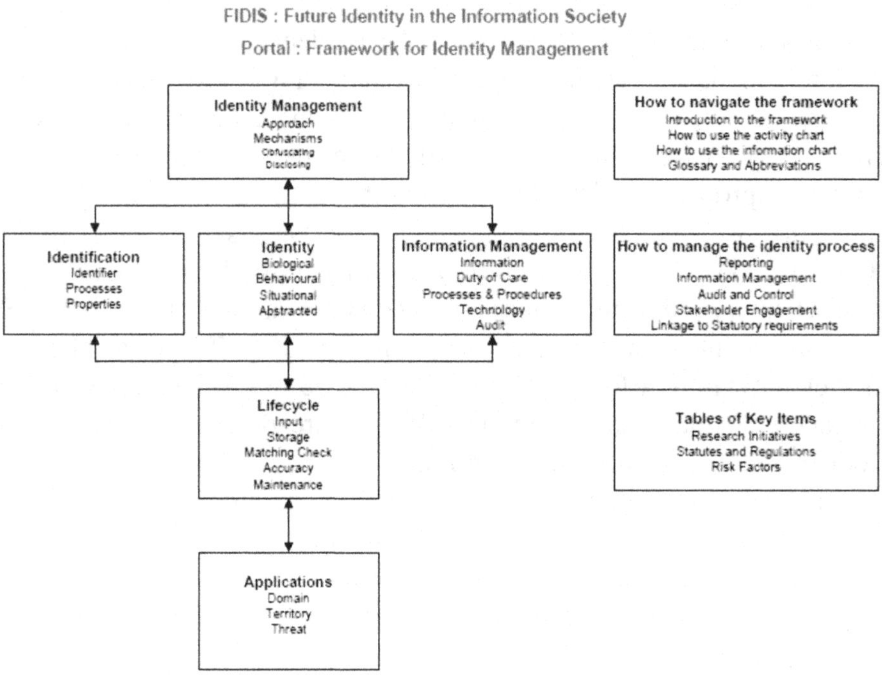
FIDIS : Future Identity in the Information Society
Portal : Framework for Identity Management
Identity Management
Approach
Mechanisms
Obfuscating
Disclosing
How to navigate the framework
Introduction to the framework
How to use the activity chart
How to use the information chart
Glossary and Abbreviations
Identification
Identifier
Processes
Properties
Identity
Biological
Behavioural
Situational
Abstracted
Information Management
Information
Duty of Care
Processes & Procedures
Technology
Audit
How to manage the identity process
Reporting
Information Management
Audit and Control
Stakeholder Engagement
Linkage to Statutory requirements
Lifecycle
Input
Storage
Matching Check
Accuracy
Maintenance
Tables of Key Items
Research Initiatives
Statutes and Regulations
Risk Factors
Applications
Domain
Territory
Threat

Figure 2 describes a 5-layer identity management architecture model adopted by PICOS which consists of: Services and Applications, Content Handling, Member Administration, Communication, and Audit, Control and Reporting component.

Figure 2. High-level view of PICOS architecture (Crane, 2010)

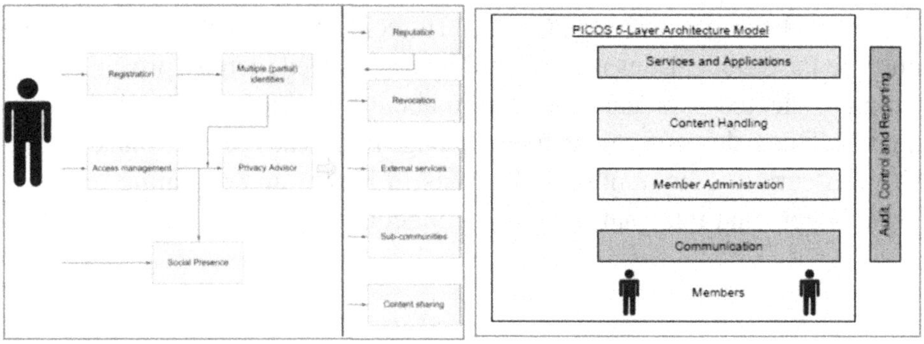
Registration
Access management
Privacy Advisor
Social Presence
Reputation
Revocation
External services
Sub-communities
Content sharing
PICOS 5-Layer Architecture Model
Services and Applications
Content Handling
Member Administration
Communication
Members
Audit, Control and Reporting

The SWIFT Consortium has the goal of leveraging identity technology to integrate service and transport infrastructures on extending identity oriented services and federation to address network usability and privacy concerns across layers.

Research results from Daidalos were adopted by SWIFT to target the following functionality (Lutz, 2010):

- SAML-based Payment Identity Federation architecture;
- Identity aggregation different identity accounts;
- Web and Network Services Authentication using virtual identities and the SWIFT framework;
- Cross-Layer Single-sign-on service;
- SWIFT Credential Bootstrapping authentication mechanisms;
- Deductive Policies language and architecture for authorisation decisions;
- Service Bound Access for service providers to deliver device/network/ location independent service experience to the users,;
- IdM Card to combine IdM functionality and secure storage of personal data into a smart card;
- Enabling Service Architecture for an enabler to interact with access control and identity management functions;
- Identity Transfer function to allow the exchange of security tokens between devices belonging to the same user, and Cross Layer Pseudonymity to provide network privacy through the use of Virtual Network Stacks in conjunction with SAML based pseudonyms.

The SWIFT architecture (Azevedo, 2009) depicted in Figure 3 shows the *Identity Aggregator* as the centerpiece in providing identity federation, authentication, discovery, charging, session admission control, data gateway, and lifecycle management functions. Another important piece is the *Identity Provider lite* providing identity attributes discovery and lifecycle management functions.

PRIME and its follow-on organisation PrimeLife have contributed all their work to the Open Source community with focus on protecting privacy in emerging Internet applications and maintaining life-long privacy (PrimeLife, 2008). *Anonymous credential* is one of the core elements to enable privacy enhancing identity management. Another major contribution from PRIME/ PrimeLife is the Identity Mixer anonymous credential technology donated by IBM Research (Bichsel & Camenisch, 2009).

Figure 3. SWIFT architecture overview (Azevedo, 2009)

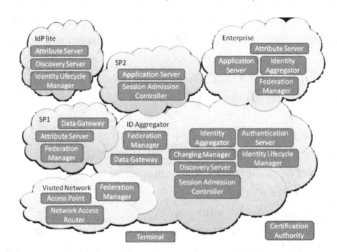

Figure 4 captures the PrimeLife's Anonymous Credential System how the PRIME's Federation Engine supports Identity Mixer technology as well as alternative OpenPGP (Pretty Good Privacy) technology to handle anonymous credential. One point to note is OpenPGP lacks the advanced features provided by Identity Mixer such as Pseudonyms, Partial Credentials and Relational Proofs functionalities.

LIBERTY ALLIANCE, OASIS, AND KANTARA INITIATIVE IDENTITY FEDERATION, GOVERNANCE, AND ASSURANCE FRAMEWORK

Apart from FIDIS, PICOS, PrimeLife and SWIFT, there are other special study groups for Identity and Access Management research founded within standards organisations.

There are two main groups of standardisation effort. The first group is driven by the Liberty Alliance, the Organization for the Advancement of Structured Information Standards (OASIS) and the Kantara Initiative. This group focuses on the federation and interoperability aspects in identity management using a decentralise architecture through efforts in standardisation of Web Services and XML related standards.

The Liberty Alliance architecture is composed of 3 independent modules:

Figure 4. PRIME architecture (Bichsel & Camenisch, 2009)

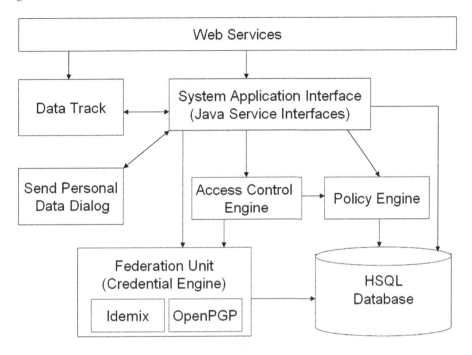

- Liberty Identity Federation Framework (ID-FF) which is the basis of Liberty Single Sign On and Federation framework.
- Liberty Identity Web Services Framework (ID-WSF) which is the federation framework for Web services, allowing providers to share users identities in a permission-based model.
- Liberty Identity Services Interfaces Specifications (ID-SIS) which defines service interfaces for each identity-based Web service for providers to exchange different parts of identity in an interoperable way.

Another key deliverable from this group is Extensible Name Service (XNS), an XML-based digital identity architecture which became part of the XRI (Extensible Resource Identifier) and XDI (XRI Data Interchange) open standards for digital identity addressing and trusted data sharing developed at OASIS. XDI graph is optimised for describing relationships between shared resources and can be used in conjunction with XRI to enable individuals and organisations to establish persistent, privacy-protected Internet identities (Reed & Strongin, 2004).

The Liberty Alliance Identity Federation and Web Services Frameworks paved the way for the proliferation of XML technologies in building identity centric Web services. Liberty Alliance donated its ID-FF specification to OASIS, which became the basis of the Security Assertion Markup Language 2.0 (SAML 2.0) specification (Lockhart & Campbell, 2008).

SAML 2.0 is the key version of the OASIS standard for exchanging authentication and authorisation data between security domains using XML-based security tokens containing assertions to pass information about an end-user between an identity provider and a Web service including SSO. SAML included a set of protocols to handle situations such as: *Assertion Query and Request, Authentication Request, Artifact Resolution, Name Identifier Management & Mapping, and Single Logout.* A review of Web Services Security standards can be found in O'Neill et al. (2003).

The work of Liberty Alliance was donated to the Kantara Initiative in 2009. According to the web page of (2016), The Kantara Initiative is a community of vendors such as: CA Technologies, Experian and ForgeRock; policy and governance organisations such as: Internet Society, OECD-ITAC; research organisations such as: Nomura Research Institute (NRI); standards-setting organisations such as: IEEE; ISO & ITU-T; and government agencies from around the world. The work of Kantara Initiative has been focusing on the development of relationship based identity management solutions.

The Connected Life initiative has set up working groups to look into issues in the following areas:

- User Managed Access (UMA) approved recommendation UMA v1.0.1 issued in 2015 acting as profile of OAuth 2.0. UMA defines how resource owners control their resource from access by clients through arbitrary requesting parties;
- Consent and Information Sharing;
- Identities of Things (IoT); and
- Identity Relationship Management (IRM)(Glazer and Brennan, 2015).

Another initiative, the Trusted Service, initiates works in leveraging the strengths for provision of services among different organisations. This track is more focused in the following areas:

- Health Identity Assurance;
- An implementation profile for eGovernment use of SAML V2.0;
- Federation Operator Guidelines (Furr & Wasley, 2011); and

- The Kantara Initiative Identity Assurance Framework (Soutar & Brennan, 2010).

SHIBBOLETH TOOPHER

Shibboleth is one of the widely deployed open source federated identity solutions. Shibboleth implements the OASIS SAML standard, to provide a federated SSO attribute exchange framework. The Shibboleth Multi-Context Broker Toopher Authentication is a plugin for the Shibboleth Multi-Context Broker. It provides support for Toopher multi-factor authentication as well as multi-context authentication and assurance profiles.

The basic structure of a Shibboleth system is depicted in the following Figure 5. A user request access to the resources managed by a Shibboleth Service Provider. The SP Resource manager will issue a request to the SSO

Figure 5. Shibboleth system structure

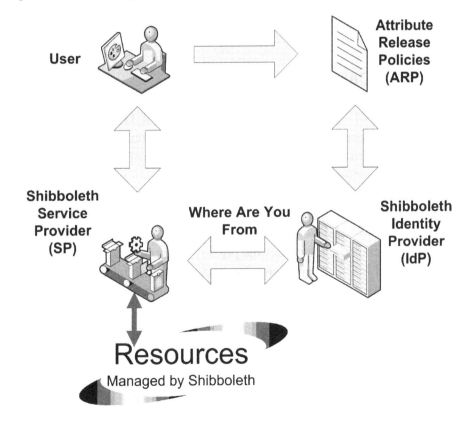

handler of the corresponding Shibboleth IdP using the Where Are You From (WAYF) service. If the user is known to the IdP, the user's attributes will be sent back to the SP with a handle using SAML. This handle has a URL about the current user which can be used to locate the user's attributes.

Otherwise, the user will be asked to perform authentication. The user specifies how much information is sent to the IdP with the help of the Attribute Release Policies (ARP's). The Shibboleth SP consists of 3 components: Assertion Consumer Services, Shibboleth Daemon (shibd) and Resource Manager. The Shibboleth IdP also has three main parts: the attribute query handler, the SSO handler and the directory service.

The Assertion Consumer Services takes care of the returned handle by sending it to "shibd". shibd will request the user's attributes from the Attribute query handler of the IdP. The Attribute query handler determines what attributes should be revealed to shibd according to the user-defined ARP's, and informs the Directory Service on IdP to send the attributes to shibd accordingly.

The user's attributes are relayed back to the Resource Manager to decide whether or not the user should be granted the access basing on the Attribute Acceptance Policies kept at the Resource Manager.

ITU-T AND ISO/IEC

The other group of standardisation effort consists of ITU-T and ISO/IEC where they collaborated on many projects and contributed promising work concerning federation standards for the general information system sector and the telecom sector.

The International Standards Organization / International Electrotechnical Commission Joint Technical Committee 1 Sub-committee 17 Working Group 5 (ISO/IEC JTC 1 /SC 27 WG5) developed methods, techniques and standards to address the identity management and privacy technologies issues. The "ISO/IEC 24745:2011 Information Technology – Security Techniques – Biometric Information Protection" standard has been published as a guideline on the management and processing of biometric data used for authentication.

ISO/IEC 24745 outlines specific measures to protect individuals; among them are:

- Analysis of threats and countermeasures inherent in a biometric and biometric-system application models;
- Security requirements for binding between a biometric reference and an identity reference;
- Biometric system application models with different scenarios for the storage and comparison of biometric references; and
- Guidance on the protection of an individual's privacy during the processing of biometric information.

One of the key deliverables from ISO/IEC is the ISO/IEC 24760 standard which has been developed over a number of years until 2016 (ISO/IEC, 2011, ISO/IEC, 2015, ISO/IEC, 2016).

ISO/IEC 24760 provides in depth discussions on terminology, concepts, reference architecture, requirements and practices for identity management framework.

ISO/IEC 24760-1:2011 defines the terms used in identity management, and some core concepts of identity and identity management and their relationships.

SO/IEC 24760 defines and establishes a framework for identity management, and the management of information associated with the identification of an entity within some context. It covers issues such as identity lifecycle management, provisioning of identities, attribute, implementations and information access management.

ISO/IEC 24760-2:2015 establishes the guidelines how to implement the IAM solution and describes some requirements for the implementation and operation of an IAM solution which adhere to the ISO/IEC 24760 standard.

ISO/IEC 24760-3:2016 details the guidelines for the management of identity information and how an IAM solution conforms to ISO/IEC 24760-1 and ISO/IEC 24760-2.

The work of ISO/IEC concentrates on the use of the proposed framework in the context of Information Security with work in conjunction with other IS/IEC standards such as: ISO/IEC NP 29100 Privacy Framework, ISO/IEC NP 29101 Privacy Reference Architecture, ISO/IEC 20008 Anonymous digital signatures, and ISO/IEC 20009 Anonymous entity authentication.

Furthermore, the International Telecommunication Union, Study Group 17 (ITU-T, 2009a) joint effort with ISO/IEC SC27 on several projects in order to publish common standards. These projects include ISO/IEC 15816: Security information objects for access control (ITU-T X.841), ISO/IEC 14516: Guidelines on the use and management of Trusted Third Party services (ITU-T X.842), and ISO/IEC 29115: Entity authentication assurance (ITU-T X.1254).

The ISO/IEC organisation has formed another Joint Technical Committee 1 Subcommittee 37 (ISO/IEC JTC1 SC37) in 2002 to deal with biometrics specific issues. The JTC 1/SC 37 is responsible for the standardisation of biometric technologies pertaining to human beings to support interoperability and data interchange among applications and systems. Since then, ISO/IEC JC1 SC37 has expanded into the following 6 Working Groups:

- JTC 1/SC 37/WG 1 Harmonized biometric vocabulary
- JTC 1/SC 37/WG 2 Biometric technical interfaces
- JTC 1/SC 37/WG 3 Biometric data interchange formats
- JTC 1/SC 37/WG 4 Biometric functional architecture and related profiles
- JTC 1/SC 37/WG 5 Biometric testing and reporting
- JTC 1/SC 37/WG 6 Cross-Jurisdictional and Societal Aspects of Biometrics

A summary of some of the standards published by JTC 1/SC37 are available on the web site of ISO/IEC JTC 1/SC 37 Biometrics. As at November 2016 (JTC1/SC37, 2016), there are 118 ISO/IEC standards published under the direct responsibility of JTC 1/SC 37.

Some of the representative standards offered by ISO/IEC are included in the following:

- **ISO/IEC 19794-1:2011 Information Technology -- Biometric Data Interchange Formats -- Part 1:** Framework.
- **ISO/IEC 19795-1:2006 Information Technology -- Biometric Performance Testing and Reporting -- Part 1:** Principles and framework.
- **ISO/IEC 24745:2011 Information Technology – Security Techniques – Biometric Information Protection:** Which is a guideline with advice on the management and processing of biometric data used for authentication.
- **ISO/IEC DIS 24779-1 Information Technology -- Cross Jurisdictional and Societal Aspects of Implementation of Biometric Technologies:** Pictograms, icons and symbols for use with biometric systems.
- **ISO/IEC 29109-1 - 2009 - Information Technology -- Conformance Testing Methodology:** For biometric data interchange formats defined in ISO/IEC 19794

- **ISO/IEC PDTR 29156:** Guidance for specifying performance requirements to meet security & usability needs in applications using biometrics
- **ISO/IEC 29164:2011 Information Technology – Biometrics:** Embedded BioAPI
- **ISO/IEC 29794-1:2009 Information Technology -- Biometric Sample Quality -- Part 1:** Framework
- **ISO/IEC 30106-1:2016 Information Technology -- Object Oriented BioAP -- Part 1:** Architecture

BioAPI

The BioAPI (Biometric Application Programming Interface) is developed by the BioAPI Consortium (JTC 1/SC37 in cooperation with other standards bodies) which has been adopted by many standards organisations. ANSI INCTIS has adopted BioAPI as the ANSI INCITS 358 standard. The ISO/IEC adopted BioAPI as the 19784 standard.

The BioAPI standard defines the biometric enrolment and verification (or identification) interfaces between modules that enable software from multiple vendors to be integrated together to provide a biometrics application within a system, or between one or more systems using a defined Biometric Interworking Protocol (BIP). The BioAPI specification has version 2.0 and 2.1 both covering the basic biometric functions of enrolment, verification, and identification and includes a database interface to support the management of the storage of biometric records. The main difference of BioAPI 2.1 from BioAPI 2.0 is the support for *"BioAPI Graphical User Interface" (BioGUI)* for 2.1 applications to control the display of graphics at enrolment, verification, and identification, as an alternative to using the graphical user interface provided by BSPs. BioAPI 2.1 also aligns the values of the type definition BioAPI_BIR_BIOMETRIC_TYPE with those specified in ISO/IEC 19785-1:2006. (Podio, 2010)

The basic architecture of BioAPI 2.0 is illustrated in Figure 6. There are multiple possible (independent) biometric applications that interact with a BioAPI Framework, which in turn routes their *Service Provider Interface (SPI)* messages to *Biometric Service Providers (BSPs)* that support the various biometric capture devices, image enhancement modules, feature extraction, matching, searching, etc. BioAPI architecture also includes the

Figure 6. BioAPI architecture

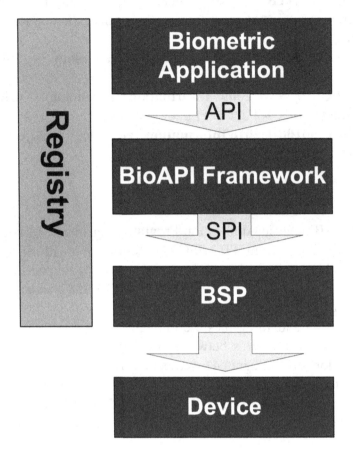

concept of a *Biometric Function Provider (BFP)* and defines further lower-level interfaces between a BFP and a controlling BSP in order to reduce the software development effort for biometric device vendors, allowing (other) software vendors to do most of the work of producing the BSP with an interface to the framework. The BioAPI Registry contains information about the framework, information about the available BSPs ("BSP schemas"), and information about the available devices managed by those BSPs ("device schemas").

In BioAPI 2.0, the Registry is hidden within the framework and accessible only via a small number of standard functions. The only users of the standard who will need to be concerned with the internals of the Registry (or use binary libraries) are those who will implement the framework. (BioAPI.org, 2013)

CBEFF (COMMON BIOMETRIC EXCHANGE FORMATS FRAMEWORK)

Another core biometric standard is the Common Biometric Exchange Formats Framework (CBEFF), a joint effort of JTC 1/SC37 with other orgnaisations such as INCITS (adopted as INCITS 398 standard) and NIST (adopted as NISTIR 6529 standard). The CBEFF specifies a common set of data elements in supporting multiple biometric technologies and to promote interoperability of biometric-based application programs and systems by allowing for biometric data exchange. These common data elements can be placed in a single file, record, or data object used to exchange biometric information between different system components and applications. CBEFF 2.0 is an ISO/IEC JTC 1 standard (ISO/IEC 19785-1:2006). Subcommittee 37 of JTC 1 (SC 37 Biometrics) developed CBEFF 2.0 based upon CBEFF 1.0 with participation by more than a dozen different national standards bodies.

CBEFF 2.0 consists of 4 parts. *Part 1: Data element specification*, specifies abstract data elements for use in biometric record headers, including definitions for biometric identifiers. *Part 2: Procedures for the operation of the Biometric Registration Authority*, defines the authority for this registry and web site and specifies additional biometric identifier data elements beyond those in Part 1. Parts 3 and 4 specify several patron formats (BIRs) and security block formats (SBs).

CBEFF (ISO/IEC 19785-2) defines a *"Biometric Identifier Owner"* entity which has a unique Biometric Organisation value, has the ability to define one or more biometric objects. To become a recognised Biometric Identifier owner (as defined by ISO/IEC 19785-2) and have a unique Biometric Organization value assigned, the entity is required to register with the Biometric Registration Authority (as managed by IBIA). In addition, there are ten types of specific biometric object identifiers. CBEFF defines *"Biometric Identifier"* with two parts: (1) the Biometric Owner identifier and, (2) the specific object identifier.

CBEFF specifies four objects that have owners and identifiers:

1. **The Biometric Data Block (BDB) Format:** Contains the actual biometric data, as opposed to the CBEFF header, which contains fields that describe attributes of the BDB;
2. **The Patron Format:** A specification for a CBEFF header (also called a BIR header or Biometric Information Record header);

3. **The Security Block Format:** A specification for the optional part of a biometric record that describes its encryption and integrity attributes; and

4. **The Product:** A software or hardware object that is associated with the creation or processing of a BDB.

A CBEFF format type or product type represents a specific data format or product defined by the format/product owner. These may be proprietary, unpublished formats (or products) or formats that have been standardised by an industry standards group. The owning entity may optionally register the format/product type value, but is not required to do so. IBIA is the registration authority for CBEFF Format/Product Owner and Format/Product Type values for organisations and vendors that require them. Registration of format owner is required to populate the various format-owner/product-owner fields of the CBEFF header.

According to the National Institute Of Standards And Technology Internal Report (NISTIR) 6529-A specification (Podio et al., 2004), biometric data elements are assembled into data structures that are defined by CBEFF Patron Format Specifications or standards. Each CBEFF-compliant Patron Format Specification defines which CBEFF data elements are present in its format and how the data elements are extracted and processed. CBEFF does not specify the content or format of the actual biometric data contained within a CBEFF biometric data record.

Figure 7 shows that A CBEFF basic data structure is consists of 3 blocks. The *Standard Biometric Header* (SBH) contains 2 mandatory fields: the *BDB Format Owner* which specifies the ID of the Group or Vendor which defined the BDB; and *BDB Format Type* which specifies the BDB Format Type as specified by the Format Owner. The *Biometric Data Block* (BDB) is mandatory which contains raw and processed data defined by the Format

Figure 7. CBEFF basic data structure

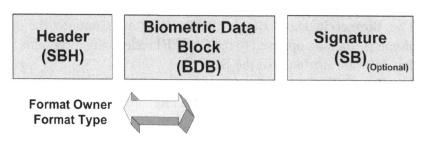

Owner. The data content may be plain or encrypted. The *Signature Block* is optional (only present if the SBH Security Options value is "Integrity-Only" or "Privacy-and-Integrity") which contains the Signature or MAC.

CBEFF Patron is an organisation that has defined a specification incorporating the biometric data object that complies with CBEFF requirements. Example Patrons are BioAPI, ISO 7816-11, and SC37 (19784-3). CBEFF Client is an entity that defines a specific biometric data structure (e.g., a BDB format owner) that meets CBEFF requirements. This would include any vendor, standards committee, working group, or industry consortium that has registered itself with The International Biometrics & Identification Association (IBIA) and has defined one or more BDB format types.

FIDO (FAST IDENTITY ONLINE), OPENID, OPEN GROUP, AND HIGGINS

Fast IDentity Online (FIDO) Alliance started in early 2013 with only six founding members and has gained over 50 members in the first eight months. This rapid movement is indicative of the industry's need for strong authentication standards as the mainstream world is pulled into the post-password paradigm. FIDO members including MasterCard, Google, PayPal, Lenovo, NXP, Nok Nok Labs and Validity, among others, to identify and set a strategy on how to eliminate consumers' reliance on passwords.

This initiative will focus on creating an open, scalable, interoperable set of mechanisms to easily and securely authenticate users of online services. The FIDO Alliance is working in a new open industry standard for online authentication which claims is the beginning of the end of passwords and PINs - and a future ecosystem with biometrics as the key component. The following Figure 8 is an extract from the FIDO Web Site explaining how it works by the use of FIDO Plugins in a browser or a FIDO compatible Authenticator in accessing Web resources.

Apart from FIDO, OpenID is another non-commercial organisation initiated to establish a single identifier, profile and password for easy and secure logging on to multiple web sites. The OpenID Framework (Recordon and Reed, 2006) is started as an HTTP-based URL authentication protocol based on a 3-parties process: *The end user, The Identifier Provider* (host the end user profile information, identifier and associated password) and *The Service Provider*.

Figure 8. FIDO: how does it work?
(Source: http://www.fidoalliance.org/how-it-works.html)

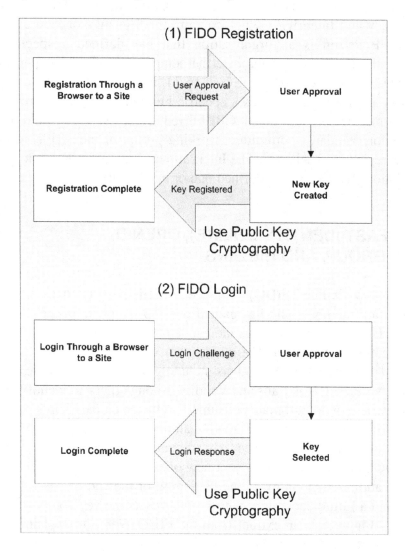

OpenID is a Web registration and SSO protocol that lets users register and login to OpenID-enabled websites using their private choice of OpenID identifier. An OpenID takes the form of a unique URL, and is managed by some *"OpenID providers"* (such as Yahoo, Google, or IBM) that handles authentication. OpenID has evolved to embrace the Open Trust Frameworks for Open Government (Thibeau & Reed, 2009) using *Information Cards* as digital identity for certification programs that enable a relying party to trust the identity, security, and privacy assurances from an identity provider.

After OpenID, we like to mention Open Group which is one of the open source organisations working jointly with the US InterNational Committee for Information Technology Standards (INCITS CS1) to develop an International Standard Framework for Identity Management. The Open Group Identity Management Architecture Guide G072 (Harding et al., 2007) addresses the key issues that an enterprise architect needs to consider in the process of developing an enterprise identity management architecture.

Lastly, the Eclipse Foundation (Higgins, 2009) is another framework that enables users and other systems to integrate identity, profile, and relationship information across multiple heterogeneous systems. Higgins is compatible with SAML 2.0 making use of *Security Token Service IdP solution* to implements the OASIS WS-Trust standard. Higgins unifies all identity interactions (regardless of protocol/format) under a common user interface metaphor called *i-cards*.

A SUMMARY OF IDENTITY AND ACCESS MANAGEMENT CONTRIBUTING ORGANISATIONS

In the private sector, the findBiometrics.com portal contains a list of vendors supplying identity management solutions with or without using the biometric technology. Fujitsu has ventured with ImageWare Systems (a provider of a multimodal biometric security solutions called CloudID) to enable the deployment of a new multi-modal biometric identity management solution and model certified on Fujitsu's NuVola Private Cloud Platform for the enterprise. HP provides ArcSight Correlation Optimized Retention and Retrieval Engine (CORR-Engine) to address the fast data retrieval for forensic analysis and compliance reporting requirements.

On the other hand, IBM offers its Tivoli IAM solution using business-driven approach starting with analysing business roles for customers, employees and business partners. Define access roles for each entity, to map against four universal processes of IAM: Provisioning, Productivity, Access and Audit. IBM IAM solution consists of (a) the Tivoli IdM to support the provisioning of business focus view, automate account setup, removal and management; (b) the Tivoli Access Manager for productivity management of the enterprise SSO, federated IdM productivity, business-focused view and consistently apply an access control policy across entire business environment; (c) the Tivoli Security Information and Event Manager for auditing, monitoring and reporting on user behaviour across entire infrastructure. The next chapter will provide more detail about the IBM Security Identity Manager and Cloud Identity Service.

Table 1 is a summary of organisations which are active in identity and access management researches.

Table 1. Identity management contributing organisations

Organisation	Active Areas	Key Deliverables
1. Privacy and Identity Management for Europe (PRIME)	privacy-enhancing Identity Management System	• idemix (identity mixer), an anonymous credential system • OnionCofee, a Java module for exchange of information over the Net anonymously No further update after 2008
2. PrimeLife	Follow-on project of PRIME from March 2008	• MediaWiki Privacy enhanced access control / reputation • Scramble!-for users to enforce access control over their own data in a social network
3. Future of Identity in the Information Society (FIDIS)	Identity profiling, Interoperability of Ids and IdMS & Forensic	• Identity in the Information Society Journal • Use cases and scenarios (Jaquet-Chielle et al., 2006) No further update after 2009
4. Privacy and Identity Management for Community Services (PICOS)	Mobile application identity management	Trust and Privacy Assurance of the Platform and Community (Vivas and Agudo, 2011)
5. Secure Widespread Identities for Federated Telecommunications (SWIFT)	Transport infrastructures for identity federation	• Scenarios and use cases (Scholta, 2010) • SWIFT Authentication Framework • Prototype Specification (Marx, 2009)
6. GUIDE	IdM for eGovernment	Pan-European architecture for identity interoperability (2005) No update after 2009
7. Center for Applied Identity Management Research (CAIMR)	IdM in Public and individual safety	Research Agenda for confronting Global Identity Management Challenges (Gordon et al., 2009)
8. International Telecommunication Union (ITU-T)	Telecommunication security & identity management	Recommendations ITU-T Y.2720, X.1250,
9. The Open Group Identity Management Forum	Framework for Identity Management.	• Identity Management Architecture Guide (G072) • Identity Management Design Patterns
10. ISO/IEC JTC1 SC17 ISO/IEC JTC1 SC27 ISO/IEC JTC1 SC37	Standards Body	• ISO/IEC 24760 Framework for Identity Management • ISO/IEC 24745:2011 Information Technology – Security Techniques – Biometric Information Protection • ISO/IEC 19784-x BioAPI • ISO/IEC 19785-x Common Biometric Exchange Formats Framework (CBEFF)

continued on following page

Table 1. Continued

Organisation	Active Areas	Key Deliverables
11. The OpenID Foundation	Adoption of OpenID in identity privacy & security on the web	• The OpenID authentication protocol • Open Trust Frameworks for Open Government
12. The Liberty Alliance	Build interoperable and secure federated identity management services	• Identity Systems and Liberty Specification, Version 1.1: Interoperability • Liberty Identity Federation Framework • Liberty Alliance Identity Web Services Framework • Liberty Alliance Governance Framework • Liberty Alliance Identity Assurance Framework
13. Kantara Initiative	Shape the future of digital identity	Follow-on of the Liberty Alliance Project
14. National Institute of Standards and Technology (NIST)	Models and metrics for identity management	• SP: 800-103 Ontology of Identity Credentials • IR 6529 – Adopted ISO/IEC CBEFF standard
15. Fast IDentity Online Alliance (FIDO)	Formed in 2012	Still in planning stage as at 2013o develop security specifications for devices and browser plugins that supplant reliance on passwords to securely authenticate users of online services.
16. Biometrics Identity Management Agency (BIMA)	Leads the DoD activities to program, integrate, and synchronise biometric technologies	• Participates in INCIST M1 and ISO/IEC JC1 SC37 • Editor of the DoD Electronic Biometric Transmission Specification (EBTS)
17. National Science & Technology Council (NSTC) Subcommittee on Biometrics and IdM	Advise and coordinate the Executive Office of the President of USA on policies, procedures and plans	• NSTC Policy for Enabling the Development, Adoption and Use of Biometric Standards • Privacy & Biometrics Building a Conceptual Foundation
18. InterNational Committee for Information Technology Standards Biometrics Technical Committee (INCITS M1)	Biometric standards for data interchange formats, common file formats, API, profiles, and performance testing and reporting.	• Conformance Test Architecture (CTA) and Conformance Test Suites (CTSs) for Biometric Data Interchange Format • INCITS 358: BioAPI • INCITS 398: CBEFF • INCITS 442: Biometric Identity Assurance Service • INCITS 377 to 396: Finger Pattern Based Interchange Format to Iris Interchange Format to Hand Geometry Interchange Format
19. Department of Homeland Security Biometrics Coordination Group (DHSBCG), USA	Develop biometric standards for DHS and coordinates DHS biometrics representation to national and international bodies	Under INCITS/M1 standards: Facial and Photo standard; Fingerprint and Iris standards; and Biometric Profiles for Border Control and Airport Access Control
20. BioAPI Consortium	A consortium of over 120 companies and organisations to develop the BioAPI specifications	BioAPI
21. OASIS Biometric Technical Committee	Create specifications for biometrics multi-factor authentication	The NIST Specification for WS-Biometric Devices (WS-BD) Version 1

Table 2 highlights some of the underlying technologies used by the different identity management frameworks. It shows that most of the frameworks use SAML as the underlying technology but with their private add-on components to address similar issues in trust, privacy and interoperability.

Therefore, using SAML as one of the standard technologies in managing federated identities seems to be a viable choice together with suitable solutions in enabling interoperable identity management functions amongst different identity management frameworks. As for the biometrics market, we observed that the existing commercial market is evolving from the offering of single factor single-modal authentication method into multi-factors multimodal biometric authentication techniques with fingerprinting and facial recognition are two of the most widely adopted biometric measures.

Table 2. Underlying technologies used by different identity management frameworks

Framework Name	Underlying Technologies	Target Protection Area
FIDIS	n/a	Interoperability of identities and identity management systems
PICOS	Partial Identity and Pseudonyms	Trust, privacy and identity management aspects of community services
SWIFT	Daidalos (virtual Ids), IdM Card, Virtual Network Stacks and SAML pseudonyms.	Generic
PrimeLife	Identity Mixer, OpenPGP	Privacy enhancing identity management
Liberty Alliance architecture	SAML 2.0, Liberty Single Sign-On and Federation, Liberty Web Services, XNS and XDI	Federation and interoperability aspects in identity management
ITUT Y.2720 NGN identity management framework	Packet-based Next Generation Network	Assurance of identity information and enable secured business applications
OpenID Framework	HTTP-based URL authentication Information Cards	Web registration and single sign-on
Open Group Identity Management Architecture	Universally Unique Identifier (UUID), and the Globally Unique Identifier (GUID). SAML 2.0	Directory Interoperability, Messaging, Mobile Management, and Security
Higgins Open Source Identity Framework,	SAML 2.0, OpenID and IMI compatible	Personal Data Store
FIDO	Web and Biometric	Remove the need for Password/PIN in Web online applications
ISO/IEC ISO/IEC JTC1 SC17, SC27, SC37	BioAPI, CBEFF	Biometric Identification
OASIS	XRI and XDI SAML 2.0	Digital identity addressing and trusted data sharing
Fujitsu PalmSecure™	Biometric - Palm Vein Pattern	Financial, healthcare and general market

OTHER BIOMETRIC STANDARDS
BODIES RELATED TO IAM

Apart from the ISO/IEC, there are also a number of standard bodies and organisations with interest in developing and promoting the use of biometric technologies. Some of the organsiations are discussed in the following:

- Department of Defense Biometric Standards Working Group (DoD BSWG)

The DoD BSWG is established to coordinate the efforts of stakeholder organisations within the DoD and the US government in playing a vital role to leverage joint expertise, build consensus, and coordinate activities and participation in standards bodies.

So far, the DoD had published a number of specifications for applications in the defense. Such as the *DoD IDD* (DoD, 2011b) which defines the data standards acting as the authoritative source for DoD biometrics data elements that are to be used to exchange among DoD Biometric Systems. Another example is the *DoD EBTS* (DoD, 2011a), which is closely aligned to the FBI Electronic Biometric Transmission Specification (FBI EBTS) v9.3.

- National Science & Technology Council (NSTC) Subcommittee on Biometrics and IdM

The NSTC Subcommittee on Biometrics and IdM has been in operation since 2003. This NTSC Subcommittee on BioIdM acts as an advisor and coordination body to the Executive Office of the President of USA on policies, procedures and plans for federally sponsored biometric and IdM activities that are of interagency importance as well as strengthening international and public sector partnerships to foster the advancement of biometric technologies.

- Department of Homeland Security (DHS) Biometrics Coordination Group (BCG)

The main function of DHS BCG is to develop biometric standards for DHS and coordinates DHS biometrics representation to national and international bodies (NSTC, INCITS, ISO, ICAO, OASIS). Some of the standards under the umbrella of DHS BCG are INCITS/M1 Facial and Photo standard;

Fingerprint and Iris standards; and Biometric Profiles for Border Control and Airport Access Control.

- InterNational Committee for Information Technology Standards Biometrics Technical Committee (INCITS M1)

INCITS is one of the major standards organisations in the US responsible for the development of Information and Communication Technology (ICT) standards. The INCITS/M1, Biometrics Technical Committee program of work includes biometric technical interfaces standards, biometric data interchange format standards, conformance testing methodology standards for the biometric technical interfaces, conformance testing methodologies for the biometric data interchange formats, biometric profiles, and biometric performance testing and reporting standards. INCITS/M1 also serves as the U.S. Technical Advisory Group (U.S. TAG) for the ISO/IEC JTC 1/SC 37.

- Biometrics Identity Management Agency (BIMA)

The Biometrics Identity Management Agency is set up to lead the DoD activities to program, integrate, and synchronise biometric technologies and capabilities and to operate and maintain DoD's authoritative biometric database to support the National Security Strategy. The BIMA participates in the INCIST M1 and the ISO/IEC JC1 SC37 as well as serving as editor of the DoD Electronic Biometric Transmission Specification (EBTS) and is responsible for the DoD EBTS change control.

- International Biometrics & Identification Association (IBIA)

The IBIA is a trade association founded in 1998 in Washington to promote the effective and appropriate use of technology to determine identity and enhance security, privacy, productivity, and convenience for individuals, organisations, and governments.

- findBiometrics

findBiometrics is an online portal dedicated for the biometrics and identity management industry since 2002. The portal contains thousands of articles, video clips and press releases for the subscribers. Companies choose to place advertisements and webinars through the portal.

- The BioAPI Consortium

The BioAPI Consortium is founded to develop a biometric Application Programming Interface (API) that brings platform and device independence to application programmers and biometric service providers. The Consortium consists of over 120 companies and organisations in developing the BioAPI specification and reference implementation for a standardised API that is compatible with a wide range of biometric application programs and a broad spectrum of biometric technologies.

- The Organisation for the Advancement of Structured Information Standards (OASIS) Biometric Technical Committee

OASIS formed the Biometric Technical Committee in Feb 2013 with the goal to create specifications that make biometrics more viable within multi-factor authentication which include biometrics as well as other technologies, such as cryptographic certificate use and management.

ACTORS AND ROLES

After having an overview of the landscape of contemporary IAM frameworks and the contributing organisations, the following sections will discuss some aspects of the IAM frameworks in greater details. One of the aspects to look at is how different frameworks define their actors and roles.

The actors and roles aspects of five different IAM frameworks have been studied.

SWIFT specified a set of roles (Scholta, 2010) which rely on SAML-based Service Oriented Architecture. Apart from the typical *End-user* and *Service Provider* roles, SWIFT defined the *Identity Provider* role which may combine any of three other sub-roles of *Identity Aggregator* (manage profiles and virtual identities), *Attribute Provider* (manager identity attribute), and *Authentication Provider* (verify user identity authenticity). SWIFT also defined the *Identity Management Subscriber* role which will maintain at least one subscription with an Identity Provider.

The second framework is the NIST Identity Ontology (MacGregor et al., 2006) as showed in Figure 9. The NIST Identity Ontology defines a set of *"models"* or *"planes"* representing different projections of the Identity Credential Ontology. It uses the *Actor Plane* to describe actors and relationships

Figure 9. NIST identity ontology: actor plane
(MacGregor et al., 2006)

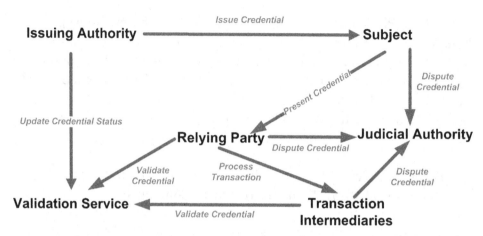

in the domain of identity credential systems. There are other planes such as, the *Issuance Plane* to describe the relationships between the Issuing Authority and other parties that are relevant to identity credential issuance, the *Maintenance Plane* to describe to describe the relationships of the Issuing Authority with other parties after issuance of an identity credential, and the *Transaction Plane* which describes the use of an identity credential in a transaction between the Subject and a Relying Party. There is also a *Life Events Plane* which illustrates events in the life of a Subject.

There are six actors define in the NIST framework: *Issuing Authority, Subject, Validation Service, Relying Party, Judicial Authority,* and *Transaction Intermediaries*. These actors defined in NIST have similar roles to other frameworks but may have different meanings. For example, in NIST the *Subject* presents the identity credential to the *Relying Party*. The Relying Party combines information from the identity credential with other transaction-relevant information, and communicates a transaction record to a *Transaction Intermediary*. Other frameworks may have different actors to perform the intermediary role.

Figure 10 shows that ITU-T X.1250 defines a five party identity management model (ITU-T, 2009b) which consists of the following:

- *Identity provider* to maintain and manage trusted identity information of other entities (e.g., end user, organisations, and devices) and offers identity-based services;

Figure 10. ITU-T five party identity management model (ITU-T, 2009b)

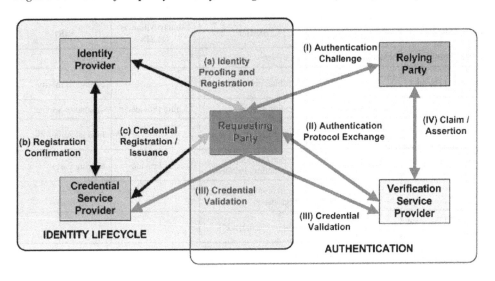

- *Credential service provider* to serve activities related to the issuance of credentials and tokens (e.g. credentials that bind tokens to verifiable identifiers and attributes);
- *Verification service provider* to assess identity information (e.g. claims and credentials) and classifying its validity;
- *Relying party* that relies on an identity representation or claim by a requesting/asserting entity within some request context; and
- *Requesting party* where all queries/responses are directed through the requesting party.

The OpenID Authentication Framework (OpenID, 2007) defines four actors from the platform perspective, *User-Agent* which is the end user's Web browser, *Relying Party* which is the Web application that wants proof that the end user controls an Identifier, *OpenID Provider* which is the OpenID Authentication server on which a Relying Party relies for an assertion that the end user controls an Identifier, and *OpenID Endpoint URL* which is the URL which accepts OpenID Authentication protocol messages.

Table 3 is a summary of the actors and roles defined by the five different frameworks. It should be noted that different frameworks define their actors differently although with similar roles. It is observed that the OASIS framework used the Service Oriented Architecture 3-party model to generalise into identity management which seems odd to other frameworks.

Table 3. Summary of actors and roles defined in 5 different frameworks

OpenID	ITU-T X.1250, Y.2720	SWIFT	Liberty Alliance/ OASIS	NIST
User Agent	Requesting Party	End User	User	Subject
OpenID Provider	Credential Service Provider	Attribute provider		Issuing Authority
	Identity Provider	Identity Aggregator	Identity Provider	Validation Service
	Verification Service Provider	Authorization Provider		Judicial Authority
Relying Party	Relying Party	Service Provider (Accounting, Payment)	Service Provider	Relying Party
		Agent (configure Id Aggregator)		Transaction Intermediaries
OpenID Endpoint URL		Identity Subscriber		

Also, the OpenID authentication framework is platform specific and may be difficult to integrate with other solutions. Interoperability across different contexts requires a common semantic. After consolidating the actors from different frameworks, we propose the following set of actors for the consideration of our readers:

- **User:** Which is the end-user who owns the identity and initiate service request.
- **Identity Issuing Authority/Credential Service Provider:** Which is the body who governs the issuance of credentials.
- **Identity Provider:** Which manages profiles, virtual identities, identity attribute, and verify user identity authenticity.
- **Service Provider:** Which is the party who provides end service to the user and relies on an identity claim by the requesting user.
- **Judicial Authority:** Which is the government body who will use the services of the Issuing Authority and Validation Services during dispute resolution.
- **Intermediary Agent:** Which is the hybrid actors who are the middlemen between the user and the other different actors.
- **Identity Subscriber:** Which is the body who subscribes to the service provided by different Identity Providers and provide agent service to other Service Providers.

INTEROPERABILITY

Interoperability is always an issue for all IAM frameworks and systems as interoperability across different contexts is impossible without a common semantic. The issue of interoperability of IAM frameworks requires agreeing on appropriate technical standards to deal with issues of technical platform, operating system, database standards and formats, and communication protocols.

The FIDIS (Backhouse & Vanfleteren, 2005) survey result is showed in Figure 11. There are three main areas of concern for interoperability issue of identity management, which are: *Cultural* (which is related to trust, usability, and semantic issues); *Legal* (which is related to compliance & privacy issues); and *Technical* (which is related to standards, protocols, hardware & software, and networking issues). Culture and legal barriers are considered even more difficult to overcome than the technical issues.

Multifactor authentication involving biometrics poses several security challenges because of the inherent features of the biometric data itself. The probabilistic nature of the biometric matching process and the issue of

Figure 11. FIDIS requirements for identity management interoperability (Backhouse & Vanfleteren, 2005)

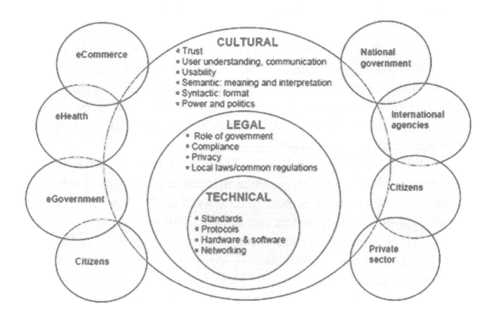

protecting biometric data in the time of enrolment or verification process demand vendors usually come up with their specific template solution and encryption technology because in case biometric data are compromised, it is difficult to revoke.

Almost all the frameworks that have been studied claim that interoperability and openness are their primary goals. However, as the author has stressed in the earlier discussions, the interoperability nature offered by different frameworks have their own target user groups in mind which may be characterised by the nature of the target business model, limited by the relying technologies and lack of a common semantic across different identity management frameworks. These frameworks in many cases make use of a suite of protocols to connect a number of identity management repositories with numerous service providers and the client-side identity management frontends.

PrimeLife's target platform is Web HTTP. Web 2.0 and AJAX programming style imparts complexity on the client as well as on the server side because more generic APIs are required to be invoked by complex applications running on the client. This implication is also valid to other identity management frameworks relying on the Web HTTP protocol.

The Liberty Alliance and OASIS SAML 2.0 federated identity management approach is based on the XML technology with focus on identity-based Web services building trust relationships between business and the ability to federate isolated accounts of users among well-defined trust circles. Identities are represented by different accounts that the user may have at different identity providers.

Koschinat et al. (2009) commented that the Liberty Alliance framework has a complex interaction scheme, which requires the introduction of multiple services at different entities which could lead to problems in the adoption by users. Furthermore, the use of standard SOAP and XML structures increases interoperability but requires other, additional entities are also compatible with Liberty Alliance framework.

The ITU-T and ISO/IEC framework (ITU-T, 2009c) stressed the importance of clearly defined data model and schemas to facilitate interoperability between heterogeneous identity management systems within an NGN provider domain, between different NGN providers and web-services providers.

The OpenID Initiative provides the interoperable Open Identity Solutions Trust Frameworks for federal use. At the moment, OpenID seems not compatible to other identity management frameworks. Furthermore, the framework does not provide rules for the security of the identification process the user's choice of the OpenID provider which is essential for the overall integrity of the system. In theory, one OpenID is required for a physical person only. In reality, a person can register with multiple OpenID providers and the registration and security and privacy-related process do not provide much possible countermeasures.

Table 4 provides a summary of the interoperability issues encountered by some of the identity management frameworks.

The author observed that the federation effort in interoperability between different authentication mechanisms and processes has been addressed by the OASIS/Liberty Alliance group. On the other hand, the federation standards for the general information system sector and the telecom sector are offered by ITU-T and ISO/IEC. What we can expect to see is the issue of interoperability of the different federation frameworks to be achieved by establishing a common semantic and a simplified common protocol stack.

In the biometric arena, the interoperability issue has been dealt with by the BioAPI and CBEFF standards using CBEFF Patron and Client model. The CBEFF framework defines the Patron entity as an organisation that has the ability to define a specification incorporating the biometric data object that complies with CBEFF requirements. An example is the ISO 7816-11, and SC37 (19784-3). CBEFF also defines the CBEFF Client entity that defines a specific biometric data structure (e.g., a BDB format owner) that meets CBEFF requirements.

Table 4. Interoperability issues of some identity and access management frameworks

Identity Management Framework	Interoperability Underlying Technologies	Interoperability Issues
PrimeLife	Web HTTP. Web 2.0 and AJAX	More generic APIs are required on the server side
Liberty Alliance and OASIS	XML SAML 2.0	Focus on identity-based Web services building trust relationships
ITU-T and ISO/IEC	NGN domain	Clearly defined data model and schemas between different NGN provider and web-services providers
OpenID	Open Identity Solutions Trust Frameworks	Registration and security and privacy-related process do not provide rules for the security of the identification process the user's choice of the OpenID provider
BioAPI & CBEFF	CBEFF Patron and CBEFF Client model	Registration with IBIA is required

FEDERATION

Federation and interoperability closely resemble each other as federated frameworks need to interoperate across organisational boundaries and work on common processes utilising different technologies, identity storage, security approaches and programming models. A federated framework requires identities and their associated credentials to be stored, owned and managed in a distributed manner with each individual member of the federation able to manage its own identities, with the ultimate capability to securely sharing and accepting identities and credentials from other sources.

A federated framework requires a standardised and secure way of expressing not only the services it makes available to trusted partners and customers, but also the credentials and policies by which it support.

(Poetzsch et al., 2009) highlighted that there are two layers to deal with the security aspects for a federated framework: infrastructure layer and communication layer, which emphasised for a secured and trusted communication environment. At the moment, the challenge for the federation area of identity management seems to be the interoperability and harmonisation of the different federation standards and solutions.

(Naderi et al., 2008) follow and build on the work of FIDIS to propose the Federated Global Identification Management Framework (FeGIMa). The FeGIMa framework makes identity and entitlements portable across autonomous policy domains within the global framework.

(Poetzsch et al., 2009) define Identity Federation Management systems should have three core features: *Identity Provisioning, SSO,* and *Attribute Exchange* (linkage of several attributes of the user to one digital identity to facilitate authorisation).

(Maler, 2005) proposed a federated identity management system using widely deployed solutions of SAML and Liberty Alliance standards. Liberty Alliance Project have developed SAML based on the Liberty Alliance Identity Federation Framework (ID-FF) 1.2 Specifications, 2007 which focuses on maintaining trust relationships between business and the federation of isolated accounts of users among well-defined trust circles. This framework mandates a third party authentication model, where individual services rely upon assertions generated by an identity provider using XML Web services. Thus, the service relies on an entity whose sole responsibility is to identify the user based on direct authentication which requires a trusted relationship be established between the service provider and the identity provider.

SAML assertions carry statements about a principal that an asserting party claims to be true. Attribute Profiles define how to exchange attribute information using assertions in a number of common usage environments (e.g. X.500/LDAP directories). SAML Metadata defines a way to express and share configuration information between SAML parties. SAML Authentication Context detailed information regarding the type and strength of authentication that a user employed when they authenticated at an identity provider.

SAML supports the establishment of pseudonyms established between an identity provider and a service provider to protect privacy. Liberty Alliance framework supports the use of multiple identities, pseudonyms and anonymity. However, it seems there is no standard available for logging and exchange of the use of personal data. Such a function relies on the Identity Provider and Service Provider. This may hinder the future development in the signalling and control aspect of a federated identity theft monitoring mechanism. From the user-empowerment perspective, Liberty Alliance framework does not provide the end-user with specific privacy support.

From the ITU-T/ISO/IEC group, ITU-T developed the X.1500 CYBEX Cybersecurity information exchange framework (ITU-T, 2010a) which defines the federation of cybersecurity information such as vulnerability, incident, and heuristics, identification and discovery information.

So far, the ITU-T CYBEX architecture is one of the most recent developments in addressing the needs for cybersecurity operations principally consist of three domains: *Incident Handling, ICT Asset Management and Knowledge Accumulation.*

The CYBEX architecture makes use of a suit of other specifications such as, Discovery Mechanisms in the Exchange of Cybersecurity Information, Common Vulnerabilities and Exposures (CVE), Common Vulnerability Scoring System (CVSS), Common Weakness Enumeration (CWE), Common weakness scoring system (CWSS), Open Vulnerability and Assessment Language (OVAL), Incident object description exchange format (IODEF), Asset Reporting Format (ARF), Common Event Expression (CEE), Common Attack Pattern Enumeration, Malware attribute enumeration and classification (MAEC) and Classification (CAPEC). The author believes this work will make impact to the future development of the federation aspect in identity management.

Table 5 highlights some of the federation issues exhibited by three IAM frameworks. For a successful adoption of a federated identity management framework, the following capabilities are suggested:

Table 5. Federation issues of some identity management frameworks

Identity Management Framework	Underlying Technologies Used in Federation	Federation Issues
FIDIS FeGIMa Framework	Three core features required: Identity Provisioning, Single-Sign On, and Attribute Exchange	Limited to FeGIMa only
Liberty Alliance Identity Federation Framework (ID-FF)	SAML 2.0	XML Web Services required Does not provide the end-user with specific privacy support
ITU-T/ISO/IEC group X.1500 CYBEX Framework	Use of a suit of other ITU-T specifications (CVE, CWE, CVSS, CWSS, OVAL, ARF, IODEF, CEE, MACE & CAPEC)	Focused on Cybersecurity operations only

- A common extensible vocabulary regarding the actors, roles, and actions of different identity actors;
- A common assertion and authentication protocol framework;
- A common negotiation protocol for privacy security and trust model; and
- A universal data representation and semantic definition.

Unfortunately, it seems none of the IAM frameworks that the author has reviewed so far are offering these features to accommodate interoperable federation with other frameworks.

SECURITY, PRIVACY, AND TRUST

Security, privacy and trust are closely related topics because trust is releasing one self's private details to another party in a given situation with a feeling of relative security. Furthermore, storing biometric information in repositories along with other personally identifiable information raises security and privacy concerns because the identity databases are vulnerable to attacks by insiders or external adversaries.

At present, Kerberos security together with PKI/X.509 mechanisms is considered a viable solution to privacy because PKI identities combined with the Transport Layer Security (TLS) protocol can provide secured point-to-point interactions. However, for security, privacy and trust aspects in identity management, the author considers that finer grain of control mechanisms should be available in allowing a particular user-id's role and preconditions pair to access a particular set of identities as well as providing role-precondition specific views to safeguard identity information from being viewed and modified by unauthorised system users.

This review study shows that all the IAM frameworks that have been reviewed in this chapter provide comprehensive security, privacy and trust functionalities using different technologies, for example, OASIS eXtensible Access Control Markup Language (XACML), IETF Common Policy, W3C Platform for Privacy Preferences (P3P), and Liberty Alliance SAML. However, most of these technologies seem not able to interoperate with other frameworks.

OASIS enhanced Liberty Alliance's work to establish the XACML standard to become one of the core technologies in delivering privacy functionalities in identity management frameworks. Liberty Alliance treats privacy as security policy applied to a principal. Liberty Alliance's framework specifies *"opaque handlers"* to allow for an *"Anonymous Identity Protocol"*. As for policy handling, this framework does not cater for policy negotiation and enforcement between users and identity/service providers. It does not provide history management, nor context detection as well. User Data are stored on different identity provider servers, each containing only partial data.

XACML defines the syntax and semantics of a language for expressing and evaluating access control policies through a network of XACML Policy Enforcement Points and XACML Policy Decision Points. The author's comment to XACML is that, although XACML may enable some type of federated access management where policies are "negotiated" based upon user roles and environmental factors, we still in need of an identity model that can meet the flexibility, and dynamic nature of user behaviour, device and applications heterogeneity.

W3C's work in identity management is represented by their involvement with the PrimeLife consortium in the development of the P3P specification to enable websites to express their privacy practices. In theory, P3P should be compatible with XACML because P3P allow users to define simple privacy policies for point-to-point interactions. P3P expresses privacy policies at a high level in generic terms while XACML expresses privacy policies in terms of more specific user identities or system-assigned resources.

PrimeLife (Bichsel & Roessler, 2010) extends the XACML language to embed its privacy-enhancing features such as credential-based access control, sanitised policy dialog, two-sided data handling policies with automated matching, and downstream usage control.

OpenID is a decentralised authentication framework which relies on the HTTP/S protocol for Web site authentications. According to (Meints and Zwingelberg, 2009) secure authentication is not part of the OpenID specification and does not provide for a trust network. Hence, OpenID may suffer phishing attacks as a stolen OpenID offers access to numerous services. Another issue is the majority of OpenID Providers (AOL, Microsoft, and Yahoo!) are only providers and not Relying Parties. This means these services only let other sites authenticate against their infrastructure with IDs that they issue, they do not allow users with OpenIDs from other providers to authenticate to their infrastructure. Unless we see the identification of the user with the OpenID provider to be coupled with other more secure systems of identification, the author do not think OpenID will be adopted widely.

ISO 24745 Biometric Template Protection standard provides assurance of privacy for biometric information. The ISO 24745 relies on the Biometrics Security Framework (ISO 19092) and the ISO JTC1 SC27 WG5 Identity Management Privacy Framework as two the vital building blocks. The framework defines the entities Pseudonymous Identifiers (PI), Auxiliary Data (AD) and Supplementary Data (SD). The PI is an entity using the renewable biometric reference that represents an individual within a certain context by means of a protected identity that can be verified by means of a captured biometric sample and AD.

ISO/IEC defines the Privacy Framework (ISO/IEC 29100) to safeguard personally identifiable information and a Privacy Reference Architecture (ISO/IEC 29101) to provide a reference model to describe best practices for a consistent technical implementation of privacy requirements in information and communication systems. ISO 29100 consists of the following components to handle different aspects of privacy management: *Privacy Preferences, Privacy Requirements, Privacy Principles, Internal Rules and Privacy Safeguarding Controls*. The PII receiver issues privacy policies to a Privacy Safeguarding Controls unit to manage the Privacy Requirements, and assuring Privacy Safeguarding Controls to the PII provider. Table 6 provides a summary of the privacy issues for some identity management frameworks.

Table 6. Privacy issues of some identity management frameworks

Identity Management Framework	Underlying Technologies	Privacy Issues
OASIS / Liberty Alliance	XACML	Privacy of authorisation entities not preserved
W3C / PrimeLife Abstract Privacy Framework	P3P + XACML Anonymous Credential System, Identity Mixer	Target platform is Web 2.0 and AJAX Point-to-point interaction
OpenID	Decentralised authentication using HTTPS	OpenID specification and does not provide for a trust network, May suffer from phishing attacks
ISO/IEC	ISO/IEC 29100 ISO/IEC 20101	Privacy Preferences, Privacy Requirements, Privacy Principles, Internal Rules and Privacy Safeguarding Controls

CONCLUSION

The author believes the information provided in this chapter about the development of different IAM frameworks are exhaustive and trust the readers find the information useful. However, there are many other relevant IAM solutions offered by commercial software vendors should be included in the discussion. Therefore, the next chapter will study some of the IAM solutions offered by the commercial software vendors.

REFERENCES

Azevedo, R. (2009). *SWIFT mobility architecture*. Secure Widespread Identities for Federated Telecommunications.

Backhouse, J., & Dyer, B. (2007). *D4.7: Review and classification for a FIDIS identity management model*. Future of Identity in the Information Society.

Backhouse, J., & Vanfleteren, M. (2005). *D4.2: Set of requirements for interoperability of Identity Management Systems*. Future of Identity in the Information Society.

Bichsel, P., & Camenisch, J. (2009). *First contribution to open source*. Privacy and Identity Management in Europe for Life.

bioapi.org. (2013). *Version 2.0 of the BioAPI specification — international version*. BioAPI Consortium. Available: http://www.bioapi.org/Version_2.0_Description.asp

Crane, S. (2010). *D4.2 platform architecture and design 2*. Privacy and Identity Management for Community Services.

DOD. (2011a). *Department of defense electronic biometric transmission specification version 3.0*. Author.

DOD. (2011b). *Department of defense integrated data dictionary version 5.0*. Author.

Emerging Opportunities in Global Biometrics and FIDO's Impressive Push for Standards. (2013). Available: http://findbiometrics.com/emerging-opportunities-in-global-biometrics-and-fidos-impressive-push-for-standards-findbiometrics-industry-news-roundup-oct-29-nov-1/

Furr, R., & Wasley, D. (2011). *Federation operator guidelines*. Kantara Initiative.

Glässer, U., & Vajihollahi, M. (2010). Identity management architecture. *Security Informatics*, *9*, 97–116.

Glazer, I., & Brennan, J. (2015). *The design principles of relationship management*. Kantara Initiative.

Gordon, G. R., Barber, S., & Cate, F. H. (2009). *An applied research agenda for confronting global identity management challenges*. Center for Applied Identity Management Research.

Guide Trial Specification - Form E101 Summary. (2005). Available: http://istrg.som.surrey.ac.uk/projects/guide/documents/trial_specification.html

Harding, C. J., Mizumori, R. K., & Williams, R. B. (2007). *Architectures for identity management*. The Open Group.

Higgins Open Source Identity Framework. (2009). Available: http://www.eclipse.org/higgins/

ISO/IEC. (2011). ISO/IEC 24760-1:2011 information technology -- security techniques -- a framework for identity management -- part 1: terminology and concepts.

ISO/IEC. (2015). ISO/IEC 24760-2:2015 Information technology -- security techniques -- a framework for identity management -- part 2: reference architecture and requirements.

ISO/IEC. (2016). ISO/IEC 24760-3:2016 Information technology -- security techniques -- a framework for identity management -- part 3: practice.

ITU-T. (2009a). *ITU-T Study group 17 (study period 2009-2012)*. International Telecommunication Union. Available: http://www.itu.int/ITU-T/studygroups/com17/index.asp

ITU-T. (2009b). Recommendation ITU-T X.1250: Baseline capabilities for enhanced global identity management and interoperability. International Telecommunication Union.

ITU-T. (2009c). Recommendation ITU-T Y.2720: NGN identity management framework. International Telecommunication Union.

Jaquet-Chielle, D., Benoist, E., & Anrig, B. (2006). *Identity in a networked world use cases and scenarios*. Future of Identity in the Information Society.

JTC1/SC37. (2016). *ISO/IEC JTC 1/SC 37 Biometrics*. Available: http://www. iso.org/iso/home/standards_development/list_of_iso_technical_committees/ iso_technical_committee.htm?commid=313770

Kantara Initiative. (2016). Available: http://kantarainitiative.org/

Koschinat, S., Rannenberg, K., & Bal, G. (2009). *Identity Management Infrastructure Protocols for Privacy-enabled SOA*. Privacy and Identity Management in Europe for Life.

Lockhart, H., & Campbell, B. (2008). Security assertion markup language (SAML) V2.0 technical overview. *OASIS*.

Lutz, D. (2010). *SWIFT deliverable D504 simulation, modelling and prototypes*. Secure Widespread Identities for Federated Telecommunications.

Macgregor, W., Dutcher, W., & Khan, J. (2006). *An Ontology of Identity Credentials Part 1: Background and Formulation. October: Draft Special Publication 800-103*. National Institute of Information and Technology.

Maler, E. (2005). *Federated Identity Management: An Overview of Concepts and Standards*. Sun Microsystems, Inc.

Marx, R. (2009). *SWIFT deliverable D503 prototype specification*. Secure Widespread Identities for Federated Telecommunications.

Meints, M., & Zwingelberg, H. (2009). *D3.17: Identity Management Systems – recent developments*. Future of Identity in the Information Society.

Naderi, M., Siddiqi, J., Akhgar, B., Orth, W., Meyer, N., Tuisku, M., & Pipan, G. (2008). Towards a Framework for Federated Global Identity Management. *International Journal of Network Security, 7*, 88–99.

O'Neill, M., Hallam-Baker, P., Mac Cann, S., Shema, M., Simon, E., Watters, P., & White, A. (2003). *Web services security*. Osborne McGraw Hill.

OPENID. (2007). *OpenID Authentication 2.0 - Final*. Available: http://openid. net/specs/openid-authentication-2_0.html#toc

PICOS. (2011a). *Achievements*. Privacy and Identity Management for Community Services. Available: http://www.picos-project.eu/ Achievements.190.0.html

PICOS. (2011b). *Concepts & features*. Privacy and Identity Management for Community Services. Available: http://www.picos-project.eu/Concepts-Features.204.0.html

Podio, F. (2010). *Published biometric standards developed by ISO/IEC JTC 1/SC 37 – biometrics and adopted by INCITS as INCITS/ISO/IEC standards*. INCITS.

Podio, F. L., Dunn, J. S., Reinert, L., Tilton, C. J., Struif, B., Herr, F., & Wirtz, B. et al. (2004). *NISTIR 6529-A common biometric exchange formats framework (CBEFF)*. National Institute Of Standards And Technology.

Poetzsch, S., Meints, M., Priem, B., Leenes, R., & Husseiki, R. (2009). D3.12: Federated Identity Management – whats in it for the citizen/customer? *Future of Identity in the Information Society*.

PrimeLife. (2008). *PrimeLife - Bringing sustainable privacy and identity management to future networks and services*. Available: http://www.primelife.eu/

Recordon, D., & Reed, D. (2006). *A framework for identity management*. Second ACM Workshop on Digital Identity Management, Fairfax, VA.

Reed, D., & Strongin, G. (2004). *The dataweb: An introduction to XDI*. OASIS XDI Technical Committee.

Scholta, P. (2010). *SWIFT deliverable D505 refined SWIFT scenarios, use cases and business models*. Secure Widespread Identities for Federated Telecommunications.

Soutar, C., & Brennan, J. (2010). *Identity assurance framework: overview*. Kantara Initiative.

Thibeau, D., & Reed, D. (2009). *Open trust frameworks for open government: enabling citizen involvement through open identity technologies*. OpenID Foundation.

Chapter 6

An Introduction to Commercial Identity and Access Management Solutions

ABSTRACT

This chapter exhibits an objective third party evaluation on a number of commercially available IAM solutions, including Microsoft Identity Manager & Microsoft Azure Active Directory, IBM Security Identity Manager and Cloud Identity Service, Okta, Centrify, Ping Identity, Oracle Identity and Access Management, and Salesforce.com. A summary of the functionalities and capabilities exhibited by those commercially available IAM solutions will be presented in this chapter to assist the readers in selecting and evaluating contemporary IAM systems for both the Cloud and on-premises environments.

INTRODUCTION

According to Ping Identity (www.pingidentity.com), system security has been evolving to become dynamic, responding to a user's location, time, behaviour, network and device. All users and devices are required to be continuously verified as authentic and trusted, starting at all entry points into all business and system applications. This means security is required to instantly respond to changes in user behaviour and context.

This chapter will provide a snapshot of the present landscape of the commercially available IAM solutions. The author has compiled this collection

DOI: 10.4018/978-1-5225-4828-7.ch006

of resources on the subject of IAM solutions based on the whitepapers, IAM Buyer's Guides, vendor reviews and market reports from leading enterprise technology analysts such as Gartner and Forrester. The goal is to provide an objective view about the functions and features available from commercially available IAM solutions and trust the readers will find the information resourceful in helping them, as IAM practitioners, can make IAM related decisions with high level of confidence.

A SUMMARY OF PRESENT IAM LANDSCAPE

The Gartner 2016 Report on Magic Quadrant for Identity and Access Management as a Service, Worldwide (Kreizman & Wynne, 2016) has named 14 vendors, amongst them Microsoft, Okta and Centrify are listed in the Leaders Quadrant while IBM, Salesforce, SalePoint, OneLogin, PingIdentity, Covisint, and EMC(RSA) being classified in the Visionaries Quadrant. The report estimates that by 2020, 40% of new IAM purchases will use the IDaaS delivery model — up from less than 20% in 2016.

A summary of the vendors surveyed by Gartner is listed in Table 1.

Forrester conducted similar evaluation in 2016 and the result is presented in the Forrester Wave for Privileged Identity Management, Q3 2016 Report (Cser, 2016). Forrester has surveyed 10 vendors in the Privileged Identity Management market and has named Centrify, BeyondTrust, and CyberArk are the leaders.

The survey has studied the following features offered by the vendors:

- A privileged password (credential) vault;
- Users, roles, and help desk integration;
- Privileged session management and recording;
- Host access control and privilege delegation/escalation;
- Cloud support;
- Reporting;
- Largest number of managed endpoints;
- Overall solution complexity;
- Overall user interface intuitiveness; and
- Application-to-application password management.

Forrester reports that Centrify is the first vendor who offers the first SaaS PIM password safe in the industry. BeyondTrust excels with its privileged

Table 1. Vendors surveyed in the Gartner 2016 magic quadrant for identity and access management as a service, worldwide (Kreizman & Wynne, 2016)

Quadrant	Vendor	Strengths	Cautions
Leaders	Okta	Multitenant, with lightweight on-premises components for repository and target system connectors. Supports adaptive multifactor authentication capabilities.	Limited reporting capabilities. Need to enhance user provisioning functionality.
	Microsoft	High scalability Broad and deep marketing, sales and support capabilities. Low Enterprise Mobility Suite (EMS) pricing.	Azure Active Directory B2C and B2B Collaboration still need time to mature.
	Centrify	Strongest Enterprise Mobility Management (EMM) features and integration with IDaaS amongst the vendors. Added biometric and wearable authentication options.	Limited social media attribute retrieval and customisation of the registration and consent workflow. No governance feature.
Visionaries	IBM	IBM's Cloud Identity Service (CIS) offers deep functional offerings. IBM's breadth of resources around the globe provides good support to smaller venture-funded vendors.	Complex effort required to implement the CIS solution. Pricing is amongst the highest.
	Salesforce	Strong contextual multifactor out-of-band authentication service. Strong social media and identity standards support, including SAML, OAuth2, OIDC (OpenID Connect) and SCIM	Lacks a password vault and the service has few provisioning connectors available. Does not support proxy-based access to on-premises web applications.
	SalePoint	Strong on-premises IGA features. Strong fulfilment capabilities to a wide variety of identity repositories and target systems.	Does not support social identity use cases. Missing access certification functionality, and approval workflow.
	OneLogin	Supports virtual LDAP services that enable multiple devices to perform LDAP authentication and attribute retrieval using OneLogin as an LDAP server.	Provides the rudiments of mobile device management (MDM). Basic reporting capabilities. Lacks user administration and provisioning and identity governance functionalities.
	PingIdentity	Multitenant web-centric IDaaS offering. Provide SSO by integrating with a variety of identity repositories. Strong leadership in identity standards development, as well as openness.	Missing user self-service access request, provisioning workflow and other identity governance features.
	Covisint	Leadership in support of IoT initiatives for the automotive industry. Strong entity relationship management capabilities.	Focused on enterprise B2B and B2C use cases.
	EMC(RSA)	RSA Via Access provide SSO, multifactor authentication and full IGA functionality.	Does not support OAuth and OpenID Connect (OIDC) or social identity integration.
Niche Players	Simeio Solutions	Deep functional support for web and legacy applications. Continues to enhance its administration and user interfaces as abstraction layers.	Simeio's pricing is high for pure web applications.
	Fischer International	Strong user provisioning focus. In particular granular provisioning functions for legacy applications	Access management is limited to SSO only, lack of authorisation enforcement capabilities.
	Ilantus	Experience with traditional large-vendor IAM stacks. Supports SSO to thick-client applications, in addition to the web applications.	Focused on workforce use cases that require identity governance, provisioning and SSO to legacy targets.
	iWelcome	IDaaS in a dedicated single-tenant delivery model. Strong capabilities in access management: authentication, federation protocol and identity repository support.	Lacks core identity governance features (such as access certification and re-certification). Offers basic provisioning approval workflow capabilities.

session management capabilities and CyberArk has the largest PIM market presence.

The Forrester report named CA Technologies, Thycotic, ManageEngine, and Lieberman Software are the Strong Performers, while Balabit, Dell, and Bomgar are the Contenders.

Table 2 provides a summary of the features offered by some of the commercial IAM vendors.

Table 2. Summary of features provided by selected commercial IAM solutions

	Microsoft	IBM	Okta	Centrify	Ping Identity	Oracle	Salesforce
Single Sign-On	Yes, Cloud & On-premises	Yes, Cloud & On-premises	Yes, Cloud & Web-based On-premises	Yes, Cloud & On-premises	Yes	Yes. Cloud & On-premises	Yes, Cloud only
Self-service Identity Management	Yes	Yes	Yes	Yes	Yes	Yes	No Info.
Privileged Identity Management	Yes	Yes	No Info.	Yes	No Info.	Yes	No Info.
Multi-Factor Authentication	Yes	Yes	Yes	Yes	Yes	Yes	Two Factors Only
Enterprise Mobility Management	Yes	Yes	Yes	Yes	Yes	Yes	Yes
Threat Analytics Tool	Yes	Yes	No Info.	No Info.	No Info.	Yes	No Info.
User Defined Audit Reporting	Yes, through SQL Server	Yes, Cognos Reporting Tool	No Info.	No Info.	No Info.	Yes	Yes
SAML 2.0 Support	Yes	Yes	Yes	Yes	Yes	Yes	Yes
OAuth 2.0 Support	Yes	Yes	Yes	Yes	Yes	Yes	Yes
OpenID Connect Support	Yes	Yes	Yes	Yes	Yes	Yes	Yes
3rd Party SaaS Connector(s)	Yes, RESTful API	Yes, over 160 as at December 2016	Yes, over 5000	Yes	Yes	No Info.	No Info.

The following sections will discuss the features and capabilities provided by some of the commercially available IAM solutions. It is beyond the effort and scope of this book to cover all the IAM products discussed in the Forrester and the Gartner reports. The author has selected some of the market leading products and look at the features and capabilities of each of the product.

MICROSOFT IDENTITY MANAGER AND MICROSOFT AZURE ACTIVE DIRECTORY

The KuppingerCole Leadership Compass report for Cloud User and Access Management (Kuppinger, 2014) named Microsoft and Ping Identity are the leaders in the Cloud IAM market.

Microsoft offers full range of IAM software for both on-premises and cloud environments. Microsoft Azure Active Directory is the IAM solution for the cloud. Microsoft Identity Manager (MIM) is for on-premises identity and access management. The current version is MIM 2016, which replaces the previous Microsoft IAM product known as the Microsoft Forefront Identity Manager.

Azure AD offers SSO to any cloud and on-premises web app and offers a number of pre-integrated apps with third party cloud vendors such as Salesforce.com, Office 365, Box, and many more. Azure AD enforces multi-factor authentication (MFA) with SaaS and works with multiple platforms and devices.

On the other hand, MIM 2016 binds multiple on-premises authentication stores like Active Directory, LDAP, Oracle, and other applications with Azure Active Directory. This provides unified user experiences to on-premises line-of-business mission critical applications and SaaS solutions.

Microsoft Identity Manager, and Microsoft Azure Active Directory enables organisations to manage their hybrid infrastructure with a full range of services, such as federation, identity management, device registration, user provisioning, application access control, and data protection.

Figure 1 Shows that MIM 2016 provides the following features:

- Self-service identity management. Self-service scenarios now include Account Unlock and multifactor authentication gate for Password Reset;
- Dynamic group membership;

Figure 1. Features offered by Microsoft identity manager 2016

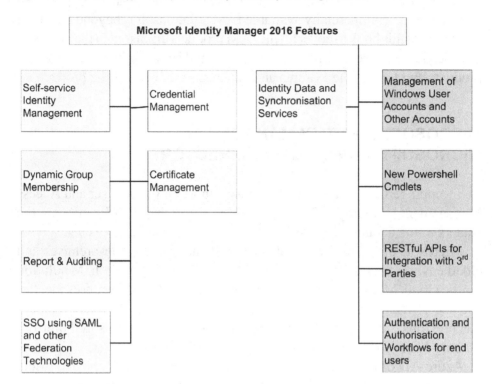

- Reporting and Auditing. The reports enable administrators can review the history of privileged access, and see who performed an activity. The administrator can verify whether the activity is legitimate or not and easily identify unauthorised activities. to identify malicious software attacks and also for tracking "inside" attackers;
- SSO using SAML and other federation technologies;
- Identity data and synchronisation;
- Credential Management;
- Certificate Management. In Certificate Management there is support for multi-forest topologies, a Windows store app for virtual smartcard and certificate lifecycle management;
- Creation of Windows accounts and other accounts;
- Additional Powershell Cmdlets;
- RESTful APIs for integration with third parties for identity related tasks. Privileged Identity Manager are supported in Certificate Management for REST API access; and
- Authentication and Authorisation Workflows for end users.

MIM 2016 offers Privileged Access Management (PAM) that helps organisations restrict privileged access within an existing Active Directory environment. PAM can re-establish control over a compromised Active Directory environment by maintaining a quarantine environment that is known to be unaffected by malicious attacks and isolate the use of privileged accounts to reduce the risk of those credentials being stolen.

Figure 2 is a sample screenshot of an MIM Admin Console. The console allows an administrator to manage *Distribution Groups, Security Groups, User Profiles, Passwords, and User Requests*. The difference between Distribution Groups and Security Group is that members in a Distribution Group can be allowed only to distribute messages. On the other hand, members in a Security Group can be allowed to distribute messages as well as to grant access permissions to resources in Active Directory.

PAM performs four steps to prepare, protect and monitor the use of privileged accounts. The first step is to *identify which groups in the existing forest have*

Figure 2. A sample Microsoft identity manage admin console

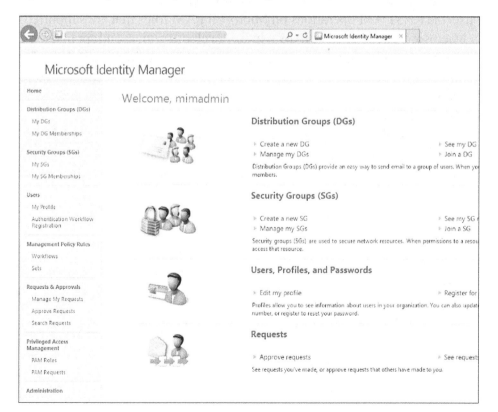

significant privileges and recreate those groups without members in the bastion forest. The second step is *set up a lifecycle and authentication protection strategy*, such as MFA, for when users request just-in-time authentication and administration. The third step is after a request is authenticated and approved, a *user account gets added temporarily to a privileged group* in the bastion forest for a pre-set amount of time. After that time, the account is removed from the group. The fourth step is *auditing, alerts, and reports* of privileged access requests.

PAM offers a set of REST APIs that operate on the PAM Role: PAM assigns users to privileged roles that can activate as needed for JIT access. These PAM roles are defined manually in the bastion environment. The role associates a collection of users with a collection of privileged access rights. The access rights are defined by reference to security groups. Every PAM role has a list of user accounts, called candidates. The candidates can be elevated to the PAM role.

A simple way to define roles for privileged access management is to compile all the information in a spreadsheet, list the roles in the rows, and identify governance requirements and permissions in the columns. The following Table 3 lists the REST API operations on Microsoft PAM roles that are supported:

Microsoft Azure AD is the IAM solution for cloud services and applications. Azure AD provides identity authorisation capabilities (including SSO) for cloud applications such as Office 365 and other SaaS applications. Azure AD shows good direct acceptance and builds the foundation for widely used Microsoft Office 365.

Azure AD offers other features such as Self-Service Password Reset, Group Management, and Multi-Factor Authentication (MFA). New cloud capabilities such as Azure Rights Management Services enable customers to

Table 3. The supported REST API operations on PAM roles of MIM 2016

Get PAM Roles	
• Create PAM Request • Get PAM Requests • Close PAM Request	A user who wants to elevate to a PAM role access rights has to submit a PAM request and get the approval for the request in order to elevate. The PAM Request object tracks the lifecycle of this request in the MIM Service.
Get Pending PAM Requests	
Approve or Reject a Pending PAM Request	Pending PAM Request APIs are used to approve or reject PAM requests that have been submitted by users.
Get PAM Session Info	When using the PAM REST API, the client establishes a session with the PAM REST API endpoint and the client is authenticated to the REST API endpoint.

protect data at the document level, across all document types and platforms. Custom made applications can use this this capability to protect data from any applications on any platform.

The Microsoft Azure platform constantly changes and enhances with proven scalability and performance, providing broad number of preconfigured integrations to Cloud services.

Azure AD offers the following four different editions:

1.   Azure AD Free Edition

This Free Edition manages users and groups, synchronise with on-premises directories, get SSO Azure domains, Microsoft Office 365, and a number of SaaS applications.

2.   Azure Active Directory Basic Edition

The Basic Edition provides cloud centric application access and self-service identity management solutions. This edition supports group-based access management, self-service password reset for cloud applications, and Azure Active Directory Application Proxy (to publish on-premises web applications using Azure Active Directory).

3.   Azure Active Directory Premium P1 Edition

The Premium P1 Edition provides features that are competitive with other web-centric IDaaS providers and supports Multi-Factor Authentication (MFA). It also includes licenses for Microsoft Identity Manager (MIM) that manages the customers' on-premises systems.

The Premium P1 Edition enables users to seamlessly access on-premises and cloud applications. This edition adds enterprise-level identity management capabilities for end users and identity administrators to perform hybrid environments across application access, self-service IAM, identity protection and security in the cloud.

This edition supports advanced administration and delegation resources such as dynamic groups and self-service group management. It includes Microsoft Identity Manager (MIM 2016) and provides cloud write-back capabilities enabling solutions like self-service password reset for on-premises users.

4.   Azure Active Directory Premium P2 Edition

Microsoft also offers Azure Active Directory Premium as part of its Enterprise Mobility Suite (EMS), along with Microsoft Intune EMM and Azure Rights Management, and the on-premises-based Advanced Threat Analytics tool.

This Premium P2 Edition contains all the capabilities in Azure AD Premium P1 as well as Microsoft's new Identity Protection and Privileged Identity Management. Azure AD Identity Protection connects with a number of threat signal providers to provide risk-based conditional access to all applications and critical company data. This edition helps the clients to manage and protect privileged accounts with Azure Active Directory Privileged Identity Management. Senior managements can work with Azure AD PIM to discover, restrict and monitor administrators and their access to resources and provide just-in-time access when needed.

Microsoft Intune is the EMM solution for managing mobile app providing functions such as:

- Publishing mobile apps;
- Configuring mobile apps;
- Controlling how corporate data is used and shared in mobile apps;
- Removing corporate data from mobile apps;
- Updating mobile apps;
- Reporting on mobile app inventory; and
- Tracking mobile app usage.

A mobile app is supported with the following features and data protections:

- Single Sign-on;
- Multi-Factor Authentication;
- JIT app conditional access;
- Isolation of corporate data from personal data inside the same app;
- App protection policy (PIN, encryption, save-as, clipboard);
- Corporate data wipe from a mobile app; and
- Rights management support.

IBM SECURITY IDENTITY MANAGER AND CLOUD IDENTITY SERVICE

Traditionally, IBM's pricing for several use-case scenarios was among the highest. However, IBM's product offering is deep and aligns with the functionality provided by its software deployed on both the Cloud and on-premises. IBM's breadth of resources, with geographically expanded data centre locations, appeals to both SME and multi-national organisations that are risk-averse and have concerns with smaller venture-funded vendors.

IBM also has set up a large number of third party support and professional services organisations in supporting its products. OnWire, with headquarters in Raleigh, North Carolina, is one of the companies offering professional consulting, engineering, and cloud Identity and Access Management solutions for IBM Security products. Their focus is on design, implementation, deployment, customisation, and maintenance of integrated IAM systems.

IBM offers a comprehensive range of security solutions that work independently or interact with one another to provide complete protection, for example:

- IBM Security Identity Manager
- IBM Security Access Manager for Web
- IBM Security Federated Identity Manager
- IBM Security Privileged Identity Manager
- IBM Security Access Manager for Enterprise SSO
- IBM Security Directory Integrator
- IBM Security QRadar SIEM

IBM Tivoli Identity Manage (TIM) was released in 2003 with the release of IBM Tivoli Identity Manager Express in 2006. The product was rebranded in early 2013 to IBM Security Identity Manager (ISIM) with the release of version 6.

The IBM Security Identity Manager (ISIM) combines an automated approach with policy-based programming to help manage users' credentials and access rights. The User Interface for IBM Security Identity Manager is called Identity Service Centre (ISC). ISC lets end users to perform self-service functions such as access rights, user roles and group memberships. It also allows an administrator to review the rights and entitlements an employee has and to make requests to add/change/revoke the access rights.

ISC makes use of the "Shopping Cart" metaphor. The Administrators click on the rights and roles they want to assign to users so that multiple options can be picked and added to a "cart". The Administrators then submit their requests in a batch check-out mode.

The ISIM self-service options provide end users the ability to handle tasks such as requests for new access rights, updates to a user's profile, and password changes. IBM QRadar is a security information and event management (SIEM) tool used for collecting and analysing security log data. ISIM works with other IBM Security products to provide integrated services to the customers, such as IBM QRadar SEIM, IBM Security Governance, and IBM Security Access Manager. ISIM utilises the closed-loop capabilities of IBM Security QRadar SIEM to monitor and reconcile the closed-loop user activities. This enables ISIM to correlate data to determine what is an actual threat, and what is a false positive.

IBM Security QRadar has been named the winner of the 2015 SANS Best Security Information and Event Management (SIEM) solution Award (2016). QRadar provides top features such as:

- A single architecture for analysing log, flow, vulnerability, user and asset data;
- Detect attacks in real time using historical security data correlation and behavioural anomaly detection rules to identify high-risk threats;
- Short start up time;
- High-priority incident detection among billions of daily incoming data points;
- Integrate with third-party security solutions for all security events, alerts and workflows;
- Ability to monitor and secure cloud-based services with full visibility into cloud, network, application and user activities; and
- Compliance data collection and reporting using automation to meet internal and external regulatory requirements.

ISIM interacts with IBM Security Governance Foundation to perform campaign management, business activity-focused access, recertification, and role mining. The functionalities are delivered in virtual appliance form for stand-alone or integrated deployments.

The ISIM uses IBM Security Access Manager appliances to provide intelligent identity and access assurance. The appliances provide risk-based access control capabilities such as: *Silent Registration* (where no user interaction is required); *Known User on Unknown Device Request Verification; Enforce Specific Authorisation for Given Resource*, and *Configure and base Decisions on Access Manager Risk-scoring Engine* (which enables dynamic decision making based on cumulative Risk Score). The virtual appliance provides the following features:

- A configuration wizard for the first-time configuration and for creating clusters;
- A console for monitoring system status, such as disk usage, and notifications, interfaces, middleware status, and partition status and control;
- Diagnostics tools in memory, CPU and storage statistics, SNMP monitoring, and troubleshooting;
- System controls for the virtual appliance settings such as updates and licensing, network settings, and system settings.

The aim of IBM Security Identity Governance and Intelligence (ISIGI) is to mitigate access risks and access policy violations. ISIGI integrates with IBM Security Identity Manager and third-party tools to provides user lifecycle management, provisioning and workflow management. Two types of workflows can be defined in ISIM: *entitlement workflows* that apply to provisioning activities, and *operational workflows* that apply to entity types.

An organisational role is controlled by a provisioning policy. Provisioning policies can be mapped to a distinct portion or level of the organisational hierarchy. System administrators can create RABC provisioning policies and assign users to roles and that define sets of entitlements to resources for these roles. RBAC extends the software-based processes and reduce manual interventions in the provisioning process.

ISIGI provides two methods of integration with target systems to achieve third party integration:

1. Identity Brokerage Adapters

This framework is used to develop a custom adapter to integrate with target systems that are currently not supported by IBM Identity Governance and Intelligence.

2.   Enterprise Connectors

This framework is used to develop a custom adapter to integrate with target systems that are currently not supported by IBM Identity Governance and Intelligence.

ISIM also supports a native IBM Cognos reporting tool that allows users to define their reports on the changes in access rights, workflow consolidation, and an edit/audit history.

The IBM Security Privileged Identity Manager (ISPIM) is available as a virtual appliance providing automated creation and management of user privileges, supports agent-less access to shared credentials, as well as agent-based and manual credential access. The purpose of ISPIM is to provide centralised privileged identity management to address insider threats, improve control and reduce risk. It also provides automated password management and SSO to access enterprise resources

In addition to the enterprise centric IAM solutions, IBM also provides the IBM Cloud Identity Service (CIS) in a multitenant model to address the cloud-based IAM requirements. The CIS is core to IBM's IAM Strategy for offering clients a cloud based Identity as a Security Service. CIS is heralded underpinned by IBM's SoftLayer infrastructure as a service (IaaS), and IBM's IAM software that delivers identity administration, approval workflow, user provisioning and access certification; along with authentication and access enforcement functionality.

IBM CIS provides user self-service console to perform self-registration, user profile management, password reset, and username recovery activities.

Figure 3 shows a sample IBM CIS Administration Console. The Administration Console provides the following functions for the administrator to manager the system:

- Company Information
- Directory Management
- Application Management
  - **Branding:** Customising the look-and-feel for user-facing web pages of the system (e.g. login, self service, etc.)
  - Content Management
  - Password Reset
  - Security Questions

Figure 3. A sample IBM CIS admin console

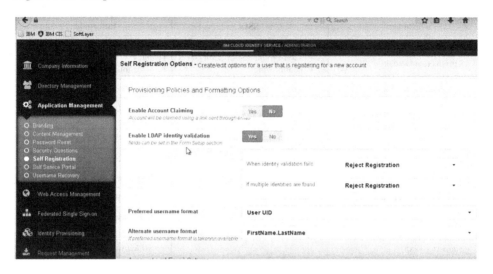

- ◦ Self Registration
- ◦ Self Service Portal
- ◦ Username Recovery
- • Web Access Management
- • Federated SSO
- • Identity Provisioning
- • Request Management

IBM has integrated CIS with Fiberlink's MaaS360 EMM capabilities to provide access enforcement that can use device registration and security posture to render access decisions. IBM has also developed a variant solution to cater for down-market customers with web-centric needs.

The following Table 4 shows IBM CIS offers three levels of services (Starter, SSO & Enterprise).

According to Gartner (Kreizman & Wynne, 2016), customers report that CIS can take significant effort to go live. This is due to the complex nature of projects that IBM takes on for larger customers and new sales are not readily translated into references. Although IBM had put great effort to transform its deep on-premises IGA functions (obtained as part of the CrossIdeas acquisition) to the CIS offering, it seems there is delay in a cloud-ready derivative of the CrossIdeas integration.

Table 4. Three levels of IBM CIS offering

Starter	SSO	Enterprise
1 Non-Production Domain 1 Production Domain	Includes Starter Features +1 Non-Production Domain + the following:	Includes Starter and SSO Features + the following:
Disaster Recover Site	Enterprise Directory	Risk Based Access Control
Site-to-Site VPN Support	Multiple Directory Integration	Identity Lifecycle and Provisioning
Cloud Directory	SSO for Unlimited Apps	Delegated User Management
Single Directory Integration	Social Login Support	Access Request and Approval
SSO for 10 Apps	MFA/OTP Support	Recertification/ Attestation
Standard User Self Suite	Support – 24x7	REST API Integration
Reporting		Multi Instance User Self Service Suite
Support – 12x5		SIEM/Audi Feed Integration

OKTA

Identity as a Service (IDaaS) is Okta's core business. Okta's identity management service is built for the cloud and is compatible with many on-premises applications. Okta offers a network of pre-integrated applications called the Okta Application Network (OAN). The OAN provides integration options for end users to conduct SSO for every app they need to access. Okta's IDaaS offering is delivered multitenant, with lightweight on-premises components for repository and target system connectors. IT can manage any user's access to any application or device.

Okta features include Provisioning, SSO, Active Directory and LDAP integration, the centralised de-provisioning of users, MFA, mobile identity management, and flexible policies for organisation security and control. Okta delivers identity administration and provisioning capabilities, access management for web architected applications using federation or password vaulting and forwarding. The MFA capability of Okta includes its own phone-as-a-token solution and an integrated mobility management product.

Okta has demonstrated a significant increase in customer base in 2016. Its market penetration and implementations have greatly outpaced most competitors. According to Gartner (Kreizman & Wynne, 2016), Okta clients have continued to report predominantly positive experiences with rapid implementation, reliability and support. A significant portion of its business supports integrations with customers' applications and workflows. Okta has enhanced its user provisioning functionality to add multilevel approval workflow, and is trying to replace the traditional on-premises IGA tools.

Some of the Okta products are discussed in the following sub-sections.

Okta Single Sign-On

Okta offers reliable integration for SSO to over 5000 pre-integrated web & mobile apps and over 700 SAML integrations. The integration is fulfilled by a federation engine and flexible access policy.

Okta provides access to cloud apps with the Okta Application Network (OAN). The applications in the OAN can use SWA, SAML or OpenID, or proprietary APIs.

Okta provides a user portal which is both useful and user-friendly, allowing for features like automatic app launching and tabbed application groups. An example is showed in Figure 4 that users can make use of the Okta App Integration Wizard to configure how to integrate any web app to Okta in an instant. The user can specify which platform the application is hosted: Web, or Mobile or On Premises. The user can choose from different sign-on

Figure 4. Okta integration wizard

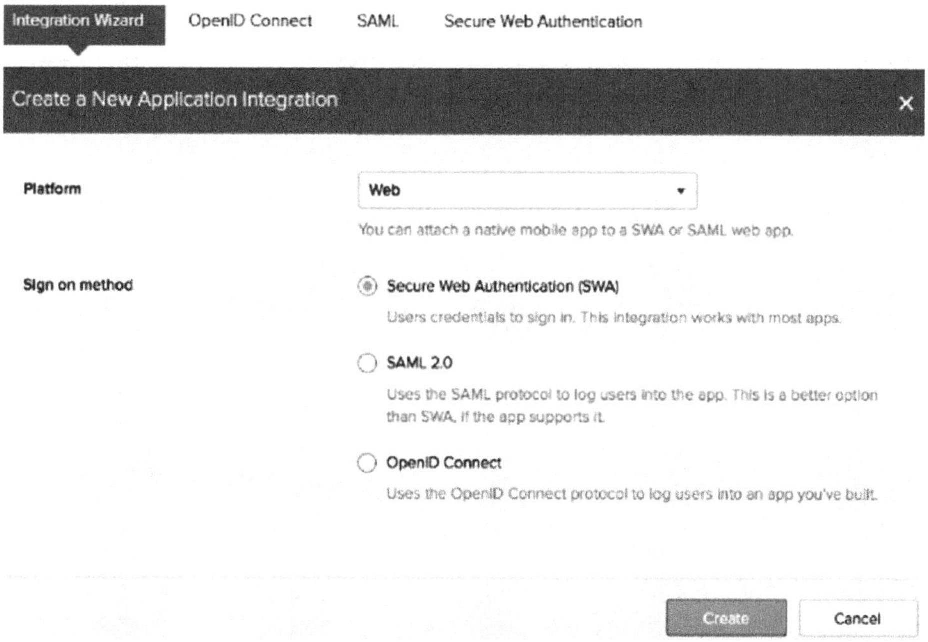

methods: whether it be Secure Web Authentication (SWA), SAML 2.0 or OpenID or proprietary APIs.

Okta SWA Plug-in is a browser extension that is designed to provide the end user SSO security for apps that do not support federated SSO.

Figure 5 shows the Okta SWA Plug-in provides the user with a mini dashboard to access all their Okta applications quickly with a single click.

When an end user enables SWA for an app, Okta stores the end user's credentials in an encrypted format using strong AES encryption combined with a customer-specific private key. When end users click an application icon, Okta securely posts their credentials to the app login page over SSL and the user is automatically signed in.

An user can configure his/her Okta user's sign-in options to make their SWA credentials match their Okta credentials so additional sign-ins are not required after the user have signed into Okta. The following different sign-in options are supported in setting up SWA:

- User sets username and password
- Administrator sets username and password
- Administrator sets username, user sets password

Figure 5. A sample screen capture of Okta secure web authentication plug-in

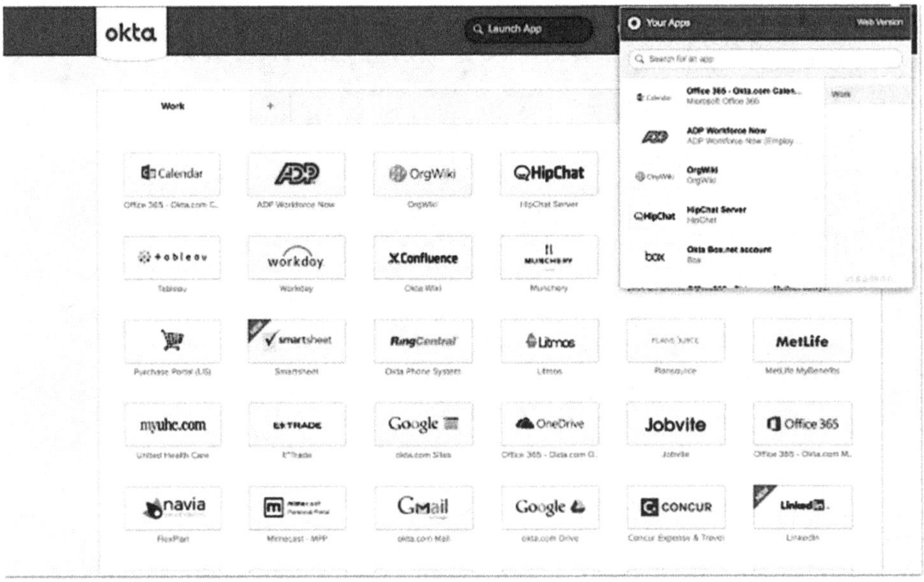

- Administrator sets username, password is the same as user's Okta password
- Users share a single username and password set by administrator

However, SWA sign-in options are not configurable when Sync Password is configured as a provisioning option in Okta.

The way Okta provides integrations for on-premises web-based applications is by SWA, SAML toolkits, and support for provisioning and de-provisioning into applications that expose provisioning APIs publicly.

Different types of mobile apps whether they are HTML5 web apps optimised for mobile platforms, native iOS, or Android apps, can access any web application in the Okta OAN with SSO from any mobile device using the SAML 2.0 or Okta's SWA SSO technology. Native applications like Box Mobile can be integrated using SAML 2.0 authentication for registration and OAuth for subsequent usage.

Okta Mobility Management

At $4 per month, per user (as of June 2017), Okta provides mobile users to access native mobile applications using Okta's SAML based mobile app SSO solution. The Okta Mobile App can securely authenticate the user to web apps on mobile devices through the Okta Mobile dashboard and the Okta Extension for iOS. A sample of the Okta Mobile dashboard is illustrated in Figure 6.

Okta Mobile SSO requires users to enrol their devices in Okta Mobility Management in order to authenticate. Okta Mobile will check the enrolment status to protect access to critical cloud applications through device-based contextual access management.

Okta Mobile SSO for native and web apps, protected access for cloud applications through device based contextual access. The app will automatically keep Exchange ActiveSync accounts up to date when users change their Active Directory passwords. This means when users are deactivated in Okta Active Directory, mobile access to cloud applications can be automatically terminated and access rights to enterprise data will be removed immediately. The app supports user self-service enrolment so that users can manage their mobile access to all their applications on the mobile device.

Figure 6. Okta mobile dashboard

Okta Adaptive Multi-Factor Authentication

Figure 7 shows that Okta Adaptive Multi-Factor Authentication employs a policy framework that supports contextual access management. There are policies to allow, deny, or require step-up authentication for access to applications and on-premises systems based on contextual data about the location, user group, network IP address, device, and application resource.

There are over 500 SAML and Radius enabled applications defined in the Okta Application Network. This allows Okta can centrally manage MFA to a broad set of cloud applications and on-premises systems. The Factor Enrolment Policies allow the users to define which factors are required, optional, and disabled based on the user type.

Okta supports a number of user friendly native factors such as Okta Verify with Push, Okta Verify with One-time-password (OTP), SMS, Voice, Security Questions, and Third Party Factors (which includes YubiKey, Google Authenticator, RSA, Symantec, and Duo).

Figure 7. Okta adaptive multi-factor authentication

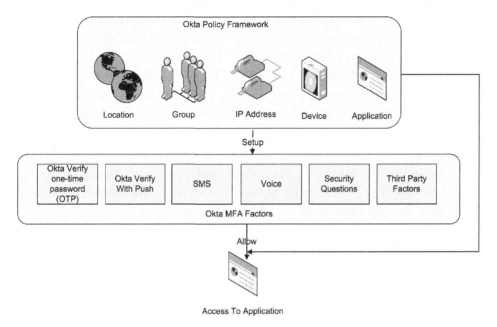

Okta employs an adaptive, risk based authentication mechanism which retrieves third-party IP reputation data, identity data, device data, breached credentials, threat feeds, as well as location data to quickly identify suspicious and unusual behaviour.

Okta Lifecycle Management

Okta Lifecycle Management charges $4 per month, per user (as of June 2017) to manage the identities across different lifecycle states with automated rules, policies, workflows, and APIs for full customisation.

Okta defines identities into seven lifecycle stages:

- Activated
- Pending Activation
- Password Reset
- Password Expired
- Deactivated
- Suspended
- Locked out

Okta offers over 80 pre-integrated applications to handle provisioning and de-provisioning of identities in real-time. User defined applications including Workday, UltiPro, BambooHR, SuccessFactors, and Google for Work can trigger the provisioning activities.

Okta provides integration to Active Directory or LDAP including extended rich profiles, group push, and license and role assignment to perform automatic detection of users attributes in the context of the applications that the users are working in along with application entitlements.

Okta supports the System for Cross-domain Identity Management (SCIM) protocol to enable custom applications to perform provisioning using the cloud or on premise provisioning SDK. Okta APIs are available to make any application the profile master,

Okta Universal Directory

Okta Universal Directory service is offered at $1 per month, per user (as of June 2017). This is the one place for administrators to manage all the users, groups and devices registered in Okta or from other sources.

According to PC Magazine's review (Ferrill, 2015), Okta Active Directory agent is easy to set up, and requires no ongoing configuration at the server. Okta demonstrates strong capabilities in integrating with multiple directories, allowing an organisation can work with multiple identity providers while maintaining secured and high-fidelity on users profiles and policies.

Okta Universal Directory can sync with different sources of identities and provides the ability to configure which data source should be the master for particular attributes. Okta can pull the information from another source, massage the formatting by using their expression engine, and push it into another application or directory. The potential for this functionality enables high degree of automation.

Okta also offers an optional password synchronisation tool to update the passwords for Okta user accounts, and potentially SaaS application account passwords, when AD passwords are changed. However, the password sync tool need to be installed on each of the domain controllers in the organisation in order to fully eventuate the password changes.

CENTRIFY

Centrify was founded in 2004 with headquarters in Santa Clara, California. Centrify offers Identity-as-a-Service (IDaaS) to enterprises charging at US $4 per user per month as a start (as of June 2017).

Figure 8 highlights that Centrify products include the following three main groups:

- Centrify Identity Service;
- Centrify Privilege Service; and
- Centrify Server Suite.

These three products are working collectively in providing the following solutions:

- Cloud and On-Premises Apps;
- Multi-factor Authentication;
- Privileged Access Security;
- Secure Hybrid Cloud;
- Big Data Security;
- Mac and Mobile Management;
- Internal and External Users;
- Regulatory Compliance; and
- Federal Compliance.

Figure 8. Product groups of Centrify (Source: www.centrify.com)

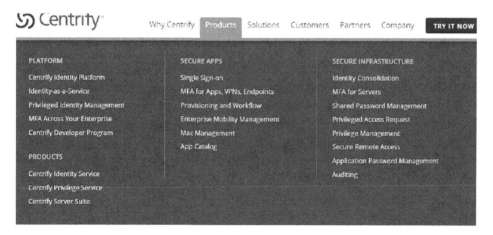

Centrify has been gaining success with over 5,000 customers, including more than half of the Fortune 50 organisations. In November 2016, the Computing, a leading weekly magazine specialising in information technology resources in the UK has awarded the Centrify Identity Service (CIS) as the best Identity and Access Management solution in the inaugural 2016 Security Excellence Awards. The award follows further recent industry recognition for Centrify, including being named a Leader in Gartner's 2016 Worldwide Magic Quadrant for Identity and Access Management as a Service (IDaaS) and a leader in The Forrester Wave for Privileged Identity Management, Q3 2016.

Centrify Identity Service controls internal and external users to access to cloud, mobile and on-premises apps via SSO employing a range of techniques such as federation standards, password vaulting and forwarding, user provisioning and multi-factor authentication (MFA). Centrify Identity Service provides the following services: Single Sign-On, Provisioning & Workflow, Multi-Factor Authentication, Enterprise Mobility Management (EMM), Mac Management, and App Catalog.

Centrify SSO supports social identity integration to allow a user to link and sign in with a social identity with limited social media attribute retrieval, registration and consent workflow capabilities. Centrify Identity Service is able to manage apps, mobile devices and Macs via Active Directory, LDAP and/or cloud identity stores. The Centrify identity provisioning function can automatically route application requests, create accounts, manage entitlements within those accounts, and revoke access.

Centrify EMM features and integration with IDaaS are the strongest among vendors in the IDaaS market. The EMM features are capable to integrate mobility capabilities include security configuration and enforcement, device X.509 credential issuance and renewal, remote device location and wiping, and application containerisation. EMM provides simple BYOD enrolment and integrated SSO to business apps and include remote lock and wipe capability across devices.

Biometric and wearable authentication options have been added, and Centrify added SSO support without requiring use of a specialised mobile SSO application. Centrify also added B2B and B2C use-case support in 2016. The service and on-premises proxy component can be configured to keep some or all identity data on-premises in Active Directory and not replicate it to the cloud.

According to Ferrill (2016), Centrify has the limitations that require extra steps to perform user import from Active Directory and there is no support for third-party MFA vendors.

Centrify Privilege Service manages the access to infrastructure with shared account password management, self-service privileged access request, conduct forensic investigations and prove compliance with privileged session monitoring and auditing of shared administrative accounts, and secure, granular remote access to enterprise infrastructure without VPN.

The Centrify Server Suite has an integrated set of tools which are able to consolidate identity authentication and access management activities for the Mac, Linux and UNIX platforms within the Microsoft Active Directory in a Windows environment. The reporting and analysis features for all events handled by the service are wide-ranging and customisable.

Figure 9 shows that Centrify Server Suite comes with three different editions: Standard, Enterprise and Platinum Editions. The figure also shows that MFA component requires Server Suite plus either Privilege Service Suite or Identity Service Suite and the App Password Management component require both Server Suite and Privilege Service Suite.

Figure 9. Different Centrify service suite editions (Source: www.centrify.com)

	Server Suite Standard Edition	Server Suite Enterprise Edition	Server Suite Platinum Edition	Privilege Service
Identity Consolidation	●	●	●	
MFA for Servers [1]	●	●	●	●
Privilege Management	●	●	●	
Auditing and Compliance		●	●	
Server Isolation			●	
Secure Remote Access				●
Identity Broker				●
Shared Password Management				●
Privileged Access Request				●
App Password Management [2]	●	●	●	●
Privileged Session Monitoring				●

[1] Requires Server Suite plus Privilege Service or Identity Service
[2] Requires both Server Suite and Privilege Service

Centrify defines a *Zone* as a collection of attributes and security policies that define the identities, access rights and privileges shared by a group of users. Zones may also contain:

- A set of UNIX management data that defines policies for those users' UNIX profile;
- The set of computers or devices to which these users can be granted access;
- An inventory of the access rights that users in that Zone need, and the discrete tasks that they can perform;
- A set of computer roles that characterize the function of a subset of computers;
- A set of user roles that specify the rights (access and privileges) granted to users in that role; and
- Role assignments that associate Active Directory users or groups with the user roles.

Centrify uses this Zone technology to consolidate complex and heterogeneous non-Windows identities into a single, definitive identity centrally stored and managed in Active Directory

Figure 10 shows an example how a UNIX profile is defined in Centrify. The profile contains some UNIX attributes such as UID, Primary Group, GECOS, Home Directory, Shell, and State.

Centrify has added single-layer, role-based approval workflow, and integrates with ServiceNow for more advanced workflows. Centrify has added the ability to integrate on-premises and cloud directories, such as Google's and Microsoft's. However, Centrify does not provide the governance features found in traditional on-premises IGA vendors.

PING IDENTITY

Ping Identity was found in 2002 with headquarters in Denver, Colorado. Ping Identity is one of the leaders in Identity Defined Security (IdDS) and a leader in identity management by focusing on secure access to seamlessly connecting all users - employees, partners and customers - to all applications, whether mobile, cloud or legacy. Ping Identity has demonstrated active involvement setting in identity standards, as well as openness in working with clients and other organisations to improve those standards.

Figure 10. Centrify UNIX profile

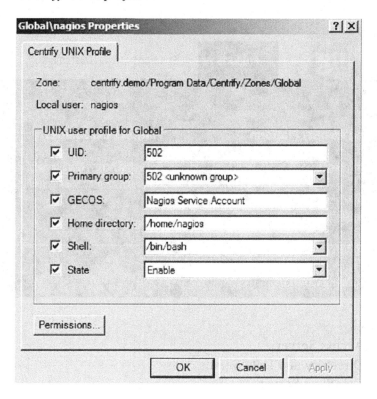

On 1 June 2016, Ping Identity announced that it was acquired by Vista Equity Partners. Vista Equity Partners is a U.S.-based private equity firm with more than $24 billion in cumulative capital commitments, currently invests in software, data and technology-based organisations. This acquisition has enabled Ping Identity to accelerate growth and innovation through strategic acquisitions and focused investment in its leading enterprise IDaaS capabilities.

Subsequently, in August 2016, Ping Identity acquired UnboundID, which is a leader in customer identity and access management solutions. This acquisition adds UnboundID's highly scalable user directory for social login, customer preference and profile management to Ping Identity's multi-factor authentication, SSO and secure access capabilities, making Ping Identity's offering one of the comprehensive IAM solutions in the market.

Figure 11 shows a screenshot of PingIdentity offering Federated Access and Identity Management software consists of the following products:

- PingFederate (SSO) Server

Figure 11. PingIdentity platform products

- PingAccess Server
- PingDirectory and Data Server
- PingDataSync Server
- PingDataGovernance Server
- PingOne Cloud, which consists of the following:
  - **PingID:** Multi-factor Authentication Solution
  - PingOne Directory
  - PingOne SSO

The PingFederate SSO Server is recognised as one of the leading federation servers integrating with a variety of identity repositories in providing secure SSO, API security and provisioning for enterprise customers, partners, and employees. The server acts as an on-premises bridge component for customers supporting most of the current identity protocol and directory standards; including SAML, WS-Federation, WS-Trust, OAuth and OpenID Connect.

The PingAccess Server is a Web and API Access Management solution which makes use of the following to define policies:

- Identity Attributes (ABAC/RBAC)
- Authentication Levels
- Network Ranges

- Web Session Attributes
- OAuth Attributes
- OAuth Scopes
- Time Ranges
- Groovy Scripts
- Custom Services (via SDK)

The PingAccess Server is able to integrate with existing applications through HTTP header authentication or token mediation, and support migration of legacy applications. PingAccess can be configured as a standalone policy server, access can be controlled through a gateway or lightweight agents for on premise Web access management (WAM) solutions. PingAccess can be deployed to support proxy access to internal web applications and APIs

The PingDirectory Server securely stores and manages customer data such as credentials, profiles, preferences and privacy choices. PingDirectory is able to support a unified customer profile to serve a broad range of structured and unstructured data. The server employs newer algorithms like PBKDF2, Scrypt and Bcrypt to hash passwords and is able to integrate with third-party security monitoring tools.

The PingDataSync Server creates a unified profile from multiple disparate data sources to migrate and consolidate identity data for one-time migrations or ongoing bi-directional synchronisations of identity data. PingDataSync is able to support real-time or scheduled data synchronisation relying on multiple connection methods and protocols as well as preserving data security and protect PII while syncing.

An enterprise uses the PingDataGovernance Server to govern, control, and secure access to customer profiles, personal identity information and preference data. PingDataGovernance allows users to self-manage their own identity information, preferences and privacy directives. It also supports centralised data access governance control and delegate account management as well as REST APIs.

The PingOne Cloud service is a multitenant web-centric IDaaS offering for large organisations. A lightweight self-service bridge component is available in PingOne Cloud to integrate a customer's Active Directory to the service. PingOne Cloud is one of the services with strong access features. However, the IGA features are considered lightweight and are lacking user self-service access request, provisioning workflow and most identity governance features.

The PingID Multi-factor Authentication Solution is able to utilise contextual data for authentication, such as location, network, biometric and device data.

Users of PingID install an app on their phone and self-register that device with the PingID service. After the registration process, users can perform strong authentication for all of the apps they need. The usage of smart phone do away with the expensive overheads required by hardware tokens that need to be issued, shipped, replaced and maintained.

PingID offers strong connectivity capabilities. PingID can connect to systems like RSA SecureID, Symantec VIP, Safenet, and Google Authenticator. It can be used to authenticate VPN clients or any remote access clients that support the RADIUS protocol. PingID supports a wide variety of devices, applications and methods for authenticating. Mobile application is one of the most widely used methods, users can use swipe or fingerprint to authenticate using their phone. One-time password can be programmed in the app for offline authentication. The other methods are USB token, voice call, SMS to any registered device, Email, and Desktop Applications.

PingID supports the following types of authentication policies:

- Group;
- Application;
- Geofence: when a particular user is physically outside of a pre-set geofence;
- Rooted or Jailbroken: when a user's device is rooted or jailbroken; and
- Network IP: when a particular device is out of a specific IP range.

PingOne Directory and PingOne SSO offer a facility to all of an organisation's applications with centralised user management based entirely in the cloud. PingOne Directory supports flexible user management features such as full user-lifecycle reporting (although PingOne's reporting capabilities are considered as weak when compared with most competitors), enforceable complex password policies, and customisable user attribute schema attributes.

ORACLE IDENTITY AND ACCESS MANAGEMENT

After many years of onslaughts from Microsoft SQL Server, IBM DB2, and the Amazon's Relational Database Service (RDS), Oracle still leads the database market with more than 350,000 customers run Oracle database in their own data centres (Darrow, 2016).

Oracle Identity Management (OIM) is the software suite offered by Oracle in answering the IAM requirements. Oracle offers 2 bundled suites: Oracle Identity & Access Management Suite Plus; and Oracle Access Management Suite Plus. Table 5 is a list of the components of OIM.

The current version of Oracle Identity Management suite is 12c (12.2.1.3.0) (as of September 2017). Oracle Access Manager 12c provides support for OAuth in a Multi Data Centre environment and supports multiple password policies for setting up varied levels of password based complexity protection for users belonging to different groups. OIM is part of the Oracle Fusion Middleware Identity Management pillar. As we can see from Table 6.5, OIM provides the following functionalities:

- **Core Services for Access Management:** On premise or cloud support in authentication, SSO, coarse-grained enterprise application access authorisation.
- **Identity Federation:** Supporting SAML, OAuth and OpenID for delegated social network identities log-on.
- **Mobile Security:** Supporting OAuth for mobile clients to access backend infrastructure for adaptive authentication, SSO, fine-grained authorisation and fraud prevention.

Table 5. Oracle identity management solutions (Source: http://www.oracle.com/technetwork/middleware/id-mgmt/overview/index-089914.html)

Access Management Oracle Access Manager Oracle Mobile and Social Access Service Oracle Identity Federation Oracle Access Portal Service Oracle Adaptive Access Manager Oracle Entitlements Server Oracle Web Services Manager Oracle Security Token Service Oracle API Gateway Oracle Enterprise Single Sign-On Suite Plus Oracle Information Rights Manager	**Directory Services** Oracle Unified Directory Oracle Internet Directory Oracle Virtual Directory Oracle Directory Server Enterprise Edition Oracle Authentication Services for Operating Systems Oracle Directory Integration Platform (meta-Directory)
Identity Governance Oracle Identity Manager Oracle Identity Analytics Oracle Privileged Account Manager Oracle Role Manager	**Mobile Solutions** Oracle Mobile Security Suite
Oracle - Sun Oracle Waveset Oracle OpenSSO	**Security Toolkits** Oracle Security Developer Tools

- **Portal Service:** A web-based interface for end users to federate their applications supported with SAML,OAuth, or Form-Fill SSO service.
- **Access and Risk Analysis:** Supports MFA and heuristic one-touch notification fraud detection service.
- **Fine-Grained Authorisation:** XACML compliant attribute-based authorisation.
- **API Security:** Supports RESTful APIs and Web Services protocol transformation, API firewalling, authentication and authorisation.
- **SOA Security:** To protect man-in-the-middle attacks.
- **Security Token Service:** Supports SAML assertions and Kerberos tokens trusted brokerage between infrastructures.
- **Thin and Rich-Client SSO:** Oracle provides components to be installed on a Microsoft Windows PC to provide SSO to rich client applications. Browser based Enterprise SSO is available through Oracle Access Portal.

Oracle Identity Cloud Service (OICS) is delivered by Oracle to meet the needs of the cloud: supporting both on-premises and cloud resources to be secured from a single set of controls), mobile access (providing sign on for native or browser -based apps), intranet and extranet access.

OICS provides the following services:

- **User Authentication Service:** Implementing the OpenID Connect 3-legged User Authentication flows on top of the standard OAuth2 protocol. Interactive web-based and native applications leverage standard browser-based OpenID Connect flows to request user authentication, receiving standard JSON-based identity tokens (JSON Web Token – JWT) conveying the user's authenticated identity.
- **Identity Federation Service:** Supporting SAML 2.0, Browser POST Login & Logout Profiles.
- **Token Service:** Supporting standard 2-legged and 3-legged interactions covering User Authentication, User Consent, Identity Propagation and Web Service Authorization patterns.
- **Reporting Service:** Generating dashboard information and reports

Although OICS provides integration with any service that can be integrated via SAML and OpenID Connect for SSO, and Administrations can be managed via a single control panel; it seems there is a lack of off-the-self third party SaaS Connectors available for the clients to use.

SALESFORCE.COM

Salesforce.com is one of the world leaders in Customer Relationship Management (CRM) platform. Salesforce.com launched Salesforce Identity Service in October 2013.

Salesforce offers two levels of services: *Classic* and *Lightning Experience*. Lightning Experience comes with a newer and more modern user interface than the Classic version. Lightning Experience includes many new feature and entirely redesigned pages when compared to Classic.

Lightning Experience supports extra features such as Performance Chart, Assistant, News, Top deals, Activity Timeline, Enhanced Notes, Reference Page Layout, and the Opportunity Kanban, which is a visualisation tool for opportunities, to review deals organised by each stage in the pipeline.

The Salesforce Identity Service provides the following features:

- Cloud-based user directories;
- Authentication services with granular control over user access by selecting the apps specific users can use, two-factor authentication, and how often individual users need to log in to maintain their session;
- Access management and authorisation for third-party apps, including UI integration;
- Provisioning and de-provisioning of apps;
- API for viewing and managing deployment of Identity features;
- Reporting on the use of apps and services; and
- Salesforce Identity Connect: an on-premises Connector for provisioning and SSO integration with directory services like Microsoft Active Directory.

Salesforce Identity supports SAML for SSO into Salesforce from a corporate portal or identity provider, OAuth 2.0 for secure authorisation between applications using RESTful APIs, and OpenID Connect authentication for users to log in to an external service, like Gmail, and then access their Salesforce application without logging in again.

Salesforce also supports users to define their own domain name within the Salesforce domain (for example, https://companyname.my.salesforce.com). This user own domain allows users to manage their login authentication and allows the users to customise their login page.

Furthermore, Salesforce supports Connected Apps to use SAML and OAuth protocols to authenticate, provide SSO, and provide tokens for use with Salesforce APIs. Salesforce admins can set various security policies and have explicit control over who can use the corresponding apps.

Figure 12 shows a sample Salesforce App Launcher that allows users to access their apps in one interface. Users use the App Launcher to launch Salesforce and third-party apps without having to log in again. Salesforce Classic users must have the "Use Identity Features" permission and the App Launcher option in their profile set to Visible before they can use the App Launcher. In Salesforce Classic, the App Launcher appears as an app in the Force.com App menu.

The Identity License component grants users access to Identity features. Salesforce Classic users must have the *"Use Identity Features"* permission to use the App Launcher. On the other hand, Lightning Experience users have the App Launcher by default. Identity licenses are included with Enterprise, Performance, and Unlimited Editions. Ten free Identity user licenses are included with each new Developer Edition org.

An External Identity license grants Identity features such as the App Launcher and SSO to external users. With External Identity, external customers and business partners can access the organisation's internal resources through an external identity community. The license is included with all user licenses in Enterprise, Performance, and Unlimited Editions. Five free External Identity user licenses are included with each new Developer Edition org.

Salesforce Identity can be set up as an identity provider and define one or more service providers. Salesforce users can access other applications directly from Salesforce using SSO by configuring the external applications

Figure 12. A sample salesforce app launcher menu

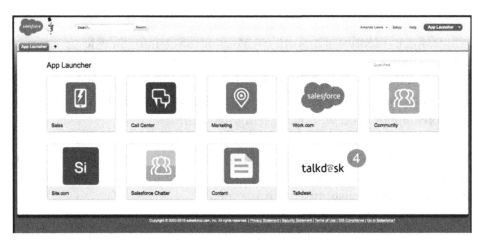

as tabs to your Salesforce organisation, so that users don't have to switch between programs.

Salesforce Identity Connect integrates Microsoft Active Directory with Salesforce via a service that runs on either Windows or Linux platforms. This allows AD users SSO access to Salesforce. Salesforce supports Two-Factor Authentication. Users need to log in with two pieces of information, such as a username and a one-time password (OTP). Salesforce supports user-defined OTPs and OTPs generated from software or hardware devices.

Salesforce has provided detail steps in setting up the identity server (Salesforce.com, 2016) to support Connected App and App Launcher:

1. Define the organisation Domain
2. Customize the organisation Login Page
3. Add Identity Providers on a Login
4. Configure the organisation's Domain Login Policy
5. Enable the App Launcher with a Profile in Salesforce
6. Enable the App Launcher with a Permission Set in Salesforce Classic
7. Set up Single Sign-on to Google Apps
8. Get a Salesforce Identity Provider Certificate
9. Set the External App (e.g., Google Administrator SSO Options)
10. Create a Connected App for External App (e.g., Gmail)
11. Set Two-Factor Authentication Login Requirements
12. Connect a One-Time Password Generator App or Device for Identity Verification

Salesforce Identity Connect provides AD integration using a service which runs on either Windows or Linux platforms. This integration can sync Active Directory users with either Salesforce or Identity Connect acting as the Identity Service Provider for SSO Active Directory integration when logging into Salesforce. Identity Connect is available for an additional cost in: Enterprise, Performance, and Unlimited Editions. Developer Edition includes 10 Identity Connect permission set licenses.

CONCLUSION

This chapter has discussed the product features of seven different IAM solutions available in the market. The purpose is not to give a score to each of the products saying which one is better than the others but to present an unbiased picture of how the IAM market is being served by different traditionally well-established software vendors and the start-up companies specialising in this IAM market.

After finish reading this chapter, in conjunction with the knowledge acquired from reading the previous chapters, the readers should have an in-depth understanding of the technological knowhow in selecting, evaluating and managing a contemporary IAM system for both the Cloud and on-premises environments.

The next chapter will look at issues surrounding how an effective IAM solution can help identify and prevent the loss of identities.

REFERENCES

Cser, A. (2016). *The Forrester Wave™: Privileged identity management, Q3 2016*. Forrester Research, Inc.

Darrow, B. (2016). *For Oracle it still boils down to the database*. Available: http://fortune.com/2016/03/15/oracle-database-earnings/

Ferrill, T. (2015). Okta identity management review & rating. *PCMag Australia*. Available: http://au.pcmag.com/okta-identity-management/37375/review/okta-identity-management

Ferrill, T. (2016). Centrify identity service. *PC Magazine*. Available: http://www.pcmag.com/review/343993/centrify-identity-service

Kreizman, G., & Wynne, N. (2016). *Magic quadrant for identity and access management as a service, worldwide*. Gartner, Inc.

Kuppinger, M. (2014). *Leadership Compass: Cloud User and Access Management*. Kuppinger Cole Ltd.

Salesforce.com. (2016). *Identity implementation guide*. Author.

SANS Best of Awards. (2016). Available: http://www.sans.org/critical-security-controls/best-of-awards

Chapter 7

The Role of Identity Theft in Identity and Access Management

ABSTRACT

The Australian Federal Police (https://www.afp.gov.au/what-we-do/crime-types/fraud/identity-crime) report that identity crime has critically threatened the Australian community as this type of crime has generated significant profits for offenders and caused considerable financial losses to the Australian Government, private industry and individuals. Recent estimates by the Attorney-General's Department indicate that identity crime costs Australia upwards of $1.6 billion each year, with the majority (around $900m) lost by individuals through credit card fraud, identity theft and scams. More alarmingly, identity crime continues to be a key enabler of serious and organised crime, which in turn costs Australia around $15 billion annually. This chapter discusses how personal identities can be stolen and exploited and proposes a Self-learning Context Aware Identity Access and Management Framework (SCAIAM) for combating identity theft.

INTRODUCTION

The Australian Transaction Reports and Analysis Centre's Proof of Identity Steering Committee have defined a set of standard definitions for Identity Crime (Payneham, 2006):

DOI: 10.4018/978-1-5225-4828-7.ch007

- *Identity fabrication* is used to describe the creation of a fictitious identity;
- *Identity manipulation* is used to describe the alteration of one's own identity;
- *Identity theft* refers the theft or assumption of a pre-existing identity (or significant part thereof), with or without consent and whether, in the case of an individual, the person is living or deceased;
- *Identity crime (or Identity fraud)* is a generic term to describe activities/ offences in which a perpetrator uses a fabricated identity; a manipulated identity; or a stolen/assumed identity to facilitate the commission of a crime(s). The fraud occurs when a fraudster impersonates another person and opens accounts in that person's name, running up an account in his / her name, or obtaining goods and services in other person's name (e.g. hospital).

According to the Attorney-General's Department 2014-2015 report (2016b), the estimate of the cost of identity crime in Australia is A\$2.2billion compared to the estimate of A\$2billion from the 2013–14 report. The costs of preventing and responding to identity crime are estimated to be a further A\$390million, bringing the total economic impact of identity crime in Australia to approximately \$2.6billion in 2015.

Identity crime continues to be one of the most prevalent crimes in Australia and around the globe. Organised crime is increasingly employing information and communication technologies to facilitate their illegal activities.

Table 1 highlights that large portion (2.18%) of identity theft victims do not know how their personal identities were stolen and the majority channels

Table 1. Channels of identity theft (Source: AIC Survey 2016) (Jorna, 2016)

Different Channels of Identity Theft	Percentage
Don't Know	21.8
Hacking of a Computer / Online Device	20
Hacking of Email	18.4
Online Banking Transaction	15.8
Information Placed Online (Non-Social Media)	14.3
Unsolicited Telephone Call (exclude SMS)	11.7
Social Media	9.1
ATM Transaction	6.9
EFTPOS Transaction	5

of theft are related to online services (such as email, social media, online platforms such as chat rooms, blogs, and forums).

In most cases, online criminal activities are related to money laundering and identity crime. According to the Australian Bureau of Statistics' (ABS) first survey of personal fraud (Pink, 2008), Australians lost almost $1 billion to fraud and scams in 2007. The recent similar ABS survey in 2015 (2016a) shows an increase to $3 billion. The most common fraud type in 2015 survey was card fraud with 1.1 million persons (or 5.9% of the population aged 15 and over) experiencing card fraud. It shows an alarming increase of 200% from the 2008 figures.

We can see the trend of an increase in hacking, phishing, and malware objects is driven by identity theft and data-focused cybercrime using sophisticated social engineering techniques to malware in what appears to be legitimate email with acceptable Web links (Ahamad et al., 2008).

However, it seems the fundamental issues of how to effectively protecting identity and information privacy from the perspectives of non-computer-literate people to be overly self-deprecating. The author has a friend who finished his arts degree who, the author discovered recently, type whole URLs not in the browser's bar but in Google's search form!

This chapter will look into some of the recent developments in combating identity theft and building the awareness of protecting personal identity in the community. A framework is proposed by the author which may help combat identity crime in an effective manner.

HOW PERSONAL IDENTITIES CAN BE STOLEN AND EXPLOITED

The identities of a person are becoming valuable commodities that can be traded in the black markets. On the dark Web marketplaces such as AlphaBay and Evolution, individual identities are known as 'fullz' carrying a value vary from $1 to over $400. Credit card information with a high credit score values the highest. The values are based on a number of factors like the brand of the card, the country it comes from, the amount of the card's metadata provided, volume discounts, and how recently the card data was stolen.

The black marketplaces can buy and sell illegal goods and services, such as, stolen data, compromised online accounts, custom malware, attack services and infrastructure, fraudulent e-vouchers or e-tickets, passports and much more can be bought if we know where to hunt. According to Wueest (2015), attackers can pick up stolen data for less than a dollar. Larger services, such as attack infrastructure, can cost anything from a hundred dollars to a few thousand.

Furthermore, Wueest (2015) has listed the following items are also available in the black market:

- Scans of passports ($1 to $2);
- Stolen gaming accounts ($10 to $15);
- Custom malware ($12 to $3,500), for example tools for stealing bitcoins by diverting payments to the attackers;
- 1,000 followers on social networks ($1 to $12);
- Stolen cloud accounts ($5 to $8), which can be used for hosting a command-and-control (C&C) server;
- Sending spam to 1 million verified email addresses ($70 to $150);
- Registered and activated Russian mobile phone SIM card ($100).

There are different ways that fraudsters can steal the identity information of a person. The traditional approaches to stealing identity include:

- **Dumpster Diving:** This is to retrieve personal data from discarded credit cards, bank cards, and utility bills;
- **Mail Theft:** This refers to someone targets a victim's mailbox and removes mail that has pertinent information on it. As in dumpster diving, the thief can take the victim's credit card statements, bank statements; anything that can be used to steal a person's identity. At times, identity theft criminals have been known to re-route a victim's mail without his/her knowledge or permission by submitting a change of address to the post office, financial institutions, and utility organisations;
- **Vishing:** Also known as "*voice phishing*". It happens when the victim receives a telephone call from the fraudster using social engineering techniques to trick the victim to believe the fraudster is calling from a legitimate organisation such as a government agency, a financial institution, a payment services organization, or a well-known company. The goal is to get the victim to disclose his/her personal identification and financial information. Other tactics include making robot-calls (pre-recorded messages) urging the victim to contact a certain phone number, for confirming a prize won, or an emergency has occurred that

requires the victim to disclose personally identifiable information or credit card / debit card numbers;

- **SMiShing (Unsolicited Phone Call):** The victim receives SMS message from fraudster posses as from a legitimate government body, a financial institution or other legitimate entity. The text message has a sense of urgency to scare the victim into thinking there is a serious emergency by leading the victim to believe and follow the instruction recorded in the message with the consequence of disclosing his/her personal identity information and suffering financial losses;
- **Unsolicited Phone Calls and SMS:** The fraudsters call and send SMS to the potential victims using social engineering techniques to trick the victims to believe they are from legitimate organisations and willingly to handover their private information and even money;
- **Stealing:** This includes stealing personal financial letters from letterboxes, and stealing wallets;
- **Pretexting:** This is a way the fraudsters use false information to approach financial institutions, telephone companies, and other sources to pretend to be somebody who lost some kind of information and asked the staff to get the information for them. Then they can use the information against the victim or sell the information to someone else to use; and
- **Shoulder Surfing:** This includes skimming ATM when individuals input personal identification information, bribing insider employees to get hold of useful personal customer information, and physically stealing confidential files or computer hard drives containing confidential identity information.

In the Internet age, online fraudsters attack identity databases via numerous way, some of them include the followings:

- **Spoofing:** This is sending messages to computers from a source that pretends to be a trusted computer's IP address;
- **Phishing:** This is sending emails to targeted individuals, asking them to access a website that mimics a trusted institution and then divulge private logon identity information;
- **Spear Phishing:** This is similar to phishing scam, except it attacks businesses. Spear phishing targets to almost every employee of an organisation with an email looks like it has been sent by a division

within the organisation such as the IT or the human resources department, asking the employee to update their user name and password for verification purposes. This potentially not only gives the attacker access to personally identifiable information but also the company's private information;

- **Pharming:** This type of identity theft works in a way that a hacker hijacks the Internet traffic so when a person types in the address of a legitimate website the traffic was taken to a fake site. If the person enter personal information at the phony site, it is harvested and used to commit fraud or sold to other identity thieves;
- **Falling for "Free" Offers, Like Vacations, Gifts, and Prizes:** Some people may receive emails or SMS or phone calls that they're offered a luxury item or trip for free, and are being pressured to sign up now because the contest is almost over. Identity thieves will use this kind of urgency to get people to make wrong decisions to disclose their personal and private information they wouldn't normally make;
- **Hacking:** The intruders try to break into databases and archives in which identity information is stored. The spoofer may even masquerades as an ISP or a Theft Prevention Service Provider to gain access to internal databases; and
- **Malware:** It stands for 'malicious software'. It is a piece of software that's built with malicious intentions to cause damage to the targeted computing facilities. Malwares are designed specifically to find its way onto a device, which includes desktop PCs, notebooks, mobile phones, or tablets and to manipulate and/or damage them. The aim of the attack is usually related to financial intentions of recording and stealing the private information stored in the device, like credit card details, e-mail accounts passwords, or online banking details.

There are different types of malware:

- **Viruses:** They are attached to a file. The system has to actually download the virus infected document to be infected;
- **Worms:** They function without the attachments. Worms infiltrate networks and computers by finding gaps and soft spots in their code;
- **Trojans:** They are named after the mythological Trojan horse at the battle of Troy, they are usually harmless for a certain period and then activate once inside the system;

- **Adware:** It is a type of unwanted software with the purpose is to push ads onto a user's device;
- **Spyware:** It gathers information about the system it's on. It tracks and monitors the user's online activities, including browsing activities and keystrokes; and
- **Ransomware:** It is also known as digital extortion. This is a type of malware that restricts access to a computer system and demands that the user pay a ransom to the operators of the malware to remove the restriction. The majority of ransomware threats today are targeting the Windows operating system and has evolved to become a special track of malware commodity.

Fraudulent abuse of travel documents affects national security and social stability. After the stolen identity information are traded, identity thieves will start creating fake documents to misrepresent identity by swapping images on the documents; modifying the validation information and names. Counterfeiters will even be able to issue forged digital certificates.

According to the Australian Taxation Office (https://www.ato.org.au) website, identity thieves will target a business' AUSkey, Business Activity Statement, employee (or employees') personal information, and business records containing personal or business information. The AUSKey is a piece of valuable login information that allows a business to access and send business information to government online – from changing the Australian Business Number (ABN) details, to lodging the Business Activity Statement. As for personal identities, thieves will target the following information: a person's full name, date of birth, current address, bank account numbers, credit card details, Tax File Number (TFN), drivers licence details, passport details, and passwords.

Stolen identities can be used to open fraudulent credit-card accounts, obtain loans or social benefits, open telecommunications or utility accounts, money laundering, purchasing air-tickets, and even gaining employment with a stolen TFN.

Stolen identities may be useful in avoiding arrest as drug traffickers and money mules are caught using fake identities frequently. A crime offender may use another's identity to avoid arrest or detention, especially if the offender already has a criminal record or if there is an arrest warrant outstanding. Committing offences in another person's name means that the police will be looking for the wrong person, not the true offender.

Another way how stolen identities will be used is where a fraudster acquires a subscription to the mobile network under a false identity; and starts reselling the use of his phone to unscrupulous customers at a rate lower than the regular tariff. The fraudster cashes up a large number of calls and disappears before the bill can be collected.

Even worst, stolen identities such as Social Security Number (SSN), driver license, or TFN, may be used to apply for a rental property or to purchase/sell a house. Some thefts even target children's identities because it often takes longer time to discover this kind of crime than other identity crimes, giving the fraudster plenty of time to use the child's identity for opening up bank accounts with lines of credit because some issuers do not authenticate the age of every applicant being processed.

Other forms of abuse in identities may include:

- Stealing the victim's identity, take over his or her insurance policies, and make false claims for "pain and suffering" suffered from auto accidents;
- Taking out auto loans or mortgages under the victim's name and residence;
- Submitting fraudulent tax returns using the victim's Tax File Number, and collects the refunds;
- Submitting applications for social security using others' identities (often those of people who have died), and receive social security payments;
- Filing a change of address to utility companies, creating a new address for the victim so they can receive the victim's billing statements and use the statements to access other accounts belongs to the victim.

A CONTEXTUAL FRAMEWORK FOR COMBATING IDENTITY THEFT

(Wang et al., 2006) have proposed a contextual framework for combating identity theft. They report that many people may think that identity thefts are primarily carried out by strangers; statistics show that the fraudsters are often someone the identity owner knows. A recent study in the US shows that as much as 70 percent of personal data stolen from companies was performed by internal employees (Source: http://msnbc.msn.com/id/5015565).

This framework defines four stack holders:

- **Identity Owner:** An individual who is the subject of his or her identity and who has the legal right to own and use it;
- **Identity Issuer:** A trusted government or private institution that issues identity documents to represent certain social or financial rights to the owner of such documents. The identity documents will have a finite time period of validity.

The identity documents usually consist of six information components:

- Document Identifier (such as a Passport Number);
- The Owner's Name;
- The Purpose (such as Driver License);
- The Issuer (such as the government);
- Validation Time Period; and
- The Issuer's Signature.

Some of the Identity Documents may also contain the information necessary to verify the document holder, such as a photograph or biometric identities details (such as fingerprint), and the identity of the document issuer such as a watermark or stamp.

The Identity Document can take digital form, such as a digital certificate issued by a trusted certificate authoriser (for example, VeriSign). Private institutions may issue business identity documents or tokens such as credit cards, debit cards, and digital certificates.

The Identity Issuer has the responsibility to verify the receiver's true identity before issuing an Identity Document so that other validating institutions can then rely on this document to verify a person's identity.

The Identity Issuers is required to protect sensitive personal identifiable information held in archives or databases as well as mechanisms in data recovery and protection mechanisms when identity information is stolen:

- **Identity Checker:** A service provider that verifies the Identity Document presented by the identity holder is valid and belongs to the person who holds it. There is a strict requirement for the authentication processes. Identity checkers have the responsibility of protecting identity information against incursions and notifying identity owners if such a breach is discovered. However, it is noted that many Identity

Checkers do not carefully verify the documents physically, and as such, fraudulent Identity Documents were established;

- **Identity Protector:** A private or public organisation or government official that works to protect individuals and institutions from identity theft. Identity Protectors can be government legislators, law enforcement agencies, the legal system, public and private security-service providers, and technical security-solution providers.

The framework defines the following three collaborative categories of activity in combating identity thefts:

1. **Prevention:** Education is the first line of defence in preventing identity exposure and subsequent theft. Identity preventing education materials and programs are available from many government and public institutions. The examples are: Ontario, Canada, government pamphlet on identity theft prevention (www.cbs.gov.on.ca); the Australian Government National Crime Prevention Program (www.ema.gov.au/); and the Stop.Think.Connect global online safety awareness campaign (https://www.stopthinkconnect.org). These organisations provide simple tips for preventing identity theft, such as guarding against exposure when entering information into public online platforms, not giving out personal information to strangers over the phone or by email, and think carefully before posting about oneself and others online.

Prevention technologies such as biometrics, smart cards, smart phone apps, PKI digital certificates, database security, and advanced anti-counterfeiting techniques (such as: watermarks, chemical voids, optically variable ink, and holograms); are required to work in a homogeneous manner. However, as long as the cost for committing any kind of fraud is significantly lower than the gains, criminals will not stop their attempts to exploit technological advances to commit identity fraud.

2. **Detection:** As for identity theft detection, restrictive authentication is the best way to detect identity theft. Well-designed authentication processes aided by advanced technologies (such as fingerprints) can be effective in detecting potential thefts.

The use of business rules and scorecards in Australia is a simple and effective defence against identity crime. One business rule is the hundred-point physical identity check test which requires the person to provide sufficient point-weighted identity documents on-the-spot. Different identity documents carry different weighted points and they must add up to at least one hundred points. Another defence mechanism is known as fraud matching by verifying a transaction against a blacklist of known frauds updated periodically. The problem of fraud matching is that the recordings of frauds is highly manual and usually take long-time to report and record the frauds.

Another major area in identity theft detection is detecting fraudulent transactions. Some banks are sending SMS confirmation message to the customer's mobile phone or email when a credit card payment or bank transfer is authorised. This significantly increases the account holders' awareness of transactions. However, the identity thieves have made massive amount of false transaction alarm messages to people in laying down a smokescreen to purportedly in the name of identity theft protection, in order to steal account holders' money. We shall discuss some of the mechanisms in identity theft detection in the next section.

3. **Legal Protection and Prosecution:** These types of activities require the law enforcement agencies to take effective actions in gathering evidence of identity criminal activities. The identity criminal acts can be detected by monitoring measures when the criminals use fake identities to obtain a certain right or financial benefit. For some situations such as data fraudulently copied from a database, unauthorised access, disclosure, copying, use, or modification of data require the IAM solution to have the capability to log and lock down such criminal evidence.

A BRIEF SURVEY OF IDENTITY THEFT DETECTION MECHANISMS

One point we need to be aware of is that, there is still lacking a clear consensus how to deal with this type of theft globally, due to the fundamental disparate and federated interaction model that the Internet has formed into its current shape over the past decades.

Research in fraud detection has progressed from handcrafted methods into automated techniques. Data mining techniques and other automatic monitoring technologies are useful in monitoring online transactions continuously with a view to identifying abnormal transactional patterns that suggest fraud.

There are a number of *adaptive approaches* developed in analysing massive amount of data using profiling methods, data mining techniques and rule-learning algorithms. The goal is to combine evidence in order to generate high-confidence alarms (Fawcett and Provost, 1997a, Xu et al., 2006).

Another technique is using *Collision and Velocity Checking (CVC)* approaches (Fawcett and Provost, 1997b). CVC performs verification checks on transactions with limits being set to the number of times a consumer's high risk personal information such as credit card details can be used at single or multiple locations in a designated time period. This is a fairly basic strategy in combating against identity theft and has high error rate in stopping legitimate transactions from going through.

Another tried methodology in fraud detection is based on the *Hidden Markov Models* (Smyth, 1995) which targets recurring sequence of states and the transition between them.

Statistical Fraud Detection mechanisms (Bolton and Hand, 2002) are gaining momentum in the research of fraud detection. There are two modes of statistical detection. The supervised mode will sample both fraudulent and non-fraudulent records to construct models which allow one to assign new observations into one of the two classes. This mode is applicable to detect frauds of a type which have previously occurred. The other one unsupervised mode simply seeks those accounts, and customer details which are most dissimilar from the norm. These can then be examined more closely. Outliers are a basic form of nonstandard observation.

The statistical mechanisms that are used include Rule-based methods, Link Discovery/Analysis methods, perform correlation of complex evidence using data mining techniques, Adaptive statistical fraud detection mechanisms (Fawcett & Provost, 1997a), and Distributed approach (Chan et al., 1999).

C4.5 is an algorithm commonly used in Rule-based fraud detection. It is an algorithm used to generate a classifier decision tree. The input is a set of training data of already classified samples. Each sample consists of a p-dimensional vector representing attribute values or features of the sample, as well as the class in which the attribute falls.

At each node of the tree, the C4.5 algorithm chooses the attribute of the data that could split the set of samples into subsets. The splitting criterion is the normalised information gain and the attribute with the highest normalised information gain is chosen to make the decision. The C4.5 algorithm then recurs on the smaller sub-lists.

The *Support Vector Machines* (SVM) (Cortes and Vapnik, 1995) are statistical learning techniques useful in a variety of classification tasks. The strength of SVMs comes from two main properties: kernel representation and margin optimisation. SVM has been demonstrated to possess a higher accuracy and efficiency of credit card fraud detection compared with other algorithms.

(Phua et al., 2012) propose a multi-layered identity crime detection system using the Communal Detection (CD) layer and the Spike Detection (SD) layer to complement the existing non-data mining activities. The CD layer is a whitelist-oriented approach basing on a set of attributes. The SD layer is an attribute-oriented approach working on a variable-size set of attributes.

The purpose of CD is to find the real social relationships to reduce the suspicion score. A whitelist is constructed by ranking link-types between applicants by volume. Communal relationship is established in proportion to the volume of link-type. The CD algorithm will check every current transaction's value against a moving window of transaction's values to find links as well as checking against the whitelist to find communal relationships and reduce their link score. It will then calculate every linked previous transactions' score for inclusion into the current transaction's score. The current transaction's score will be updated as well as the State-of-Alert parameter value and the whitelist will be updated to reflect the result of the new transaction.

SD strengthens CD by providing attribute weights which reflect the degree of importance in attributes. The SD algorithm matches every current value against a moving window of previous values. It will calculate every current value's score by integrating all steps to find spikes. The next step is to calculate every current application's score using all values' scores and attribute weights. At the finish of every current mini-discrete data stream, the SD algorithm will then select the attributes for the SD suspicion score and updates the attribute weights for CD.

INCREASING AWARENESS OF CYBER FRAUD

Nowadays, cyber criminals are attacking their online victims through numerous online facilities. The ways of attack may include the followings:

- Send targeted messages online to target audiences to steal victims' private information and lure them into making financial payments to achieve a variety of purposes (money laundering, opening ghost financial accounts, stealing money from the victim's account);

- Scammers collect users' credit card information and PIN for withdrawing money from the victim's financial account;
- Use of fake websites to induce victims with information appear to be legitimate by offering fake services at low prices and with fake consumer feedbacks;
- Use of virus infected email attachments to trick users into running macros written for applications from Adobe or Microsoft. The virus macro will execute the automated task to download and install malware into the victim's online device.

Most people conduct their routine Internet activities without the level of vigilance that could expose themselves to cyber criminals. The more time spent on the Internet, the greater exposure to perpetrators. According to Van Wilsem (2011), exposures in social networking sites and online forums can increase people's visibility and provide necessary profile information for potential offenders to develop targeted strategies to scam specific individuals:

- **Protection Motivation Theory (PMT) (Rogers, 1975):** One of the promising Internet privacy protection methodologies, which is based on the assumption that people will exercise risk appraisal and coping appraisal before they engage in risk mitigation behaviours. This awareness of appraisal helps form the development of protection motivation and, subsequently, actual protection behaviours;
- **The Extended Parallel Process Model (EPPM):** Proposed by Chen et al. (2017) provides refinements to PMT by introducing two extra theories: Self-control theory (refers to one's ability to regulate emotions, behaviours, and desires) and Routine Activity theory (refers to that the possibility of being a crime victim increases when motivated offenders and targeted victims are present in the same time and physical/logical location), in the attempt to explain the antecedents of Internet scam victimisation.

Research results have shown the following online routines are major predictors of victimisation of Internet scams (Pratt et al., 2010; Reyns, 2013):

- Online shopping that increases the risk of information theft and monetary loss due to disclosure of private information;
- Information search results that lead to untrusted websites;

- Files sharing and downloading: People are habitually downloading textual, audio, video files, and software from websites. They are unknowingly bringing in malicious software that can infect their online devices from unreliable sources; and
- Opening emails from unknown senders leads to unsafe websites and result in the installation of malware.

The *Anti-Phishing Working Group* (APWG; http://www.antiphishing.org/) is an international coalition unifying the global response to cybercrime across industry, government and law-enforcement sectors and NGO communities. The APWG was founded in 2003, now has grown to membership with more than 1800 institutions worldwide.

The APWG website provides a way for people to report phishing incidence by simply copying both the message header and message body to the input form and then click on the "Submit" button in the form. The APWG collects, analyses, and exchanges lists of verified credential collection sites, like those used in phishing.

The APWG hosts an Accredited Reporter Data Submission Program which allows any brand holder that has cybercrime event data to be cleared through the URL Block List (UBL) established at APWG. The UBL is a repository serving as a central clearinghouse to receive phishing reports from brand holders and responders, and to distribute them to developers of security software, such as browser security toolbars and anti-virus systems as well as to cybercrime investigators requiring notification of attacks.

Apart from the developers of security software, the UBL has served many other purposes, such as:

- Global protection of consumers and business from frauds involving commercial enterprises and brand-holders;
- Prevention of users globally from downloading malicious software, and disclosing login/password credentials;
- Benchmarking efficacy against others in similar industries to determine if fraudsters are targeting a particular industry;
- Creation of forensic databases for researchers, industrial investigators and law enforcement; and
- Data exchange with other members of the economy or government who are being affected by similar threats (for example: phishing kits, malware distribution sites, botnet command & controls, and malicious IP addresses).

The quarterly Phishing Activity Trends Report issued by the APWG is one of the useful reports for understanding the overall trend of the online situation worldwide. In the 3rd quarter 2016 report, it was noted that the Retail/Service sector continued to be the most-attacked category of victim, suffering 43% of phishing attacks in Q3 2016 and an average of 200,000 new malware samples were discovered per day. In the 4th quarter 2016 report, it was reported that the total number of phishing attacks in 2016 was 1,220,523, a 65% increase over 2015. The country that is most affected by malware is China, where 47.09% of machines are infected, followed by Turkey (42.88%) and Taiwan (38.98%).

Furthermore, the APWG produces many useful tips and whitepapers to educate institutions and individuals about online safety. One of the most popular ways to spread malware is by email, which may be disguised to look as if it is from a familiar company such as a bank, or a personal email from a friend. We need to be wary of emails that ask us to provide passwords, or emails that seem to be from friends, but have only a message such as "check out this cool website!" followed by a link.

Other simple tips are such as:

- Be suspicious if someone contacts you unexpectedly online and asks for your personal information;
- Remember that no financial institution will email you and ask you to put sensitive information such as account numbers and PINs in your response;
- Assume that a request for information from a bank where you've never opened an account is probably a scam;
- Verify the validity of a suspicious-looking email or a pop-up box before providing personal information;
- Don't immediately open email attachments or click on links in unsolicited or suspicious-looking emails. Don't open attachments in emails unless you know who sent it and what it is;
- Install good anti-virus software that periodically runs to search for and remove malware;
- Be diligent about using spam (junk mail) filters provided by your email provider;
- Don't visit untrusted websites and don't believe everything you read;
- Scan USBs and other external devices before using them. Be careful if anyone—even a well-intentioned friend or family member—gives you a disk or USB drive to insert in your computer;

- Exercise caution when clicking on enticing links sent through emails or posted on social networks. Instead of clicking on a link in an email, type the URL of a trusted site directly into your browser;
- Don't click on popups or banner ads about your computer's performance;
- Back up your data regularly;
- Read each screen when installing new software. Decline the installation of additional programs in the "bundled" software;
- When entering personal or financial information, ensure that the website is encrypted with a Secure Sockets Layer (SSL) certificate by looking for the padlock icon or "HTTPS" in the address bar;
- Be cautious of any suspicious behaviour before submitting sensitive information online.

How to protect our systems from malware?

The answer has two parts: *Personal Vigilance, and Protective Tools.* Personal vigilance is the first layer of protection against malware, but simply being careful is not enough. Because business security is not perfect, even downloads from legitimate sites can sometimes have malware attached. This means that even the most prudent user is at risk, unless additional measures are taken.

A robust antivirus software package is the primary component of technological defences against malware. The antivirus protection software must check any newly downloaded program to ensure that it is malware-free. It should periodically scan the system to detect and remove any malware that might have slipped through. It is required to be updated regularly to recognise the latest threats. Furthermore, the antivirus protection software must also be able to recognise any previously unknown malware threats, based on technical features that are characteristic of malware. In addition, the antivirus software should also detect and warn against suspicious websites.

PROPOSAL: A SELF-LEARNING CONTEXT AWARE IDENTITY ACCESS AND MANAGEMENT FRAMEWORK FOR COMBATING IDENTITY THEFT

The author considers the methodologies that we have discussed in the above seem mostly using static architectures, which in many cases require heavy pre-implementation definition, setting up and training effort using good forensic analysis on the evidence before they become usable with reasonable accuracy.

Also, any change in the forms of identity theft by no means will induce effort to adjust to the new form of challenges. This type of challenges is not limited to a certain physical location or time of a day.

The author proposes to extend the contextual framework of (Wang et al., 2006) by incorporating self-learning context aware mechanisms for prevention, detection, and legal protection and prosecution in a generic IAM framework.

Wang have highlighted some of the issues in combating identity theft:

- Careless visual checking by front-line personnel and lack of administrative mechanism to regulate checking execution of front-line personnel;
- Lack of systematic identity theft prevention action plans and prevention policies;
- Lack of a cohesive mechanism to manage, control, and protect sensitive identity information, such as fingerprints, passwords;
- Lack of collaborative evaluation for technical solutions, such as biometrics, smart cards, and experiences in implementation;
- Lack of comprehensive restrictive authentication process or other effective methods for detecting identity theft occurrences;
- Poor cooperation between law enforcement agencies among jurisdictions both nationally and internationally;
- Data warehouses hold extensive dossiers of personal information, generally without the knowledge of the individuals concerned. Anyone able to gain access to these data banks has all the information required to steal identities.

The Self-learning Context Aware Identity Access and Management (SCAIAM) framework proposed in this chapter will address the issues listed in the above and will focus on three of the following major challenges in automated fraud detection:

1. **Self-Learning:** Self-learning requires a small set of bootstrap training data, with the help of a set of *"how to learn"* rules and conditions. The benefit of self-learning is that the system will select from the *Rules Database (RDb)* to explore different strategies and score the result automatically and making judgement in cooperating new rules into the Rules Database;

2. **Context:** The use of a particular personal identity that would be unusual for one organisation would be typical for another. There is a need to differentiate changes in behaviours that are indicative of fraud rather than static indicators. Furthermore, context help meeting the challenge for IAM in keeping track of the changes in identities for a particular person whose digital profiles are changed due to change in lifestyle, physical, social environments or age; and

3. **Granularity:** There is a trade-off between accuracy versus level of coverage. The detection algorithms will need to consider aggregated population behaviours smoothing out local variations and correlates with coarser-grained changes. Nonetheless, this granularity also applies to user-centric preferences so that online users can manage how their online profile data are being treated by the service providers.

The SCAIAM context and granularity features help meet the challenge of inter-operational issue when people access applications through multiple access points using separate security policies and identity stores.

The core components of SCAIAM framework are depicted in Figure 1. The SCAIAM framework defines a set of core context elements with coarse granularity as the starting point. These core context elements are defined in the *Bootstrap Training Dataset*. This will provide a set of rules acting as the blueprint for the *Self-learning Identity Agents* (SIA) in the SCAIAM model to extend with their relevant contexts and specific level of granularities depending on the environments that a particular Identity Agent is situated at that particular instant.

There is a *Context Database (CD)* keeping track of the changes in context sensitive history data for making real-time correlations in deciding whether the *Granularity Scope (SC)* should be expanded or contracted for that particular context.

The RDb allows the SCAIAM framework administrators to define different kinds of rules to protect the system from thefts and the processes to authenticate and authorise user access requests. New rules will be added and existing rules will be updated or made obsoleted automatically (or authorised, depending on the severity level of the rules) based on the outcomes of *the Theft Prevention, Theft Detection & Reporting*, and *Theft Responding* components. These rules will define a scoring and classification algorithm so as to inform the SCAIAM framework to make appropriate judgements in all the IAM activities monitored by this framework.

Figure 1. Core components of the self-learning context aware identity access and management framework

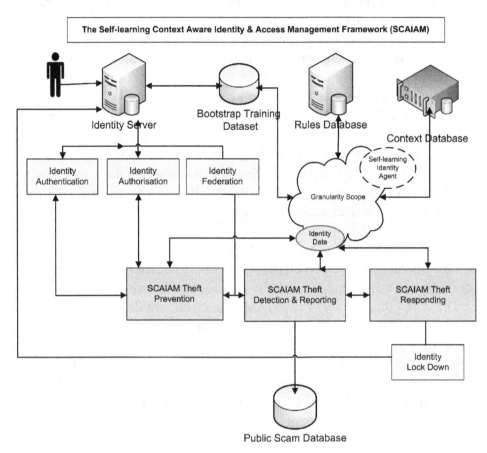

Furthermore, the SCAIAM framework adopts the federated model in avoiding the use of centralised IAM registries. *Identity Federation* can be achieved in several different ways, which may include the SAML specification, OpenID, Higgins' trust framework, and information cards. This allows companies to share applications, regardless of the need to adopt the same technologies for authentication, directory services and security. As for individuals, the SCAIAM framework allows user to use SSO to access the networks of different enterprises using their personal identification information or login credentials in a particular trusted domain. The partners in a federated system are responsible for authenticating their respective users and for vouching for their access to the networks.

Apart from enabling secure, cross-domain SSO for web and mobile applications, the SCAIAM framework will also support modern web and API access security and multi-factor authentication.

Preventing malicious creation of fake identities in the system using any other identity when the actual user has not registered is a major concern. Although we can mandate that at the time of registration the user provides the strong identifiers indicated by the rules and polices set by the framework, our framework also make use of the *Self-Learning Identity Agent* (SIA), which is a piece of application instantiated when a business transaction for a particular user is initiated, for example, a bank transfer, or new credit card application, or user login request from a remote location. The SIA will live and monitor the user's transaction, noting down the relevant context information, and determine the level of granularities required to be monitored.

A user can register his/her personal attributes with any Security Identity Providers in the federation engaging a bootstrapping procedure. After the registration is completed, a set of personal attributes are associated with the user SSO ID and with other context information are logged at the SIA. The SIA attributes are used together with the Context Database and other ordinary data to protect from identity theft. To protect against identity theft, it is important that an adversary be prevented from registering as its own personal attributes of other users; therefore this framework will include mechanisms to detect duplicates within a federation.

There are many researchers and engineers working diligently in the field of security information technologies to develop solutions for the prevention, detection, reporting and responding of identity theft. These technologies are essential for building secure IAM systems that identity issuers, verifiers, and owners can rely on. This SCAIAM framework will incorporate those existing technologies to build the following theft prevention, detection and responding inter-related constituent components.

The SCAIAM Theft Prevention Component

The onset of the information age has pushed all sorts of information to the fore, that has transformed information from the physical file cabinets locked in the office of bureaucracies (both governmental and private) into become a major product of the market place.

Therefore, the SCAIAM framework's theft prevention strategies will focus on minimising the opportunity structures (described in the above sections) that make identity crime both possible and desirable to fraudster. The techniques specified in the Situational Crime Prevention (Clarke, 1997) are suitable to the prevention of identity theft. Situational prevention divides up the possible techniques into five categories:

- Increase the effort the offender must make to complete the crime;
- Increase the risks of getting caught;
- Reduce the rewards that result from the crime;
- Reduce provocations that may encourage or otherwise tempt offenders; and
- Remove excuses that offenders may use to justify their crime.

First of all, regular audits (varied from yearly overall audit, quarterly sectional audit, monthly functional audit, down to weekly component audit) to assess organisational compliance with security-related policies and procedures are necessary.

To increase the effort of the offender to commit crime, this framework will promote the use of a password manager, so that users only need to remember one password to access the password manager itself and relying on the password manager to store and encrypt all of the user's login information.

Moreover, the author prefers to have the system requires accessing the password manager through a biometric mechanism, such as fingerprint, or through some form of MFA which requires users to have extra credentials, beyond just a password, to access the service. One of the preferred forms of MFA is that the user requires knowing something, such as a password, and having something, such as a specific mobile device with active biometric access control.

(Newman & McNally, 2005) report that identity theft of the deceased has been dubbed "Britain's largest growing identity theft related crime," which has grown from 5,000 cases in 2001, to16,000 in 2003. They also report that certain groups of victims may be more vulnerable than others because of the organisations to which they belong. In particular, higher education students and members of the armed services may be particularly at risk. This is because they are required to disclose their private information extensively among institutions of higher learning and students' increased opportunities for obtaining credit.

As such, this framework requires the security solution providers to select countermeasures to protect identity thefts from possible threats depending on the likelihood of each group of users (i.e. Students, On-line Traders, or Financial institutions).

Other security mechanisms in increasing the effort of committing theft are suggested as follows:

- Implementing ID tracking mechanisms to track location of use and who uses the device to log in;
- Requiring several forms of proof–of-Id when obtaining new ID or replacement;
- Limiting the number of persons who are able to access the identity databases; and
- Requiring MFA (password, pass phase, mobile device & biometric) to access databases.

In cryptography, Zero-Knowledge Protocol (ZKP) is a method by which one party (the Prover) can prove to another party (the Verifier) that he or she holds the answer to a given question, without revealing any information apart from the fact that the statement is indeed true (Quisquater et al., 1989).

Social-Login is implementing ZKP, which demonstrates the following three properties:

- **Completeness:** If the Prover is honest, then he or she will eventually convince the Verifier. If Facebook accepts the login of a particular email-address, the honest verifying entity will be convinced of this fact specified by Facebook in using Social-Login;
- **Soundness:** The Prover can only convince the Verifier if the statement is true. If the statement is false, no cheating Prover can convince the honest Verifier that it is true, except with some small probability;
- **Zero-Knowledge:** The Verifier learns no information beyond the fact that the statement is true. In other words, the Verifier just knows the statement (not the secret) is sufficient to prove that the Prover knows the secret.

This framework proposes using a ZKP identification scheme which enables a Prover holding a secret key to identify himself or herself to a Verifier holding the corresponding public key. Security against impersonation under active attack has been one of the major challenges of identification schemes. There is a growing trend of more sophisticated attacks than before, namely concurrent ones. Here, the attacker would play the role of cheating the Verifier prior to impersonation, but could interact with many different Prover "clones" concurrently. The clones all have the same secret key but are initialised with independent coins and maintain their own state. Security against impersonation under concurrent attack implies security against impersonation under active attack.

The Guillou-Quisquater (GQ; Guillou & Quisquater, 1988) and Schnorr (1991) identification schemes are two of the efficient schemes available. (Bellare and Palacio, 2002) have proved that the GQ identification scheme is secure against impersonation, under both active and concurrent attacks, under the assumption that RSA is secure under one more inversion. Furthermore, Bellare and Palacio (2002) have proved that the Schnorr scheme is also secure against impersonation, under both active and concurrent attacks, under the assumption that discrete exponentiation is secure under one more inversion in the underlying group.

The SCAIAM Theft Detection and Reporting Component

The SCAIAM Theft Detection and Reporting Component will conduct evidence collection, analysis and investigation, forensics, remediation, full recovery, and post-mortem activities.

The SCAIAM framework relies heavily on joint efforts and coordination among all stakeholders in every relevant activity of IAM. The SCAIAM Theft Detection & Reporting Component is responsible for the detection of any identity theft incident and reporting the incident to the related entities in world. So far, we have identified the following anti-fraud entities that this framework will report to:

- The APWG Malicious Domain Suspension Program;
- The America Federal Bureau of Investigation Internet Crime Complaint Center (IC3);
- The Australian Competition and Consumer Commission (ACCC) Scamwatch program; and
- The America Federal Trade Commission Report Identity Theft Program.

This component will utilise the CD, RDb, GC and SIA to calculate an *Individual Theft Score* (ITS) of individual case of identity breach as well as an *Aggregated Theft Score* (ATS) when GC is taken into consideration.

The SCAIAM framework requires a set of *Theft Action Plan* (TAP) to be defined in the system to deal with different breach scenarios. Different TAPs will have different ITS & ATS alert trigger levels to accommodate the variation of severity levels and scope.

The following fraud detection mechanisms will be employed in the SCAIAM framework:

- Monitoring the performance metrics and probability distributions of transactions frequencies, amount, and durations;
- Modelling different activities;
- Computing user profiles;
- Time-series analysis of different transaction context data;
- Clustering and classification techniques to identify fraud patterns and associations with other data; and
- Matching algorithms to detect anomalies in the behaviour of transactions or users as compared to previously known models and profiles.

Prodromidis and Stolfo (1999) apply agent based inductive learning algorithms and meta-learning methods as a means to compute accurate classification models for detecting electronic frauds. The author considers the application of AI into identity theft detection is the key to future development in successful combat against identity theft. The SIA acts as the agent in applying different inductive learning programs (e.g., Bayes, C4.5, ID3, CART, and Ripper).

SIA will compute effective classifiers that correctly discern fraudulent from legitimate transactions. The self-learning process of SIA works like this:

- SIA will execute a number of machine learning processes on a number of data subsets in parallel, and combine their computed classifiers through an additional phase of learning;
- An *Initial Base Classifier* (IBC) will be established first (based on the underlying data subset);
- Based on the GC result, additional machine learning tasks will be performed to integrate different independently computed *Base Classifiers* (BCs) into a *Higher Scope Classifier* (HSC). This HSC forms the detection mechanism to discover any characteristics of fraud behaviours.

The SCAIAM Theft Responding Component

Responding to an identity theft is like responding to any human-caused or natural disaster. There should be a collection of *Theft Response Procedures / Policy (TRP)* established within the organisation. The TRPs serves to outline the structures that the organisation may already have in place for emergency response.

The TRPs will identify functions and steps that need to be performed in responding to a theft. There are different roles from within an organisation and some are likely to be filled by people outside the institution.

It is important to specify in advance the person who will be in charge of an incident, a line of succession (3 to 5 people deep) of people who are trained to perform each response function, and who will provide liaison with outside agencies. After that, put into practice the response through drills, table-top exercises, etc.

The organisation may be involved in a theft-in-progress or to one that has been identified as occurring sometime in the past. In either case, the SCAIAM framework will keep with highest priority to secure the return of the organisation asset without any injuries or damage. The framework will ensure speedy recovery by quick reporting of the incident through law enforcement and other professional channels.

Angelopoulou (2007) states that the difficulty the investigators need to face when dealing with an ID Theft incident and what really makes this type of crime individually-treated is that they have to face two investigative categories: victim and perpetrator. The SCAIAM framework shall provide the law enforcement such evidential data that will be able to prove the fraud against the victim monitored by this framework as well as the related computer forensic information.

On the other hand, the way that can reveal the evidential data of the fraudster's machine and the deception's proof will be left to the investigators to devise.

As depicted in Figure 2, The SCAIAM Theft Responding Component will include the following five phases in responding to an alert received from the SCAIAM Theft Detection and Reporting Component.

Figure 2. The SCAIAM theft responding component

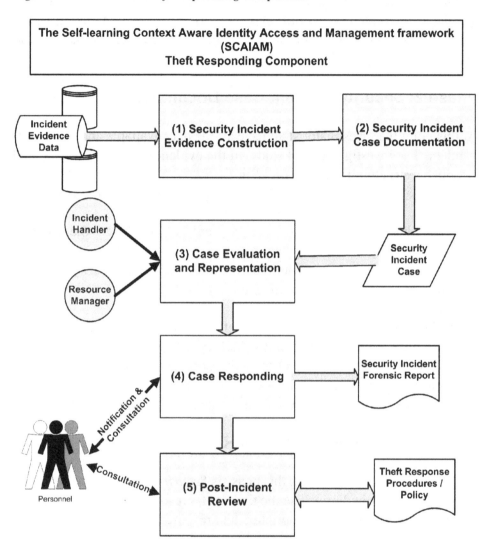

Phase 1: Security Incident Evidence Construction

All the related evidential data will be structured and formatted in way acceptable to other law enforcement organisations. The threat agent SIA profile for the victim and the fraudster's digital footprints will be analysed. There is going data collection so that the investigator can have enough information to construct the fraudster's profile.

Furthermore, the framework suggests the administrators to obtain and archive an encrypted copy of the crime report and all related records of the incident. This is to ensure all the theft evidence is secured, untouched and protected.

Phase 2: Security Incident Case Documentation

At this point the investigator shall have all the data available about the theft incident. The investigator shall study all the evidence available at hand and establish a structured *Security Incident Case*.

This phase will document the following aspects of the theft incident:

- To what extent and how the incident has impacted the existing functionality of all the systems;
- How much of the user population is affected by the security incident; who are the affected identities and are there any suspected employee has committed the theft;
- What are the possible source of theft channels and the snapshot of the complete environment when the theft occurs;
- How the incident has breached the confidentiality, integrity of any internal and external data; and
- To what extent is the reputational/financial impact of the organisation.

Phase 3: Case Evaluation and Representation

One of the important actions in this phase is *Security Incident Prioritisation*. This is to identify and prioritise the timing and resources required to deploy corrective action, resource proprietors and resource custodians.

The investigator will assess the impact of the security incident based on a number of factors that are documented in the previous phase, Security Incident Case.

Basing on the information collected in the Security Incident Case, the security incident will be assessed and assigned a high to low priority score (10 =high to 1 = low) by a designated *Incident Handler* and a *Resource Manager* component.

Apart from the current impact of the incident, the investigator shall also provide an estimation of the likely future impact of the incident if it is not immediately corrected. Any high priority incidents should be immediately reported to all the related internal and external entities (e.g. ISP, Legal Entities and Law Enforcement Entities).

Once the security incident is reported to the related entities, the priority rating will be confirmed or revised following additional analysis of the event by the other related entities. Any update to priority level shall be reviewed by local incident response team members in consultation with other external trusted security analysts.

Examples of high priority security incident include:

- Events leading to the loss of critical function to organisation wide or departmental wide user population;
- Breaches of data confidentiality affecting more than 10% user populations; and
- Financial loss worth over $10000.

Phase 4: Case Responding

The purpose of this phase is to prepare a *Security Incident Forensic Report*. The Security Incident Forensic Report will include all the evidence as well as the impact analysis of the security incident. This report will be used to stand in a court of law, ready for charging the fraudster of the case.

Additional response actions to be conducted in this phase include:

- Contacting the Identity Theft Hotline;
- Notifying the Credit Reporting Agencies;
- Placing Fraud Alert or Security Freeze to all related external entities (such as banks, creditors, utilities, insurance carriers);
- Notifying and consulting with Director Board and Trustees, as appropriate, on issues related to minimisation of risk to the institution, public relations, and other broad issues;
- Notifying the local Police Department and other law enforcement;
- In keeping with the severity of the incident, mitigating the impact of the incident by finishing containment and eradication activities, and ultimately recovering from it. During this phase, activity often cycles back to the Theft Detection & Reporting component to see if additional systems are infected by the incident while eradicating the incident; and
- Implementing safeguard procedures against additional loss or damage to people or asset of the organisation.

The Directors and other relevant team members are required to examine and determine strategies for external communications appropriate to the situation as well as reviewing and planning response policies in conjunction with the response team and board.

The response team is responsible to ensure all response operations are conducted safely and are well documented, establish timeline for resumption of internal and external business operations.

Phase 5: Post-Incident Review

After the incident is adequately handled, the incident response team shall compile a report that details the cause and cost of the incident and the suggested steps that the organisation should take to prevent similar incidents from recurring in the future.

This phase will include possible Legal reviews and approves changes to the organisation's *Theft Response Procedures / Policy*. All the related legal entities shall be invited to provide advice to the response team and board.

CONCLUSION

This chapter has served the threefold purpose of (1) explaining different ways how personal identities are stolen and exploited; (2) a discussion on how to combat identity crime; and (3) describing the Self-learning Context Aware Identity Access and Management framework proposed by the author.

In most cases, the victims of identity theft may not even know they have been fallen victim of identity thefts until long after the thefts have taken place; not until they received calls from creditors, debt collectors or solicitors about transactions they didn't enter into or debts that aren't theirs, arrival of new credit cards that they didn't ask for, unexpected denial of credit, or refusal of services or benefits because they are told they are already receiving them.

The Identity Theft Awareness Website (http://www.identity-theft-awareness.com/) and the Identity Management Institute Website (https://www.identitymanagementinstitute.org/) contain valuable resources for normal end users and IT practitioners on how to take responsibility for the protection of the information they have been entrusted with and have control over, especially, when managing the personal information of employees, employers and clients.

The author believes that collaboration and education are two of the key success factors in developing appropriate identity protection strategies, training programs, policies and procedures, and identity theft awareness programs in combating identity theft.

REFERENCES

Ahamad, M., Amster, D., Barrett, M., Cross, T., Heron, G., Jackson, D., & Traynor, P. et al. (2008). *Emerging Cyber Threats Report for 2009*. Georgia Tech Information Security Center.

Angelopoulou, O. (2007). ID theft: a computer forensics' investigation framework. *Australian Digital Forensics Conference*.

Australian Bureau of Statistics. (2016a). *4528.0 - Personal fraud, 2014-15*. Available: http://www.abs.gov.au/AUSSTATS/abs@.nsf/Lookup/4528.0Main+Features172014-15?OpenDocument

Australian Bureau of Statistics. (2016b). *Identity crime and misuse in Australia 2016*. Attorney-General's Department.

Bellare, M., & Palacio, A. (2002). GQ and schnorr identification schemes: proofs of security against impersonation under active and concurrent attacks. *Advances in Cryptology (CRYPTO 2002)*.

Bolton, R. J., Hand, D. J., Provost, F., Breiman, L., Bolton, R. J., & Hand, D. J. (2002). Statistical fraud detection: A review. *Statistical Science*, *17*(3), 235–255. doi:10.1214/ss/1042727940

Chan, P. K., Fan, W., Prodromidis, A. L., & Stolfo, S. J. (1999). Distributed data mining in credit card fraud detection. *IEEE Intelligent Systems*, *14*(6), 67–74. doi:10.1109/5254.809570

Chen, H., Beaudoin, C. E., & Hong, T. (2017). Securing online privacy: An empirical test on Internet scam victimization, online privacy concerns, and privacy protection behaviors. *Computers in Human Behavior*, *70*, 291–302. doi:10.1016/j.chb.2017.01.003

Clarke, R. V. G. (1997). *Situational crime prevention*. Criminal Justice Press Monsey.

Cortes, C., & Vapnik, V. (1995). Support-vector networks. *Machine Learning, 20*(3), 273–297. doi:10.1007/BF00994018

Fawcett, T., & Provost, F. (1997a). Adaptive fraud detection. *Data Mining and Knowledge Discovery, 1*(3), 291–316. doi:10.1023/A:1009700419189

Fawcett, T., & Provost, F. (1997b). *Combining data mining and machine learning for effective fraud detection.* AAAI.

Guillou, L., & Quisquater, J. J. (1988). A "paradoxical" identity-based signature scheme resulting from zero-knowledge. *Advances in Cryptology (CRYPTO '88).*

Jorna, P. (2016). *Australasian Consumer Fraud Taskforce: Results of the 2014 online consumer fraud survey.* AIC Reports.

Newman, G. R., & Mcnally, M. M. (2005). *Identity theft literature review.* Available: https://www.ncjrs.gov/pdffiles1/nij/grants/210459.pdf

Payneham, S. (2006). *Standardisation of definitions of identity crime terms: A step towards consistency.* The Australasian Centre for Policing Research (ACPR) and and The Australian Transaction Reports and Analysis Centre (AUSTRAC) Proof of Identity Steering Committee.

Phua, C., Smith-Miles, K., Lee, V., & Gayler, R. (2012). Resilient identity crime detection. *IEEE Transactions on Knowledge and Data Engineering, 23*(3), 533–546. doi:10.1109/TKDE.2010.262

Pink, B. (2008). *Personal fraud.* Australian Bureau of Statistics.

Pratt, T. C., Holtfreter, K., & Reisig, M. (2010). Routine online activity and internet fraud targeting: Extending the generality of routine activity theory. *Journal of Research in Crime and Delinquency, 47*(3), 267–296. doi:10.1177/0022427810365903

Prodromidis, A. L., & Stolfo, S. (1999). Agent-based distributed learning applied to fraud detection. *Sixteenth National Conference on Artificial Intelligence.*

Quisquater, J.-J., Guillou, L., Annick, M., & Berson, T. (1989). How to explain zero-knowledge protocols to your children. *Advances in Cryptology (CRYPTO '89).*

Reyns, B. W. (2013). Activity theory beyond direct-contact offenses. *Journal of Research in Crime and Delinquency, 50,* 268–238. doi:10.1177/0022427811425539

Rogers, R. W. (1975). A protection motivation theory of fear appeals and attitude change1. *The Journal of Psychology, 91*(1), 93–114. doi:10.1080/0 0223980.1975.9915803 PMID:28136248

Schnorr, C. P. (1991). Effcient signature generation by smart cards. *Journal of Cryptology, 4*(3), 161–174. doi:10.1007/BF00196725

Smyth, P. J. (1995). *US Patent 5465321 - Hidden markov models for fault detection in dynamic systems.* No. 047135 filed on 04/07/1993

Van Wilsem, J. (2011). 'Bought it, but never got it' assessing risk factors for online consumer fraud victimization. *European Sociological Review, 29*(2), 168–178. doi:10.1093/esr/jcr053

Wang, W., Yuan, Y., & Archer, N. (2006). A contextual framework for combating identity theft. *IEEE Security and Privacy, 4*(2), 30–38. doi:10.1109/MSP.2006.31

Wueest, C. (2015). Underground black market: Thriving trade in stolen data, malware, and attack services. *Symantec Official Blog.* Available from: http://www.symantec.com/connect/blogs/underground-black-market-thriving-trade-stolen-data-malware-and-attack-services

Xu, J., Sung, A. H., & Liu, Q. (2006). *Tree based behavior monitoring for adaptive fraud detection.* 18th International Conference on Pattern Recognition (ICPR'06), Hong Kong.

Chapter 8

Challenges and Future Development in Identity and Access Management

ABSTRACT

Online identity has become so pivotal to so many different aspects of a person's live and will impact all of us in one way or another. This chapter tries to post some insights to where the Identity and Access Management industry is going. This chapter discusses the future development of IAM in relation to the following new technological trends: Internet of Everything (IoE), Identity Relationship Management, Transient Identities, and Autonomous Devices.

INTRODUCTION

SMIC (Social, Mobile, Information Analytics and Cloud) is the concept that four technologies are currently driving the creation of new business design. The synergy created by SMIC working together has created a competitive advantage for the following business innovations:

- **Social Media:** Enabling businesses to reach and interact with customers;
- **Mobile Technologies:** Enabling people to communicate, shop and work without physical boundary;

DOI: 10.4018/978-1-5225-4828-7.ch008

- **Information Analytics:** Allowing businesses to capture and analyse customer behaviours (how, when and where) in conducting online goods and services; and
- **Cloud Computing:** Providing Software-as-a-Service (SaaS), Infrastructure-as-a-Service (IaaS), and Platform-as-a-Service (PaaS) delivery modes for business organisations to quickly respond to changing needs of the business.

The integration of the SMIC technologies has posed new challenges to the IAM development. Our readers should have noticed that legacy approaches to IAM are lagging because those products cannot handle access from consumer endpoints effectively, not able to support the rapid adoption of Cloud services and cannot provide secure data exchange across user populations.

The increasing trend of Bring Your Own Device (BYOD) within organisations that allows weakened authentication and authorisation has introduced many security threats associated with identity thefts. Furthermore, it requires great effort in safeguarding employees from provisioning their own software on those devices to use at work (such as, Dropbox, Box, SugarSync, Google Drive and Evernote).

Access control application is expected to play a key role in the IAM market due to the fact that identity administrators need the right tool with real-time management of all the activities with user devices such as mobile phones, tablets, and laptops along with high security against malicious threats within the enterprises. This requires clear policies and guidelines as well as management tools that can automate the access control processes.

Apart from that, Cloud-based IAM deployment is expected to benefit organisations with increased scalability, speed, 24/7 services, and enhanced management capabilities. Cloud-based IAM solutions can meet customer demand in starting or stopping any service, at will.

There are many reports and research articles detailing different visions for the future of Identity and Access Management. The Forrester Research Report prepared by (Cser et al., 2016) helps security and risk professionals understand how they can leverage IAM technologies to enable new customer functionality and business models in the coming three years. The Forrester Research report highlights that the employees' BYOD mobile applications and DevOps methodologies are increasing application releases, which has shaped the need for new approach in dealing with mobile IAM and security in mobile apps; and the slimming down and simplifying of IAM.

(Wagner, 2014) predicts that by year end 2020:

- The majority of user access will be shaped by new mobile and non-PC architectures that serve all identity types regardless of origin;
- Most digital identities interacting with enterprises will come from external identity providers through a competitive marketplace;
- Most enterprises will allow unrestricted access to non-critical assets, reducing spending on IAM by 25 percent;
- The majority of enterprises will use Attribute-Based Access Control (ABAC) as the dominant mechanism to protect critical assets; and
- The Internet of Things will redefine the concept of identity management to include what people own, share, and use.

On top of the many predictions about the future development in IAM, the author found (Maler, 2014) has made a sound observation that cross-domain user provisioning due to many different Software-as-a-Service (SaaS) applications have caused reduced security due to latency when removing authorisations due to SaaS and partner apps that rely on too-infrequent synchronisation. Maler suggests that the next generation of IAM will be "*Contextual*" based driven massively by "*mobile-fueled*" devices, often adding risk-based and biometric components and asymmetric key technology to improve both security and usability.

Maler also proposed the *Zero Trust Identity* model which supports the goal of *Identity Statelessness*, allowing *just-in-time identity data consumption* and services coming from different organisational domains that are authoritative for them. The Zero Trust Identity model is consists of the following steps:

- Mapping identity context to all the internal data;
- Enabling federation services for all the business applications;
- Preparing the internal IAM services for loose coupling and creating a developer community that promotes the goal of Identity Statelessness; and
- Pushing the edge of the envelope in externalising authorisation.

As the concluding chapter of this book, the main goal is set to discuss some of the major development challenges of IAM solutions and the trends of new technologies that will affect the future development of IAM solutions.

IDENTITY AND ACCESS MANAGEMENT OF THE INTERNET OF EVERYTHING (IOE)

Traditional IAM services were built for internal use, controlling access to data and systems behind the firewall. However, we're now entering an era known as the Internet of Things (IoT), and in the next few years the number of connected devices is going to grow exponentially.

The IoT creates both a challenge and an opportunity for companies because it represents a network of interrelated physical devices, computing devices, mechanical and digital machines, vehicles, buildings, objects, animals or people that are embedded with electronics, software, sensors, actuators, and network connectivity with unique identifiers and the ability to exchange information over a network without requiring human-to-human or human-to-computer interaction.

The demand for identity services will continue to increase as use cases expand into areas such as the IoT. The number of human identities and associated attributes will grow with the volume of connected devices as each of these devices will have associated attributes and data that must be managed in a secured manner.

The growth does not stop at IoT. The dawn of Internet of Everything (IoE) is at sight. The IoE builds on the foundation of the IoT by adding network intelligence that allows convergence, orchestration and visibility across previously disparate systems.

The development of IP-enabled devices, the increase in global broadband availability and the advent of IPv6 lead to the explosion of new connections joining the IoE. The IoE brings together people, process, data and things to make networked connections to become actions that create new capabilities and functionalities for businesses, individuals and countries. IoE embraces the intelligent connection of people, process, data and things:

- **People:** People are connected through devices and social media, such as Facebook and LinkedIn. As the IoE emerges, the interaction of people on the Internet will become common to wear sensors on our skin or in our clothes that collect and transmit data to other healthcare practitioners and friends so that people may become individual nodes that produce a constant stream of data;
- **Process:** This includes evolving technology, business, organisational and other processes that are needed to manage and automate the

explosive growth in connections. Processes play a vital role in managing how each of these entities—people, data, and things—interact with each other within the IoE to deliver societal benefits and economic value through the processes of accumulating, analysing and communicating information in the IoE world;

- **Things:** This includes almost any physical things that are capable of connecting to the Internet. There are many physical items like sensors, meters, actuators, and other types of devices that can be attached to any object, that are capable of connecting to the Internet and sharing information. These things will sense and deliver data, respond to control inputs, and provide information to assist people and machines make decisions. Examples of "things" in the IoE include smart meters, assembly line robots, and smart transportation systems;

- **Data:** Smart devices are gathering data and stream it over the Internet to a server, where it is analysed and processed. Such data has very short life span and thus, not all generated data should be stored. We anticipate that the traditional batch-oriented data analysis model by combining data into more useful information will not be able to meet the advance in data intelligence.

Rather than just reporting raw data, IoE connected things are required to send higher-level information and insights back to servers and people in real time for further evaluation and decision making.

This new wave of 'data in motion' imparts new challenges to the IAM market because the scope of entities to be managed by the IAM solutions expands beyond human and physical devices identities.

The advent of IoE will have great impact on the future development of IAM as there are important considerations in the privacy, security, energy consumption and network congestion of IoE.

The author proposes an IoE IAM stack which is shown in Figure 1. The IAM stack for IoE requires three core components to work effectively:

- The End-to-End Identity and Access Management Service of People, IoT, Processes, Data & Communication Channels;
- The Identity Relationship Management Service; and
- The IoE Identity Providers.

An End-to-End IAM solution is the enabler for real-time networked people, devices, processes and data. The existing OpenID Connect authentication

Figure 1. IoE identity and access management stack

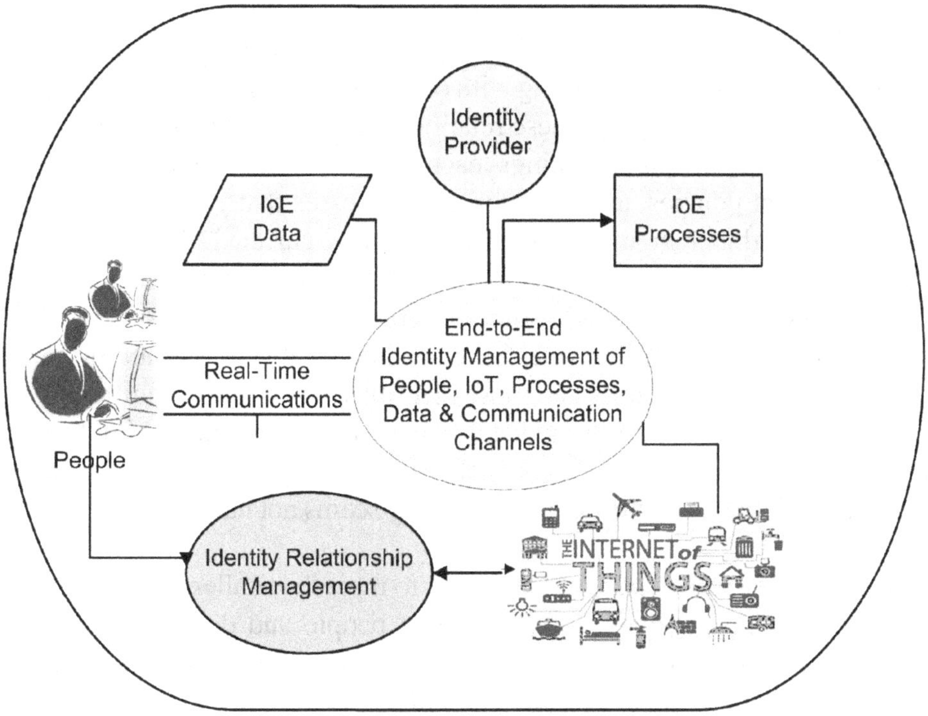

standard should be extended so as to accomplish the implementation across virtually any application or service to manage meshed network connections between people and devices through the Identity-Based Network Interactive Connectivity Establishment (ICE) standard mechanism for establishing end-to-end identity based communication between software agents running behind firewalls in a distributed and heterogeneous IoE scenario. The Cisco's Identity Services Engine (ISE) is one of the solutions which enforce identity-based access control that can be extended to mobile devices as well as Mobile-to-Mobile IoE entities.

The IoE Identity Provider extends the existing functionalities of people identities to cover the identities for device context processes and data. The Identity Relationship Management Service covers the complex relationships amongst all the IoE entities. We are going to discuss the Identity Relationship Management topic in the next section.

IDENTITY RELATIONSHIP MANAGEMENT

One of the challenges indicated by Glazer and Brennan (2015) is that things and human identities are mingling with one another in an unreasonably large number of relationships; and these relationships are among an unreasonably large numbers of people and things, each with sets of attributes.

The current policies, technologies and processes that govern IAM seem cannot handle this changing landscape. Most of the current IAM solutions are used to dealing with reasonable numbers of people with reasonable numbers of attributes. For example, IAM solutions are granting user access, segregate duties, and manage user lifecycles based on having at least one authoritative source for employee identity and those identities have a few dozen attributes.

When the world is becoming one dominated by a large number of "smart objects" and the connections between them in the world of identity is growing at a geometric rate, the current IAM industry seems not handling these types of scenarios yet.

Relationship data is part of the answer to meet the challenge. Enterprises will start to manage connections between people and devices as well as connecting devices to devices. As a result, the complexity, scale and security requirements are going to be quite difficult.

Here comes *Identity Relationship Management (IRM)* which enables the development of secure relationships for IoT across the Internet – including Cloud, social, mobile and enterprise environments. IRM shall extend identities to any 'thing' connected to the Internet and is not limited to connectivity behind the firewall. IRM shifts focus to the value of relationships that are represented by identities and not the identities themselves. This shift bringing with it the complexities of deploying IAM, including: privacy for personal data, appropriate security, access control and attribute information sharing policies (where attributes are pieces of data about a person, entity or thing).

The key security advantage of IRM is that it ties users to digital identities that an organisation can identify and interact with. This means they can securely and seamlessly deploy services to customers across different applications, devices, and things. As people, devices and "things" are assigned identities across networks, IRM services that are designed to quickly verify identities and access privileges become imperative for any business or institution to safely and efficiently engage with their stakeholders and customers.

At the same time, because it provides much greater insight into who accesses which systems from which devices and when, its benefits go far beyond security. This new data helps companies understand their customers, not just protect them. It opens up new revenue opportunities for cross-selling, upselling, and delivering personalised services to customers.

In 2014, the Kantara Initiative has established the Identity Relationship Management Working Group (https://kantarainitiative.org/groups/irm/) to develop community market driven works around the IRM, such as whitepapers, case studies, best practices, deployment profiles, user experience surveys, and APIs.

The Working Group has produced the IRM Design Principles of Relationship Management version 1.0 report (Glazer & Brennan, 2015). This report has laid the foundation for future IRM development by capturing the evolving concepts around IAM and to inform the IAM developers the design principles for consideration and adoption of future IRM innovations. The report describes the following laws of relationship that are able to describe and inform scenarios involving groups of actors in relationships with other groups of actors, person-to-person interactions as well as relationships applicable to "things.":

- Relationships must be *scalable*;
- Relationships must be *actionable* (able to do something of value and, more specifically, relationships that can carry authorisation data);
- Relationships can be *immutable* (provide the ground layer for assurance and important contextual information);
- Relationships can be *contextual* (relationships can be "triggered" by changes in context);
- Relationships can be *transferred* (the substitution can be done on a temporary basis or permanently);
- Relationships must be *provable* (this is to prove the existence of a relationship or set of relationships to establish trust between parties, provides auditability and traceability. The types of assertion may include: Single-party Asserted relationship, Multi-party Asserted relationship, and Third-party Asserted relationship);
- Relationships can be *acknowledged* (this is for participants to acknowledge that they have relationships to certain actors);

- Relationships must be *revocable* (this is related to developing legal approaches such as the Right to be Forgotten, and the ability or lack of ability for a data subject to remove personally identifiable data); and
- Relationships must be *constrainable* (all behaviours and allowable actions associated with a relationship must be able to be constrained based on the desires, preferences, and business models of the parties involved).

ForgeRock, the official stewards of the ForgeRock I3 Open Platform project, is one of the leaders in the IRM solutions. The I3 Open Platform is built upon the open source projects including OpenAM (based on OpenSSO), OpenESB, OpenIdM and OpenPortal (based on Liferay Portal). The current projects undertaken by ForgeRock include: OpenAM, OPenDJ, OpenIDM, OpenIG, OpenICF, and OpenUMA.

These projects cover areas such as:

- Access management that includes authentication, adaptive risk assessment, authorization, federation, single sign-on, social sign-on, basic self-service, privacy and consent, and high performance session management;
- REST and LDAP Directory Services;
- Multiple sources of identity together for policy and workflow based management that puts end-users in control of the data. Consume, transform and feed data to external sources in order to maintain control over identity of users, devices and things;
- Identity Gateway reverse proxy server with session management and credential replay functionality working together with OpenAM to integrate Web applications for native execution of target application;
- ICF Connector supporting the provisioning software such as OpenIDM to manage identities maintained by a specific identity provider; and
- User-Managed Access, an OAuth-2 based protocol in using, profiling, and extending OAuth 2 to enable various use cases for resource owner-managed access that enables an individual to control the authorisation of data sharing and service access made by others.

The author expects that existing IAM developments will be extended to incorporate IRM functionalities in the coming years.

IDENTITY AND ACCESS MANAGEMENT OF TRANSIENT IDENTITIES

The third driving force that shapes the future development of IAM is suggested by Walters (2016) that the future of IAM will be rooted in *Continuous Authentication*, which operates continuously in the background, unbeknownst to the user.

One of the promising forms of continuous authentication is centred around unique human behaviours. Known as behavioural biometrics, these tools can monitor things like keystroke patterns, iris patterns and more. Other behaviour profiling techniques make use of webcam to monitor the user's face, the colour of clothing, as well as micro-movement and orientation dynamics that take into account how the user grasps, holds and taps his/her mobile phone.

One of the aims for Continuous Authentication is to build a unique behaviour-based profile for each user which can be automatically and continually updated to reflect the present situation that the user is at. While Continuous Authentication is still in its early stage, businesses are adopting technologies like *context-based authentication* that define trust by contextual elements such as user role, geolocation, device type, device health and network.

The demand for continuous identity authentication services will continue to extend to the scenarios in giving birth to *Transient Identities*. Transient Identities refers to a set of attributes that uniquely define the identity of an object at a particular instance of contextual environment. The Transient Identities have short lifespans, serving a set of specific purposes, limited to a certain set of environmental conditions.

SAML 2.0 defines the concepts of Persistent NameID and Transient NameID to be used when a user tries to access a resource on a Service Provider. The user's identity shall be authenticated through SAML by a separate Identity Provider across different security domains. The federation service can be transient (one-sided) or mapped (two-sided).

The usual SAML federation flow is like this:

- After a user logging on to his/her identity provider, the user is redirected to the target service provider;
- The identity provider includes a transient name ID, e-mail address, first name, last name, and other information about the user;

- The transient name ID, e-mail address, and cost centre are mandatory in most scenarios and the use of the federation type Virtual Users can guarantee that the user exists on the user management engine (UME) of the service provider temporarily or for the length of the session.

However, the author believes that SAML 2.0 is required to be extended to accommodate the changes in requirements for Continuous Authentication at a fine granularity level.

Apart from that, the author finds the insightful claim from O'Connor (2017) about the usage of *Blockchain Technology* in enhancing security, enabling inclusion of low-value IoT to be increasingly viable and manageable.

According to *The Economist* (2015), the first Blockchain was conceptualised by Satoshi Nakamoto in 2008 serving as the public ledger for all Bitcoin (the digital currency) transactions.

A Blockchain is a chain of records arranged in data units called *Blocks* that use cryptographic validation to link themselves together. Each Block references and identifies the previous Block by a hashing function, forming an unbroken chain. This means we can use Blockchain as a peer to peer distributed ledger transactional application which maintains an unbroken growing list of cryptographically secured data blocks which can withstand against tampering and modification. Blockchain can help establish trust, non-repudiation, accountability and transparency while streamlining business transactions.

It is envisaged that Blockchain can leverage IoT/IoE IAM data flows without the need to set up sophisticated and expensive centralised IAM infrastructure. Furthermore, the Blockchain distributed replication facility shall allow business partners to share IoT/IoE private data without the need for centralised control and management. Blockchain has intrinsic strong data protection mechanism that fosters trustworthy working relationship between partners and greater efficiency as partners can trace the chain of information that is readily available.

The future IoT/IoE platforms shall be able to participate in Blockchain transactions. These types of devices shall be required to interact using private Blockchain ledgers for inclusion in shared transactions with distributed records, maintained by consensus, and cryptographically encrypted.

IDENTITY AND ACCESS MANAGEMENT OF AUTONOMOUS DEVICES

Autonomous Devices are those capable of knowing the physical and logical environment that they are currently at, their state, and incoming data; and most important is that they have the ability to learn and make decisions on their own.

Macy (2015) estimates that 50 billion IoT devices will be connected to the Internet by 2020; almost any object will become smart devices, such as, coffee makers, boilers and doors. There will be billions of devices and trillions of sensors, too many to manage through human manipulation and it will become a practical necessity for devices to operate autonomously.

No longer the realm of science fiction fantasy; autonomous cars that drive without needing a human driver behind the wheel are now a reality. The Google Car, the Mercedes-Benz F 015, Volvo XC60; and Uber are amongst the few car manufacturers offering driverless cars.

Levander (2017) paints a picture that tomorrow's robotic voyagers will be sailing without anyone on board. Ships will be controlled remotely or to navigate themselves. Levander reports that Rolls-Royce have been working on situational-awareness systems that integrate imagery from high-definition visible-light and infra-red cameras with lidar measurements, providing a detailed picture of the ship's immediate environment and the ship's on-board computer is able to generate the appropriate response action.

Apart from that, we can see some of the following new trends of development of intelligence platform that will impact the future of our society, for example:

- **Viv:** An intelligence platform that can connect millions of apps to its global brain with the flexibility to process complicated commands, countering the limitations of current voice-navigated systems;
- **Wit.ai:** A Voice interface to turn speech into actionable data for developers building applications and devices. Wit.ai is able to learn human language as it goes, building an extensive natural language platform for its community of developers;
- **Cohda:** A wireless vehicle-to-vehicle (V2X) technology enabling vehicles communicate with each other as well as with smart road infrastructures to share information on safety, mobility, and the environment;

- **Saffron:** A decision making tool that takes data from disparate sources and works quickly and intelligently through a contextual memory to identify thousands of connections;
- **IBM's Watson Developer Cloud:** The industry's largest portfolios of cognitive APIs that help developers bring their own data and engage with others to gain insights, extract value, and enhance learning. The platform has its natural language processing, computer vision, and cognitive capabilities that create an ideal platform for intelligent apps;
- **Edge3:** A vision-analytic software that monitors, tracks, and maps the behaviour of drivers and their passengers to verify identity, levels of awareness, and heart rate, among other variables. These factors will enable semi-autonomous driving to occur, while ensuring car operators are attentive and capable of decision making necessary to operate self-driving cars. Edge3's potential goes beyond self-driving cars and into robot control and object dimensioning;
- **B+B SmartWorx:** A hardware infrastructure for machine-to-machine networking; such that the network equipment can adapt and evolve into smarter, more autonomous, responsive, and decisive systems;
- **Filament:** A telecommunication system that enables users to deploy a wireless network at a range of up to 5Km. These networks work without dependency on Wi-Fi or cellular connectivity.

The challenge of managing the identity and access control services of autonomous devices lies in the fact that this paradigm has created new types of requirements that can be expressed in terms of the magnitude of the number of resources connected, density of the connections and complexity to manage all the interacting elements at the same time; and most important, the need to identify the actual owner of the autonomous device at a particular context.

The identity landscape of Autonomous Devices is complicated by the vast number of unstructured resources (the applications, the processes, the environment, and the device itself) that are exposed over the network (Internet, domestic, and corporate).

All the resources are related in groups where a particular resource may be a member of different groups simultaneously and as such may be administered and monitored by more than one entity, at times only in specific context, and sets policies for them. In term of management, some of these policies might be relevant only for a specific resource, in a particular context.

CONCLUSION

We have seen IAM services have evolved from mere using Active Directory & LDAP serving internal organisational control of access to data and systems behind the firewall into serving continuous multi-continental cross boundaries, Internet of Everything autonomous device-to-device, device-to-human, and human-to-human interactions.

As we have read from this book, the requirements on IAM had already made a number of drastic changes triggered by the advance in the Social, Mobile, Information Analytics and Cloud technologies. There are different evolving IAM deployment models using different technologies such as MFA multimodal biometric, pass phase / token based, X.509, SAML, OpenID, OAuth and SCIM.

We've also seen that IoT/IoE continuous authentication technologies are emerging for businesses to perform context-based authentication that define trust by contextual information. Furthermore, the requirements for context-based authorisation are re-shaping the features, functions and data analytics of future IAM solutions.

What's clear is IAM needs to evolve into incorporating a more fine grain and multi-dimension methodology so as to meet the future requirements of providing a secured and community-friendly environment for today's increasingly mobile workforce.

Moreover, the advent of Autonomous Devices poses new challenges to the future development of IAM solutions. We can expect a paradigm shift in IAM development will happen in the near future in order to cope with the new challenges.

Finally, as a word of advice to the readers, we, as researchers and technology developers, do our best to solve problems of value to people and the earth, taking regard to utility, sharing our responsibility and knowledge so that our work can be extended further together, and resist the temptation to offer solutions simply because they are too cool to refuse.

REFERENCES

Cser, A., Maxim, M., Balaouras, S., & Schiano, S. (2016). *The future of identity and access management*. Forrester Research, Inc.

Glazer, I., & Brennan, J. (2015). *The design principles of relationship management* (10th ed.). Kantara Initiative.

Levander, O. (2017). Autonomus ships on the high seas. *IEEE Spectrum*.

Macy, C. (2015). *'Autonomous tech' will surge in 2016 — keep an eye on these 8 players*. Available from: http://venturebeat.com/2015/12/12/autonomous-tech-will-surge-in-2016-keep-an-eye-on-these-8-players/

Maler, E. (2014). *Navigate the future of identity and access management*. Forrester Research, Inc.

O'Connor, C. (2017). *What blockchain means for you, and the Internet of Things*. Available from: https://www.ibm.com/blogs/internet-of-things/watson-iot-blockchain/

The Economist. (2015). Blockchains the great chain of being sure about things. *The Economist*.

Wagner, R. (2014, June). Identity and access management 2020. *ISSA Journal*, 26 - 30.

Walters, R. (2016). Continuous authentication: the future of identity and access management (IAM). *Network World*. Available: http://www.networkworld.com/article/3121240/security/continuous-authentication-the-future-of-identity-and-access-management-iam.html

Glossary

Access Management: Access management is the process of identifying, tracking, and controlling every valid user in a system what he/she is allowed or dis-allowed to access the resources available in the system.

Agent: A software agent is a lightweight program that runs as a service outside of the main system which helps integrating external applications with the core system.

App: App is the abbreviation of application.

Attribute-Based Access Control (ABAC): ABAC defines an access control mechanism whereby access rights are granted to users through the use of policies which combine attributes together and controls access to objects by evaluating rules against the attributes of the entities (subject and object) actions and the environment relevant to a request.

Authentication: Authentication is a process in which a person provides a certain set of credentials to an authenticating agent for the purpose of proofing that the person is who he/she claims to be.

Authorisation: Authorisation is the process of determining whether an authenticated person has a certain access rights to a particular resource (e.g. an application) according to the permissions assigned to that resource.

Biometric Application Programming Interface (BioAPI): BioAPI is the standards that support systems to perform biometric identity enrolment and identification.

Biometric Identification: Biometric Identification is using the unique physiological and/or behavioural properties exhibited by an individual to authenticate and verify the individual for access to protected resources or transactions.

Blockchain: A Blockchain is a chain of records arranged in data units called Blocks that use cryptographic validation to link themselves together.

Bring Your Own Device (BYOD): BYOD is the increasing trend of allowing the employees of an organisation to bring their own devices for work purposes.

Common Biometric Exchange Formats Framework (CBEFF): CBEFF is a set of data elements in supporting multiple biometric technologies and to promote interoperability of biometric-based application programs and systems by allowing for biometric data exchange.

Credential: A credential is the authoritative evidence of an individual's claimed identity.

Credential Management: Credential Management is the process of issuing, tracking, updating, and revoking credentials for identities within their context.

Cloud (Computing): Cloud computing refers to applications and services offered over the Internet. These services are offered from data centres spread across multi-geographic locations, which are referred to collectively as "the cloud."

Fast IDentity Online (FIDO): FIDO is an ecosystem for standards-based, interoperable authentication, which supports MFA, public key cryptography, and stores personally identifying information such as biometric authentication data locally on the user's device.

Government-to-Citizen (G2C): G2C is a term that refers to the relationships between public government services and the citizens.

Identity and Access Management (IAM): IAM concerns with the administration and identification of individual entities in a system or environment (which can be a country, a network, an IT application, or an enterprise), and controlling their access to resources within that system.

Identity Management Life Cycle: The Identity Management Life Cycle encompasses the security policies, processes, and technologies in managing a person's identity for the provisioning, auditing, governance, synchronisation across different platforms, and ongoing management of user credentials, entitlements and password establishments.

Identity Provider (IdP): IdP is a service that manages end user accounts. Some IdP applications are such as LDAP and Active Directory that can send SAML replies to Service Providers to authenticate end users.

JavaScript Object Notation (JSON): JSON is a lightweight data-interchange format derived from JavaScript object notation syntax. It is easy for humans to read and for machines to parse/generate.

JSON Web Encryption (JWE): JWE is a means of representing encrypted content using JSON data structures.

JSON Web Signature (JWS): JWS is an open standard for signing arbitrary JSON based data structures secured with digital signatures or Message Authentication Codes (MACs).

JSON Web Token (JWT): JWT is an open standard (RFC 7519) that defines a compact and digitally signed self-contained JSON based data structure for securely transmitting information between parties.

Kerberos: It is a protocol for a client to present a token to an Application Server to demonstrate the authenticity of its identity reliably over open networks.

Lightweight Directory Access Protocol (LDAP): LDAP is a simplified version of DAP for TCP/IP network distributed directory service.

Match-on-Card Technology: Combining biometric authentications with smart cards, enabling users to not only carry their biometric with them but also match it on the card. This achieves greater privacy for the cardholder and the ability to authenticate without connection to a backend biometric database.

Mobile Digital Signature (MDS): MDS is a digital signature generated either on a smartphone based on the IMEI or other user specified attributes or on the SIM card on the phone.

Mobility Management (MM): MM enables you to manage your users' mobile devices, applications, and data. MM allows users to enrol in the service and then download and use managed apps from the Apps Store.

Multi-Factor Authentication (MFA): MFA is an access control style in which a person is required to present multiple separate pieces of identity credential to an authentication mechanism.

Open Authorisation (OAuth): OAuth is an open standard for authorisation, commonly used as a way for Internet users to log into third party websites using their Microsoft, Google, or Facebook accounts without exposing their password to the third party.

OpenID: OpenID is an open standard for authentication and SSO. OpenID Connect supports end users to log in once and access multiple resources on Internet.

Remote Authentication Dial-In User Service (RADIUS): RADIUS is a client/server networking protocol that provides authentication, authorisation, and accounting services for remote users to communicate with a central server to access the requested system resource.

Repository Management: In Identity and Access Management, a repository is a central place in which an aggregation of identity profile is maintained and accessed in a secured manner.

Role-Based Access Control (RBAC): RBAC defines the access rights for a particular user to the resources of a system based on the roles of the individual user within an enterprise. Roles are defined according to the job competency, authority, and responsibility of the user within an enterprise.

Secure Web Authentication (SWA): SWA is a SSO system without using SAML for users to enter their credentials for these apps on their homepage. These credentials are stored such that users can access their apps without entering their credentials each time.

Security Assertion Markup Language (SAML): SAML is an XML-based standard for exchanging authentication and authorisation data between an Identity Provider and a Service Provider. The SAML standard addresses issues unique to the SSO solution.

Service Provider (SP): An SP is a public or private organisation or business entity providing communications, storage, processing, and a host of other services.

Single Sign-On (SSO): SSO is an authentication methodology allowing a user to log in once to the system and can access multiple systems without being prompted to sign in for each one.

Social Login: A new trend of SSO allowing users to use an existing social identity issued by a trusted third-party identity provider, such as Facebook, to access a third-party application without having to go through a new registration process.

System for Cross-Domain Identity Management (SCIM): SCIM is an application-layer protocol for provisioning and managing the exchange of user identity information between identity domains.

XML Access Control Language (XACL): XACL also known as XAC-ML (Extensible Access Control Markup Language). It is an XML-based language to specify security policies to be enforced on specific accesses to XML documents.

XML Key Management (XKMS): XKMS is a protocol for distributing and registering public keys, for use in conjunction with the proposed standard for XML Signature.

Zero-Knowledge Protocol (ZKP): ZKP is a cryptography method to allow one party (the Prover) to prove to another party (the Verifier) that he/she holds the answer to a given question, without revealing any information apart from the fact that the statement is indeed true.

Related Readings

To continue IGI Global's long-standing tradition of advancing innovation through emerging research, please find below a compiled list of recommended IGI Global book chapters and journal articles in the areas of access management, cloud computing, and biometric authentication. These related readings will provide additional information and guidance to further enrich your knowledge and assist you with your own research.

Abbasi, K. M., Haq, I. U., Malik, A. K., Raza, B., & Anjum, A. (2016). Managing Access in Cloud Service Chains Using Role-Level Agreements. In A. Malik, A. Anjum, & B. Raza (Eds.), *Innovative Solutions for Access Control Management* (pp. 224–247). Hershey, PA: IGI Global. doi:10.4018/978-1-5225-0448-1.ch008

Abdelhamid, M., Venkatesan, S., Gaia, J., & Sharman, R. (2018). Do Privacy Concerns Affect Information Seeking via Smartphones? In M. Gupta, R. Sharman, J. Walp, & P. Mulgund (Eds.), *Information Technology Risk Management and Compliance in Modern Organizations* (pp. 301–314). Hershey, PA: IGI Global. doi:10.4018/978-1-5225-2604-9.ch011

Adhikari, M. (2015). Biometrics in Cloud Computing. In G. Deka & S. Bakshi (Eds.), *Handbook of Research on Securing Cloud-Based Databases with Biometric Applications* (pp. 269–297). Hershey, PA: IGI Global. doi:10.4018/978-1-4666-6559-0.ch013

Adhikari, M., & Kar, S. (2015). NoSQL Databases. In G. Deka & S. Bakshi (Eds.), *Handbook of Research on Securing Cloud-Based Databases with Biometric Applications* (pp. 109–152). Hershey, PA: IGI Global. doi:10.4018/978-1-4666-6559-0.ch006

Ahmad, K., Kumar, G., Wahid, A., & Kirmani, M. M. (2015). Intrusion Detection and Prevention on Flow of Big Data Using Bacterial Foraging. In G. Deka & S. Bakshi (Eds.), *Handbook of Research on Securing Cloud-Based Databases with Biometric Applications* (pp. 386–411). Hershey, PA: IGI Global. doi:10.4018/978-1-4666-6559-0.ch018

Algarín, A. D., Demurjian, S. A., Ziminski, T. B., Sánchez, Y. K., & Kuykendall, R. (2014). Securing XML with Role-Based Access Control: Case Study in Health Care. In A. Ruiz-Martinez, R. Marin-Lopez, & F. Pereniguez-Garcia (Eds.), *Architectures and Protocols for Secure Information Technology Infrastructures* (pp. 334–365). Hershey, PA: IGI Global. doi:10.4018/978-1-4666-4514-1.ch013

Amini, E., & Maleki, I. (2014). A New Approach of Web Systems Modularity Increase Using Combination of Event-Driven Software Architecture and Relationship Mechanism Based on Message Passing: Case Study. *International Journal of Information Technology and Web Engineering*, *9*(3), 1–14. doi:10.4018/ijitwe.2014070101

Ampah, N. K., & Akujuobi, C. M. (2015). An Auto-Reclosing-Based Intrusion Detection Technique for Enterprise Networks. In M. Gupta (Ed.), *Handbook of Research on Emerging Developments in Data Privacy* (pp. 371–402). Hershey, PA: IGI Global. doi:10.4018/978-1-4666-7381-6.ch017

Arulogun, T., AlSa'deh, A., & Meinel, C. (2014). Mobile IPv6: Mobility Management and Security Aspects. In A. Ruiz-Martinez, R. Marin-Lopez, & F. Pereniguez-Garcia (Eds.), *Architectures and Protocols for Secure Information Technology Infrastructures* (pp. 71–101). Hershey, PA: IGI Global. doi:10.4018/978-1-4666-4514-1.ch003

Asim, Y., & Malik, A. K. (2016). A Survey on Access Control Techniques for Social Networks. In A. Malik, A. Anjum, & B. Raza (Eds.), *Innovative Solutions for Access Control Management* (pp. 1–32). Hershey, PA: IGI Global. doi:10.4018/978-1-5225-0448-1.ch001

Assis, M. R., Bittencourt, L. F., Tolosana-Calasanz, R., & Lee, C. A. (2016). Cloud Federations: Requirements, Properties, and Architectures. In G. Kecskemeti, A. Kertesz, & Z. Nemeth (Eds.), *Developing Interoperable and Federated Cloud Architecture* (pp. 1–41). Hershey, PA: IGI Global. doi:10.4018/978-1-5225-0153-4.ch001

Atzeni, A., Lyle, J., & Faily, S. (2014). Developing Secure, Unified, Multi-Device, and Multi-Domain Platforms: A Case Study from the Webinos Project. In A. Ruiz-Martinez, R. Marin-Lopez, & F. Pereniguez-Garcia (Eds.), *Architectures and Protocols for Secure Information Technology Infrastructures* (pp. 310–333). Hershey, PA: IGI Global. doi:10.4018/978-1-4666-4514-1.ch012

Atzeni, A., Smiraglia, P., & Siringo, A. (2015). Hard Clues in Soft Environments: The Cloud's Influence on Digital Forensics. In K. Munir, M. Al-Mutairi, & L. Mohammed (Eds.), *Handbook of Research on Security Considerations in Cloud Computing* (pp. 258–284). Hershey, PA: IGI Global. doi:10.4018/978-1-4666-8387-7.ch012

Augusto, A. B., & Correia, M. E. (2014). A Mobile-Based Attribute Aggregation Architecture for User-Centric Identity Management. In A. Ruiz-Martinez, R. Marin-Lopez, & F. Pereniguez-Garcia (Eds.), *Architectures and Protocols for Secure Information Technology Infrastructures* (pp. 266–287). Hershey, PA: IGI Global. doi:10.4018/978-1-4666-4514-1.ch010

Awad, W. S., & Abdullah, H. M. (2014). Improving the Security of Storage Systems: Bahrain Case Study. *International Journal of Mobile Computing and Multimedia Communications*, 6(3), 75–105. doi:10.4018/IJMCMC.2014070104

Balusamy, B., Nadhiya, S., Sumalatha, N., & Velu, M. (2017). Cloud Database Systems: NoSQL, NewSQL, Hybrid. In N. Kamila (Ed.), *Advancing Cloud Database Systems and Capacity Planning With Dynamic Applications* (pp. 225–245). Hershey, PA: IGI Global. doi:10.4018/978-1-5225-2013-9.ch010

Barać, D., Radenković, M., & Jovanić, B. (2014). Mobile Learning Services on Cloud. In M. Despotović-Zrakić, V. Milutinović, & A. Belić (Eds.), *Handbook of Research on High Performance and Cloud Computing in Scientific Research and Education* (pp. 147–172). Hershey, PA: IGI Global. doi:10.4018/978-1-4666-5784-7.ch006

Based, M. A. (2014). A Polling Booth-Based Electronic Voting Scheme. In A. Ruiz-Martinez, R. Marin-Lopez, & F. Pereniguez-Garcia (Eds.), *Architectures and Protocols for Secure Information Technology Infrastructures* (pp. 124–159). Hershey, PA: IGI Global. doi:10.4018/978-1-4666-4514-1.ch005

Belić, A. (2014). High Performance and Grid Computing Developments and Applications in Condensed Matter Physics. In M. Despotović-Zrakić, V. Milutinović, & A. Belić (Eds.), *Handbook of Research on High Performance and Cloud Computing in Scientific Research and Education* (pp. 214–245). Hershey, PA: IGI Global. doi:10.4018/978-1-4666-5784-7.ch009

Benjelloun, F., & Lahcen, A. A. (2015). Big Data Security: Challenges, Recommendations and Solutions. In K. Munir, M. Al-Mutairi, & L. Mohammed (Eds.), *Handbook of Research on Security Considerations in Cloud Computing* (pp. 301–313). Hershey, PA: IGI Global. doi:10.4018/978-1-4666-8387-7. ch014

Berhe, S., Demurjian, S. A., Pavlich-Mariscal, J., Saripalle, R. K., & Algarín, A. D. (2016). Leveraging UML for Access Control Engineering in a Collaboration on Duty and Adaptive Workflow Model that Extends NIST RBAC. In A. Malik, A. Anjum, & B. Raza (Eds.), *Innovative Solutions for Access Control Management* (pp. 96–124). Hershey, PA: IGI Global. doi:10.4018/978-1-5225-0448-1.ch004

Bhadoria, R. S. (2015). Security Architecture for Cloud Computing. In G. Deka & S. Bakshi (Eds.), *Handbook of Research on Securing Cloud-Based Databases with Biometric Applications* (pp. 47–71). Hershey, PA: IGI Global. doi:10.4018/978-1-4666-6559-0.ch003

Bhat, W. A. (2015). Achieving Efficient Purging in Transparent per-file Secure Wiping Extensions. In K. Munir, M. Al-Mutairi, & L. Mohammed (Eds.), *Handbook of Research on Security Considerations in Cloud Computing* (pp. 345–357). Hershey, PA: IGI Global. doi:10.4018/978-1-4666-8387-7.ch017

Bhatia, T., & Verma, A. K. (2015). Biometric Authentication for Cloud Computing. In G. Deka & S. Bakshi (Eds.), *Handbook of Research on Securing Cloud-Based Databases with Biometric Applications* (pp. 209–235). Hershey, PA: IGI Global. doi:10.4018/978-1-4666-6559-0.ch010

Bhatt, R., Gupta, M., & Sharman, R. (2015). Identity Management Systems: Models, Standards, and COTS Offerings. In M. Gupta (Ed.), *Handbook of Research on Emerging Developments in Data Privacy* (pp. 144–169). Hershey, PA: IGI Global. doi:10.4018/978-1-4666-7381-6.ch008

Bhattacharjee, J., Sengupta, A., Barik, M. S., & Mazumdar, C. (2018). An Analytical Study of Methodologies and Tools for Enterprise Information Security Risk Management. In M. Gupta, R. Sharman, J. Walp, & P. Mulgund (Eds.), *Information Technology Risk Management and Compliance in Modern Organizations* (pp. 1–20). Hershey, PA: IGI Global. doi:10.4018/978-1-5225-2604-9.ch001

Boehmer, W. (2015). Do We Need Security Management Systems for Data Privacy? In M. Gupta (Ed.), *Handbook of Research on Emerging Developments in Data Privacy* (pp. 263–299). Hershey, PA: IGI Global. doi:10.4018/978-1-4666-7381-6.ch013

Bogdanović, Z., Milić, A., & Labus, A. (2014). Model of E-Education Infrastructure based on Cloud Computing. In M. Despotović-Zrakić, V. Milutinović, & A. Belić (Eds.), *Handbook of Research on High Performance and Cloud Computing in Scientific Research and Education* (pp. 104–146). Hershey, PA: IGI Global. doi:10.4018/978-1-4666-5784-7.ch005

Bukač, V., & Matyáš, V. (2014). Host–Based Intrusion Detection Systems: Architectures, Solutions, and Challenges. In A. Ruiz-Martinez, R. Marin-Lopez, & F. Pereniguez-Garcia (Eds.), *Architectures and Protocols for Secure Information Technology Infrastructures* (pp. 184–213). Hershey, PA: IGI Global. doi:10.4018/978-1-4666-4514-1.ch007

Butani, B., Shukla, P. K., & Silakari, S. (2015). An Outline of Threats and Sensor Cloud Infrastructure in Wireless Sensor Network. In G. Deka & S. Bakshi (Eds.), *Handbook of Research on Securing Cloud-Based Databases with Biometric Applications* (pp. 412–432). Hershey, PA: IGI Global. doi:10.4018/978-1-4666-6559-0.ch019

Chahal, R. K., & Singh, S. (2015). Trust Calculation Using Fuzzy Logic in Cloud Computing. In K. Munir, M. Al-Mutairi, & L. Mohammed (Eds.), *Handbook of Research on Security Considerations in Cloud Computing* (pp. 127–172). Hershey, PA: IGI Global. doi:10.4018/978-1-4666-8387-7.ch007

Chaudhari, G., & Mulgund, P. (2018). Strengthening IT Governance With COBIT 5. In M. Gupta, R. Sharman, J. Walp, & P. Mulgund (Eds.), *Information Technology Risk Management and Compliance in Modern Organizations* (pp. 48–69). Hershey, PA: IGI Global. doi:10.4018/978-1-5225-2604-9.ch003

Chaudhuri, A. (2015). Governance and Risk Management in the Cloud with Cloud Controls Matrix V3 and ISO/IEC 38500:2008. In K. Munir, M. Al-Mutairi, & L. Mohammed (Eds.), *Handbook of Research on Security Considerations in Cloud Computing* (pp. 80–101). Hershey, PA: IGI Global. doi:10.4018/978-1-4666-8387-7.ch005

Cherif, A., & Imine, A. (2016). Optimistic Access Control for Collaborative Applications. In A. Malik, A. Anjum, & B. Raza (Eds.), *Innovative Solutions for Access Control Management* (pp. 125–158). Hershey, PA: IGI Global. doi:10.4018/978-1-5225-0448-1.ch005

Connolly, R. (2015). Dataveillance in the Workplace: Privacy Threat or Market Imperative? In M. Gupta (Ed.), *Handbook of Research on Emerging Developments in Data Privacy* (pp. 69–84). Hershey, PA: IGI Global. doi:10.4018/978-1-4666-7381-6.ch004

Crainic, T. G., Davidović, T., & Ramljak, D. (2014). Designing Parallel Meta-Heuristic Methods. In M. Despotović-Zrakić, V. Milutinović, & A. Belić (Eds.), *Handbook of Research on High Performance and Cloud Computing in Scientific Research and Education* (pp. 260–280). Hershey, PA: IGI Global. doi:10.4018/978-1-4666-5784-7.ch011

Csicsmann, N., McIntyre, V., Shea, P., & Rizvi, S. S. (2015). Cloud Security: Implementing Biometrics to Help Secure the Cloud. In G. Deka & S. Bakshi (Eds.), *Handbook of Research on Securing Cloud-Based Databases with Biometric Applications* (pp. 236–250). Hershey, PA: IGI Global. doi:10.4018/978-1-4666-6559-0.ch011

Čudanov, M., & Krivokapić, J. (2014). Organizational and Management Aspects of Cloud Computing Application in Scientific Research. In M. Despotović-Zrakić, V. Milutinović, & A. Belić (Eds.), *Handbook of Research on High Performance and Cloud Computing in Scientific Research and Education* (pp. 31–55). Hershey, PA: IGI Global. doi:10.4018/978-1-4666-5784-7.ch002

Das, P. K. (2015). A Practical Approach on Virtual Machine Live Migration. In G. Deka & S. Bakshi (Eds.), *Handbook of Research on Securing Cloud-Based Databases with Biometric Applications* (pp. 464–483). Hershey, PA: IGI Global. doi:10.4018/978-1-4666-6559-0.ch021

De, D., Mukherjee, A., Bhattacherjee, S., & Gupta, P. (2015). Trusted Cloud-and Femtocell-Based Biometric Authentication for Mobile Networks. In G. Deka & S. Bakshi (Eds.), *Handbook of Research on Securing Cloud-Based Databases with Biometric Applications* (pp. 320–336). Hershey, PA: IGI Global. doi:10.4018/978-1-4666-6559-0.ch015

Deka, G. C. (2015). Cloud Database Security Issues and Challenges. In G. Deka & S. Bakshi (Eds.), *Handbook of Research on Securing Cloud-Based Databases with Biometric Applications* (pp. 153–173). Hershey, PA: IGI Global. doi:10.4018/978-1-4666-6559-0.ch007

Draper-Gil, G., Ferrer-Gomila, J., Hinarejos, M. F., & Tauber, A. (2014). Towards a Certified Electronic Mail System. In A. Ruiz-Martinez, R. Marin-Lopez, & F. Pereniguez-Garcia (Eds.), *Architectures and Protocols for Secure Information Technology Infrastructures* (pp. 46–70). Hershey, PA: IGI Global. doi:10.4018/978-1-4666-4514-1.ch002

Francia, G. A. III, Hutchinson, F. S., & Francia, X. P. (2015). Privacy, Security, and Identity Theft Protection: Advances and Trends. In M. Gupta (Ed.), *Handbook of Research on Emerging Developments in Data Privacy* (pp. 133–143). Hershey, PA: IGI Global. doi:10.4018/978-1-4666-7381-6.ch007

Gangwar, H., & Date, H. (2015). Exploring Information Security Governance in Cloud Computing Organisation. *International Journal of Applied Management Sciences and Engineering, 2*(1), 44–61. doi:10.4018/ijamse.2015010104

García, S., Zunino, A., & Campo, M. (2015). Detecting Botnet Traffic from a Single Host. In M. Gupta (Ed.), *Handbook of Research on Emerging Developments in Data Privacy* (pp. 426–446). Hershey, PA: IGI Global. doi:10.4018/978-1-4666-7381-6.ch019

Ghazal, R., Malik, A. K., Qadeer, N., & Ahmed, M. (2016). Intelligent Multi-Domain RBAC Model. In A. Malik, A. Anjum, & B. Raza (Eds.), *Innovative Solutions for Access Control Management* (pp. 66–95). Hershey, PA: IGI Global. doi:10.4018/978-1-5225-0448-1.ch003

Ghazi, Y., Masood, R., Shibli, M. A., & Khurshid, S. (2016). Usage-Based Access Control for Cloud Applications. In A. Malik, A. Anjum, & B. Raza (Eds.), *Innovative Solutions for Access Control Management* (pp. 197–223). Hershey, PA: IGI Global. doi:10.4018/978-1-5225-0448-1.ch007

Gibson, M., Renaud, K., Conrad, M., & Maple, C. (2015). Play That Funky Password!: Recent Advances in Authentication with Music. In M. Gupta (Ed.), *Handbook of Research on Emerging Developments in Data Privacy* (pp. 101–132). Hershey, PA: IGI Global. doi:10.4018/978-1-4666-7381-6.ch006

Gupta, S., & Gupta, B. B. (2015). BDS: Browser Dependent XSS Sanitizer. In G. Deka & S. Bakshi (Eds.), *Handbook of Research on Securing Cloud-Based Databases with Biometric Applications* (pp. 174–191). Hershey, PA: IGI Global. doi:10.4018/978-1-4666-6559-0.ch008

Hajdu, L., Lauret, J., & Mihajlović, R. A. (2014). Grids, Clouds, and Massive Simulations. In M. Despotović-Zrakić, V. Milutinović, & A. Belić (Eds.), *Handbook of Research on High Performance and Cloud Computing in Scientific Research and Education* (pp. 308–340). Hershey, PA: IGI Global. doi:10.4018/978-1-4666-5784-7.ch013

Jaiswal, C., & Kumar, V. (2016). Highly Available Fault-Tolerant Cloud Database Services. In G. Kecskemeti, A. Kertesz, & Z. Nemeth (Eds.), *Developing Interoperable and Federated Cloud Architecture* (pp. 119–142). Hershey, PA: IGI Global. doi:10.4018/978-1-5225-0153-4.ch005

Jaiswal, S., Kumar, S., Patel, S. C., Singh, R. S., & Singh, S. K. (2015). Biometric Authentication for the Cloud Computing. In G. Deka & S. Bakshi (Eds.), *Handbook of Research on Securing Cloud-Based Databases with Biometric Applications* (pp. 1–15). Hershey, PA: IGI Global. doi:10.4018/978-1-4666-6559-0.ch001

Janković, S., Mladenović, S., & Vesković, S. (2014). Model of Interoperable E-Business in Traffic Sector based on Cloud Computing Concepts. In M. Despotović-Zrakić, V. Milutinović, & A. Belić (Eds.), *Handbook of Research on High Performance and Cloud Computing in Scientific Research and Education* (pp. 341–361). Hershey, PA: IGI Global. doi:10.4018/978-1-4666-5784-7.ch014

Jayanand, M., Kumar, M. A., Srinivasa, K. G., & Siddesh, G. M. (2015). Big Data Computing Strategies. In G. Deka & S. Bakshi (Eds.), *Handbook of Research on Securing Cloud-Based Databases with Biometric Applications* (pp. 72–90). Hershey, PA: IGI Global. doi:10.4018/978-1-4666-6559-0.ch004

Khan, N., & Al-Yasiri, A. (2016). Cloud Security Threats and Techniques to Strengthen Cloud Computing Adoption Framework. *International Journal of Information Technology and Web Engineering*, *11*(3), 50–64. doi:10.4018/IJITWE.2016070104

Khosravi, A., & Buyya, R. (2017). Energy and Carbon Footprint-Aware Management of Geo-Distributed Cloud Data Centers: A Taxonomy, State of the Art, and Future Directions. In N. Kamila (Ed.), *Advancing Cloud Database Systems and Capacity Planning With Dynamic Applications* (pp. 27–46). Hershey, PA: IGI Global. doi:10.4018/978-1-5225-2013-9.ch002

Kierkegaard, S. (2015). Cloud State Surveillance: Dark Octopus Tentacle Clouds from the Atlantic. In M. Gupta (Ed.), *Handbook of Research on Emerging Developments in Data Privacy* (pp. 1–23). Hershey, PA: IGI Global. doi:10.4018/978-1-4666-7381-6.ch001

Kirci, P. (2017). Ubiquitous and Cloud Computing: Ubiquitous Computing. In A. Turuk, B. Sahoo, & S. Addya (Eds.), *Resource Management and Efficiency in Cloud Computing Environments* (pp. 1–32). Hershey, PA: IGI Global. doi:10.4018/978-1-5225-1721-4.ch001

Krishnamachariar, P. K., & Gupta, M. (2018). Swimming Upstream in Turbulent Waters: Auditing Agile Development. In M. Gupta, R. Sharman, J. Walp, & P. Mulgund (Eds.), *Information Technology Risk Management and Compliance in Modern Organizations* (pp. 268–300). Hershey, PA: IGI Global. doi:10.4018/978-1-5225-2604-9.ch010

Kumar, R., Pattnaik, P. K., & Pandey, P. (2017). Big Data Optimization for Customer Discounts in Cloud Computing Environment. In N. Kamila (Ed.), *Advancing Cloud Database Systems and Capacity Planning With Dynamic Applications* (pp. 195–224). Hershey, PA: IGI Global. doi:10.4018/978-1-5225-2013-9.ch009

Kumar, S., Abidi, A. I., & Singh, S. K. (2015). Cloud Security Using Ear Biometrics. In K. Munir, M. Al-Mutairi, & L. Mohammed (Eds.), *Handbook of Research on Security Considerations in Cloud Computing* (pp. 39–64). Hershey, PA: IGI Global. doi:10.4018/978-1-4666-8387-7.ch003

Kumar, S., Sadhya, D., Singh, D., & Singh, S. K. (2015). Cloud Security Using Face Recognition. In G. Deka & S. Bakshi (Eds.), *Handbook of Research on Securing Cloud-Based Databases with Biometric Applications* (pp. 298–319). Hershey, PA: IGI Global. doi:10.4018/978-1-4666-6559-0.ch014

Lahmiri, S. (2018). Information Technology Outsourcing Risk Factors and Provider Selection. In M. Gupta, R. Sharman, J. Walp, & P. Mulgund (Eds.), *Information Technology Risk Management and Compliance in Modern Organizations* (pp. 214–228). Hershey, PA: IGI Global. doi:10.4018/978-1-5225-2604-9.ch008

Larson, U., Jonsson, E., & Lindskog, S. (2015). Guidance for Selecting Data Collection Mechanisms for Intrusion Detection. In M. Gupta (Ed.), *Handbook of Research on Emerging Developments in Data Privacy* (pp. 340–370). Hershey, PA: IGI Global. doi:10.4018/978-1-4666-7381-6.ch016

Loganathan, S. (2018). A Step-by-Step Procedural Methodology for Improving an Organization's IT Risk Management System. In M. Gupta, R. Sharman, J. Walp, & P. Mulgund (Eds.), *Information Technology Risk Management and Compliance in Modern Organizations* (pp. 21–47). Hershey, PA: IGI Global. doi:10.4018/978-1-5225-2604-9.ch002

Majumder, A., Roy, S., & Biswas, S. (2015). Data Security Issues and Solutions in Cloud Computing. In K. Munir, M. Al-Mutairi, & L. Mohammed (Eds.), *Handbook of Research on Security Considerations in Cloud Computing* (pp. 212–231). Hershey, PA: IGI Global. doi:10.4018/978-1-4666-8387-7.ch010

Majumder, S., & Pal, S. (2015). ECG-Based Biometrics. In G. Deka & S. Bakshi (Eds.), *Handbook of Research on Securing Cloud-Based Databases with Biometric Applications* (pp. 337–363). Hershey, PA: IGI Global. doi:10.4018/978-1-4666-6559-0.ch016

Malik, A. J., & Haneef, M. (2016). Network Intrusion Detection Using Multi-Objective Ensemble Classifiers. In A. Malik, A. Anjum, & B. Raza (Eds.), *Innovative Solutions for Access Control Management* (pp. 248–262). Hershey, PA: IGI Global. doi:10.4018/978-1-5225-0448-1.ch009

Mandal, A. K., Changder, S., Sarkar, A., & Debnath, N. C. (2014). Architecting Software as a Service for Data Centric Cloud Applications. *International Journal of Grid and High Performance Computing*, 6(1), 77–92. doi:10.4018/ijghpc.2014010105

Marinković, M., Čavoški, S., & Marković, A. (2014). Application of Cloud-Based Simulation in Scientific Research. In M. Despotović-Zrakić, V. Milutinović, & A. Belić (Eds.), *Handbook of Research on High Performance and Cloud Computing in Scientific Research and Education* (pp. 281–307). Hershey, PA: IGI Global. doi:10.4018/978-1-4666-5784-7.ch012

Marosi, A. C., & Kacsuk, P. (2016). Volunteer Clouds: From Volunteer Computing to Interconnected Infrastructures. In G. Kecskemeti, A. Kertesz, & Z. Nemeth (Eds.), *Developing Interoperable and Federated Cloud Architecture* (pp. 314–355). Hershey, PA: IGI Global. doi:10.4018/978-1-5225-0153-4.ch011

Mead, N. R., & Abu-Nimeh, S. (2015). Security and Privacy Requirements Engineering. In M. Gupta (Ed.), *Handbook of Research on Emerging Developments in Data Privacy* (pp. 199–215). Hershey, PA: IGI Global. doi:10.4018/978-1-4666-7381-6.ch010

Medlin, B. D., & Cazier, J. A. (2015). Social Engineering Techniques, Password Selection, and Health Care Legislation: A Health Care Setting. In M. Gupta (Ed.), *Handbook of Research on Emerging Developments in Data Privacy* (pp. 85–99). Hershey, PA: IGI Global. doi:10.4018/978-1-4666-7381-6.ch005

Memon, Q. A. (2015). Authentication and Error Resilience in Images Transmitted through Open Environment. In K. Munir, M. Al-Mutairi, & L. Mohammed (Eds.), *Handbook of Research on Security Considerations in Cloud Computing* (pp. 102–126). Hershey, PA: IGI Global. doi:10.4018/978-1-4666-8387-7.ch006

Meng, Y., & Kwok, L. (2014). Enhancing Intrusion Detection Systems Using Intelligent False Alarm Filter: Selecting the Best Machine Learning Algorithm. In A. Ruiz-Martinez, R. Marin-Lopez, & F. Pereniguez-Garcia (Eds.), *Architectures and Protocols for Secure Information Technology Infrastructures* (pp. 214–236). Hershey, PA: IGI Global. doi:10.4018/978-1-4666-4514-1.ch008

Mihaljević, M. J., & Imai, H. (2014). Security Issues of Cloud Computing and an Encryption Approach. In M. Despotović-Zrakić, V. Milutinović, & A. Belić (Eds.), *Handbook of Research on High Performance and Cloud Computing in Scientific Research and Education* (pp. 388–408). Hershey, PA: IGI Global. doi:10.4018/978-1-4666-5784-7.ch016

Milutinović, M., Stojiljković, V., & Lazarević, S. (2014). Ontology-Based Multimodal Language Learning. In M. Despotović-Zrakić, V. Milutinović, & A. Belić (Eds.), *Handbook of Research on High Performance and Cloud Computing in Scientific Research and Education* (pp. 195–212). Hershey, PA: IGI Global. doi:10.4018/978-1-4666-5784-7.ch008

Mishra, S. K., Sahoo, B., Sahoo, K. S., & Jena, S. K. (2017). Metaheuristic Approaches to Task Consolidation Problem in the Cloud. In A. Turuk, B. Sahoo, & S. Addya (Eds.), *Resource Management and Efficiency in Cloud Computing Environments* (pp. 168–189). Hershey, PA: IGI Global. doi:10.4018/978-1-5225-1721-4.ch007

Mohammed, L. A., & Munir, K. (2015). Security Challenges for Cloud Computing Development Framework in Saudi Arabia. In K. Munir, M. Al-Mutairi, & L. Mohammed (Eds.), *Handbook of Research on Security Considerations in Cloud Computing* (pp. 285–300). Hershey, PA: IGI Global. doi:10.4018/978-1-4666-8387-7.ch013

Mohapatra, S., & Majhi, B. (2015). An Evolutionary Approach for Load Balancing in Cloud Computing. In G. Deka & S. Bakshi (Eds.), *Handbook of Research on Securing Cloud-Based Databases with Biometric Applications* (pp. 433–463). Hershey, PA: IGI Global. doi:10.4018/978-1-4666-6559-0. ch020

Mujawar, T. N., Sutagundar, A. V., & Ragha, L. L. (2017). Security Aspects in Cloud Computing. In N. Kamila (Ed.), *Advancing Cloud Database Systems and Capacity Planning With Dynamic Applications* (pp. 320–342). Hershey, PA: IGI Global. doi:10.4018/978-1-5225-2013-9.ch013

Mulukutla, V., Gupta, M., & Rao, H. R. (2015). How Private Is Your Financial Data?: Survey of Authentication Methods in Web and Mobile Banking. In M. Gupta (Ed.), *Handbook of Research on Emerging Developments in Data Privacy* (pp. 170–197). Hershey, PA: IGI Global. doi:10.4018/978-1-4666-7381-6.ch009

Munir, K., & Mohammed, L. A. (2015). Access Control Framework for Cloud Computing. In K. Munir, M. Al-Mutairi, & L. Mohammed (Eds.), *Handbook of Research on Security Considerations in Cloud Computing* (pp. 314–325). Hershey, PA: IGI Global. doi:10.4018/978-1-4666-8387-7.ch015

Munir, K., & Palaniappan, S. (2015). Secure Architecture for Cloud Environment. In K. Munir, M. Al-Mutairi, & L. Mohammed (Eds.), *Handbook of Research on Security Considerations in Cloud Computing* (pp. 65–79). Hershey, PA: IGI Global. doi:10.4018/978-1-4666-8387-7.ch004

Murad, S. E., & Dowaji, S. (2017). Using Value-Based Approach for Managing Cloud-Based Services. In A. Turuk, B. Sahoo, & S. Addya (Eds.), *Resource Management and Efficiency in Cloud Computing Environments* (pp. 33–60). Hershey, PA: IGI Global. doi:10.4018/978-1-5225-1721-4.ch002

Nanda, A., Popat, P., & Vimalkumar, D. (2018). Navigating Through Choppy Waters of PCI DSS Compliance. In M. Gupta, R. Sharman, J. Walp, & P. Mulgund (Eds.), *Information Technology Risk Management and Compliance in Modern Organizations* (pp. 99–140). Hershey, PA: IGI Global. doi:10.4018/978-1-5225-2604-9.ch005

Nayak, S. C., Parida, S., Tripathy, C., & Pattnaik, P. K. (2017). Resource Allocation Policies in Cloud Computing Environment. In N. Kamila (Ed.), *Advancing Cloud Database Systems and Capacity Planning With Dynamic Applications* (pp. 115–132). Hershey, PA: IGI Global. doi:10.4018/978-1-5225-2013-9.ch005

Omar, M. (2015). Cloud Computing Security: Abuse and Nefarious Use of Cloud Computing. In K. Munir, M. Al-Mutairi, & L. Mohammed (Eds.), *Handbook of Research on Security Considerations in Cloud Computing* (pp. 30–38). Hershey, PA: IGI Global. doi:10.4018/978-1-4666-8387-7.ch002

Onwubiko, C. (2015). Health IT: A Framework for Managing Privacy Impact Assessment of Personally Identifiable Data. In M. Gupta (Ed.), *Handbook of Research on Emerging Developments in Data Privacy* (pp. 239–262). Hershey, PA: IGI Global. doi:10.4018/978-1-4666-7381-6.ch012

Ostermann, S., Kecskemeti, G., Taherizadah, S., Prodan, R., Fahringer, T., & Stankovski, V. (2016). Decentralised Repositories for Transparent and Efficient Virtual Machine Operations: Architecture of the ENTICE Project. In G. Kecskemeti, A. Kertesz, & Z. Nemeth (Eds.), *Developing Interoperable and Federated Cloud Architecture* (pp. 170–219). Hershey, PA: IGI Global. doi:10.4018/978-1-5225-0153-4.ch007

Patel, S. C., Singh, R., & Jaiswal, S. (2015). Security Issues in Cloud Computing. In K. Munir, M. Al-Mutairi, & L. Mohammed (Eds.), *Handbook of Research on Security Considerations in Cloud Computing* (pp. 1–29). Hershey, PA: IGI Global. doi:10.4018/978-1-4666-8387-7.ch001

Pattabiraman, A., Srinivasan, S., Swaminathan, K., & Gupta, M. (2018). Fortifying Corporate Human Wall: A Literature Review of Security Awareness and Training. In M. Gupta, R. Sharman, J. Walp, & P. Mulgund (Eds.), *Information Technology Risk Management and Compliance in Modern Organizations* (pp. 142–175). Hershey, PA: IGI Global. doi:10.4018/978-1-5225-2604-9.ch006

Paul, A. K., & Sahoo, B. (2017). Dynamic Virtual Machine Placement in Cloud Computing. In A. Turuk, B. Sahoo, & S. Addya (Eds.), *Resource Management and Efficiency in Cloud Computing Environments* (pp. 136–167). Hershey, PA: IGI Global. doi:10.4018/978-1-5225-1721-4.ch006

Petri, I., Diaz-Montes, J., Zou, M., Zamani, A. R., Beach, T. H., Rana, O. F., & Rezgui, Y. et al. (2016). Distributed Multi-Cloud Based Building Data Analytics. In G. Kecskemeti, A. Kertesz, & Z. Nemeth (Eds.), *Developing Interoperable and Federated Cloud Architecture* (pp. 143–169). Hershey, PA: IGI Global. doi:10.4018/978-1-5225-0153-4.ch006

Pflanzner, T., Tornyai, R., Gorácz, Á. Z., & Kertesz, A. (2016). Characterizing PaaS Solutions Enabling Cloud Federations. In G. Kecskemeti, A. Kertesz, & Z. Nemeth (Eds.), *Developing Interoperable and Federated Cloud Architecture* (pp. 91–117). Hershey, PA: IGI Global. doi:10.4018/978-1-5225-0153-4.ch004

Pina, P. (2015). File-Sharing of Copyrighted Works, P2P, and the Cloud: Reconciling Copyright and Privacy Rights. In M. Gupta (Ed.), Handbook of Research on Emerging Developments in Data Privacy (pp. 51-68). Hershey, PA: IGI Global. doi:10.4018/978-1-4666-7381-6.ch003

Prades, J., Campos, F., Reaño, C., & Silla, F. (2016). GPGPU as a Service: Providing GPU-Acceleration Services to Federated Cloud Systems. In G. Kecskemeti, A. Kertesz, & Z. Nemeth (Eds.), *Developing Interoperable and Federated Cloud Architecture* (pp. 281–313). Hershey, PA: IGI Global. doi:10.4018/978-1-5225-0153-4.ch010

Pungila, C., & Negru, V. (2014). Towards Building Efficient Malware Detection Engines Using Hybrid CPU/GPU-Accelerated Approaches. In A. Ruiz-Martinez, R. Marin-Lopez, & F. Pereniguez-Garcia (Eds.), *Architectures and Protocols for Secure Information Technology Infrastructures* (pp. 237–264). Hershey, PA: IGI Global. doi:10.4018/978-1-4666-4514-1.ch009

Radenković, B., & Kočović, P. (2014). From Mainframe to Cloud. In M. Despotović-Zrakić, V. Milutinović, & A. Belić (Eds.), *Handbook of Research on High Performance and Cloud Computing in Scientific Research and Education* (pp. 1–30). Hershey, PA: IGI Global. doi:10.4018/978-1-4666-5784-7.ch001

Rafiee, H., von Löwis, M., & Meinel, C. (2014). Challenges and Solutions for DNS Security in IPv6. In A. Ruiz-Martinez, R. Marin-Lopez, & F. Pereniguez-Garcia (Eds.), *Architectures and Protocols for Secure Information Technology Infrastructures* (pp. 160–182). Hershey, PA: IGI Global. doi:10.4018/978-1-4666-4514-1.ch006

Rai, R., & Sahoo, G. (2017). Advances in Dynamic Virtual Machine Management for Cloud Data Centers. In N. Kamila (Ed.), *Advancing Cloud Database Systems and Capacity Planning With Dynamic Applications* (pp. 91–114). Hershey, PA: IGI Global. doi:10.4018/978-1-5225-2013-9.ch004

Rakočević, G., & Milutinović, V. (2014). Exploiting Spatial and Temporal Patterns in a High-Performance CPU. In M. Despotović-Zrakić, V. Milutinović, & A. Belić (Eds.), *Handbook of Research on High Performance and Cloud Computing in Scientific Research and Education* (pp. 246–259). Hershey, PA: IGI Global. doi:10.4018/978-1-4666-5784-7.ch010

Rawat, A., & Gambhir, S. (2015). Biometric: Authentication and Service to Cloud. In G. Deka & S. Bakshi (Eds.), *Handbook of Research on Securing Cloud-Based Databases with Biometric Applications* (pp. 251–268). Hershey, PA: IGI Global. doi:10.4018/978-1-4666-6559-0.ch012

Regola, J. R., Mitchell, J. K. III, Baez, B. R., & Rizvi, S. S. (2015). Analyzing the Security Susceptibilities of Biometrics Integrated with Cloud Computing. In G. Deka & S. Bakshi (Eds.), *Handbook of Research on Securing Cloud-Based Databases with Biometric Applications* (pp. 192–208). Hershey, PA: IGI Global. doi:10.4018/978-1-4666-6559-0.ch009

Samra, H. E., Li, A. S., Soh, B., & AlZain, M. A. (2017). A Cloud-Based Architecture for Interactive E-Training. *International Journal of Knowledge Society Research*, 8(1), 67–78. doi:10.4018/IJKSR.2017010104

Sánchez, Y. K., & Demurjian, S. A. (2016). Towards User Authentication Requirements for Mobile Computing. In A. Malik, A. Anjum, & B. Raza (Eds.), *Innovative Solutions for Access Control Management* (pp. 160–196). Hershey, PA: IGI Global. doi:10.4018/978-1-5225-0448-1.ch006

Sangulagi, P., & Sutagundar, A. V. (2017). Resource Management in Sensor Cloud. In N. Kamila (Ed.), *Advancing Cloud Database Systems and Capacity Planning With Dynamic Applications* (pp. 158–175). Hershey, PA: IGI Global. doi:10.4018/978-1-5225-2013-9.ch007

Sanzi, E., & Demurjian, S. A. (2016). Identification and Adaptive Trust Negotiation in Interconnected Systems. In A. Malik, A. Anjum, & B. Raza (Eds.), *Innovative Solutions for Access Control Management* (pp. 33–65). Hershey, PA: IGI Global. doi:10.4018/978-1-5225-0448-1.ch002

Sathiyamoorthi, V. (2017). Challenges and Issues in Web-Based Information Retrieval System. In N. Kamila (Ed.), *Advancing Cloud Database Systems and Capacity Planning With Dynamic Applications* (pp. 176–194). Hershey, PA: IGI Global. doi:10.4018/978-1-5225-2013-9.ch008

Savić, D., Vlajić, S., & Despotović-Zrakić, M. (2014). From Software Specification to Cloud Model. In M. Despotović-Zrakić, V. Milutinović, & A. Belić (Eds.), *Handbook of Research on High Performance and Cloud Computing in Scientific Research and Education* (pp. 82–102). Hershey, PA: IGI Global. doi:10.4018/978-1-4666-5784-7.ch004

Sen, J. (2014). Security and Privacy Issues in Cloud Computing. In A. Ruiz-Martinez, R. Marin-Lopez, & F. Pereniguez-Garcia (Eds.), *Architectures and Protocols for Secure Information Technology Infrastructures* (pp. 1–45). Hershey, PA: IGI Global. doi:10.4018/978-1-4666-4514-1.ch001

Sethi, S., & Sruti, S. (2017). Cloud Security Issues and Challenges. In A. Turuk, B. Sahoo, & S. Addya (Eds.), *Resource Management and Efficiency in Cloud Computing Environments* (pp. 89–104). Hershey, PA: IGI Global. doi:10.4018/978-1-5225-1721-4.ch004

Shalan, M. (2017). Cloud Service Footprint (CSF): Utilizing Risk and Governance Directions to Characterize a Cloud Service. In A. Turuk, B. Sahoo, & S. Addya (Eds.), *Resource Management and Efficiency in Cloud Computing Environments* (pp. 61–88). Hershey, PA: IGI Global. doi:10.4018/978-1-5225-1721-4.ch003

Shukla, P. K., & Ahirwar, M. K. (2015). Improving Privacy and Security in Multicloud Architectures. In K. Munir, M. Al-Mutairi, & L. Mohammed (Eds.), *Handbook of Research on Security Considerations in Cloud Computing* (pp. 232–257). Hershey, PA: IGI Global. doi:10.4018/978-1-4666-8387-7.ch011

Shukla, P. K., & Bhatele, K. R. (2015). Networked Multimedia Communication Systems. In K. Munir, M. Al-Mutairi, & L. Mohammed (Eds.), *Handbook of Research on Security Considerations in Cloud Computing* (pp. 184–211). Hershey, PA: IGI Global. doi:10.4018/978-1-4666-8387-7.ch009

Shukla, P. K., & Dixit, M. (2015). Big Data: An Emerging Field of Data Engineering. In K. Munir, M. Al-Mutairi, & L. Mohammed (Eds.), *Handbook of Research on Security Considerations in Cloud Computing* (pp. 326–344). Hershey, PA: IGI Global. doi:10.4018/978-1-4666-8387-7.ch016

Shukla, P. K., & Singh, G. (2015). Reliability, Fault Tolerance, and Quality-of-Service in Cloud Computing: Analysing Characteristics. In K. Munir, M. Al-Mutairi, & L. Mohammed (Eds.), *Handbook of Research on Security Considerations in Cloud Computing* (pp. 358–370). Hershey, PA: IGI Global. doi:10.4018/978-1-4666-8387-7.ch018

Siddesh, G. M., Srinivasa, K. G., & Tejaswini, L. (2015). Recent Trends in Cloud Computing Security Issues and Their Mitigation. In G. Deka & S. Bakshi (Eds.), *Handbook of Research on Securing Cloud-Based Databases with Biometric Applications* (pp. 16–46). Hershey, PA: IGI Global. doi:10.4018/978-1-4666-6559-0.ch002

Singh, N., Mittal, T., & Gupta, M. (2018). A Tale of Policies and Breaches: Analytical Approach to Construct Social Media Policy. In M. Gupta, R. Sharman, J. Walp, & P. Mulgund (Eds.), *Information Technology Risk Management and Compliance in Modern Organizations* (pp. 176–212). Hershey, PA: IGI Global. doi:10.4018/978-1-5225-2604-9.ch007

Soni, P. (2018). Implications of HIPAA and Subsequent Regulations on Information Technology. In M. Gupta, R. Sharman, J. Walp, & P. Mulgund (Eds.), *Information Technology Risk Management and Compliance in Modern Organizations* (pp. 71–98). Hershey, PA: IGI Global. doi:10.4018/978-1-5225-2604-9.ch004

Spyra, G., Buchanan, W. J., Cruickshank, P., & Ekonomou, E. (2014). Cloud-Based Identity and Identity Meta-Data: Secure and Control of Data in Globalization Era. *International Journal of Reliable and Quality E-Healthcare*, *3*(1), 49–66. doi:10.4018/ijrqeh.2014010105

Stojanović, B., Milivojević, N., Ivanović, M., & Divac, D. (2014). Dot Net Platform for Distributed Evolutionary Algorithms with Application in Hydroinformatics. In M. Despotović-Zrakić, V. Milutinović, & A. Belić (Eds.), *Handbook of Research on High Performance and Cloud Computing in Scientific Research and Education* (pp. 362–386). Hershey, PA: IGI Global. doi:10.4018/978-1-4666-5784-7.ch015

Stoll, M. (2015). An Information Security Model for Implementing the New ISO 27001. In M. Gupta (Ed.), *Handbook of Research on Emerging Developments in Data Privacy* (pp. 216–238). Hershey, PA: IGI Global. doi:10.4018/978-1-4666-7381-6.ch011

Stranacher, K., Tauber, A., Zefferer, T., & Zwattendorfer, B. (2014). The Austrian Identity Ecosystem: An E-Government Experience. In A. Ruiz-Martinez, R. Marin-Lopez, & F. Pereniguez-Garcia (Eds.), *Architectures and Protocols for Secure Information Technology Infrastructures* (pp. 288–309). Hershey, PA: IGI Global. doi:10.4018/978-1-4666-4514-1.ch011

Suresh, N., & Gupta, M. (2018). Impact of Technology Innovation: A Study on Cloud Risk Mitigation. In M. Gupta, R. Sharman, J. Walp, & P. Mulgund (Eds.), *Information Technology Risk Management and Compliance in Modern Organizations* (pp. 229–267). Hershey, PA: IGI Global. doi:10.4018/978-1-5225-2604-9.ch009

Tahir, S., & Rashid, I. (2016). ICMetric-Based Secure Communication. In A. Malik, A. Anjum, & B. Raza (Eds.), *Innovative Solutions for Access Control Management* (pp. 263–293). Hershey, PA: IGI Global. doi:10.4018/978-1-5225-0448-1.ch010

Tanque, M. (2017). Cloud-Based Platforms and Infrastructures: Provisioning Physical and Virtual Networks. In N. Kamila (Ed.), *Advancing Cloud Database Systems and Capacity Planning With Dynamic Applications* (pp. 47–90). Hershey, PA: IGI Global. doi:10.4018/978-1-5225-2013-9.ch003

Tanque, M. (2017). Security for Hybrid Mobile Development: Challenges and Opportunities. In N. Kamila (Ed.), *Advancing Cloud Database Systems and Capacity Planning With Dynamic Applications* (pp. 246–288). Hershey, PA: IGI Global. doi:10.4018/978-1-5225-2013-9.ch011

Thangavel, M., Varalakshmi, P., Sridhar, S., & Sindhuja, R. (2017). Privacy Preserving Public Auditing in Cloud: Literature Review. In N. Kamila (Ed.), *Advancing Cloud Database Systems and Capacity Planning With Dynamic Applications* (pp. 133–157). Hershey, PA: IGI Global. doi:10.4018/978-1-5225-2013-9.ch006

Thomas, M. V., & Chandrasekaran, K. (2016). Identity and Access Management in the Cloud Computing Environments. In G. Kecskemeti, A. Kertesz, & Z. Nemeth (Eds.), *Developing Interoperable and Federated Cloud Architecture* (pp. 61–90). Hershey, PA: IGI Global. doi:10.4018/978-1-5225-0153-4.ch003

Tzanou, M. (2015). Data Protection in EU Law after Lisbon: Challenges, Developments, and Limitations. In M. Gupta (Ed.), *Handbook of Research on Emerging Developments in Data Privacy* (pp. 24–50). Hershey, PA: IGI Global. doi:10.4018/978-1-4666-7381-6.ch002

Varadi, S. (2016). Regulating European Clouds: The New European Data Protection Framework. In G. Kecskemeti, A. Kertesz, & Z. Nemeth (Eds.), *Developing Interoperable and Federated Cloud Architecture* (pp. 42–60). Hershey, PA: IGI Global. doi:10.4018/978-1-5225-0153-4.ch002

Veloso, B., Meireles, F., Malheiro, B., & Burguillo, J. C. (2016). Federated IaaS Resource Brokerage. In G. Kecskemeti, A. Kertesz, & Z. Nemeth (Eds.), *Developing Interoperable and Federated Cloud Architecture* (pp. 252–280). Hershey, PA: IGI Global. doi:10.4018/978-1-5225-0153-4.ch009

Veluru, S., Rahulamathavan, Y., Gupta, B. B., & Rajarajan, M. (2015). Privacy Preserving Text Analytics: Research Challenges and Strategies in Name Analysis. In G. Deka & S. Bakshi (Eds.), *Handbook of Research on Securing Cloud-Based Databases with Biometric Applications* (pp. 364–385). Hershey, PA: IGI Global. doi:10.4018/978-1-4666-6559-0.ch017

Vivas, J. L., Brasileiro, F. V., Barros, A., Farias da Silva, G., Nóbrega, M. Jr, Neto, F. G., & Ururahy, C. et al. (2016). EUBrazilCC Federated Cloud: A Transatlantic Multi-Cloud Infrastructure. In G. Kecskemeti, A. Kertesz, & Z. Nemeth (Eds.), *Developing Interoperable and Federated Cloud Architecture* (pp. 220–251). Hershey, PA: IGI Global. doi:10.4018/978-1-5225-0153-4. ch008

Vujin, V., Simić, K., & Kovačević, B. (2014). Digital Identity Management in Cloud. In M. Despotović-Zrakić, V. Milutinović, & A. Belić (Eds.), *Handbook of Research on High Performance and Cloud Computing in Scientific Research and Education* (pp. 56–81). Hershey, PA: IGI Global. doi:10.4018/978-1-4666-5784-7.ch003

Vulić, M., Petrović, P., Kovačević, I., & Živanović, V. R. (2014). Student Relationship Management Using Social Clouds. In M. Despotović-Zrakić, V. Milutinović, & A. Belić (Eds.), *Handbook of Research on High Performance and Cloud Computing in Scientific Research and Education* (pp. 173–194). Hershey, PA: IGI Global. doi:10.4018/978-1-4666-5784-7.ch007

Wahid, A., Quadri, M. P., Siddiqui, A. T., Kirmani, M. M., & Ahmad, K. (2015). Verifiable Response in Heterogeneous Cloud Storage: An Efficient KDC Scheme. In G. Deka & S. Bakshi (Eds.), *Handbook of Research on Securing Cloud-Based Databases with Biometric Applications* (pp. 91–108). Hershey, PA: IGI Global. doi:10.4018/978-1-4666-6559-0.ch005

Warren, M. J., & Leitch, S. (2015). The Security, Privacy, and Ethical Implications of Social Networking Sites. In M. Gupta (Ed.), *Handbook of Research on Emerging Developments in Data Privacy* (pp. 329–338). Hershey, PA: IGI Global. doi:10.4018/978-1-4666-7381-6.ch015

Woodside, J. M. (2015). Use of Cloud Computing For Education. In K. Munir, M. Al-Mutairi, & L. Mohammed (Eds.), *Handbook of Research on Security Considerations in Cloud Computing* (pp. 173–183). Hershey, PA: IGI Global. doi:10.4018/978-1-4666-8387-7.ch008

Yaokumah, W. (2017). Modelling the Impact of Administrative Access Controls on Technical Access Control Measures. *Information Resources Management Journal*, *30*(4), 53–70. doi:10.4018/IRMJ.2017100104

Yaokumah, W., Brown, S., & Dawson, A. A. (2016). Towards Modelling the Impact of Security Policy on Compliance. *Journal of Information Technology Research*, *9*(2), 1–16. doi:10.4018/JITR.2016040101

Yeboah-Boateng, E. O. (2017). Cyber-Security Concerns with Cloud Computing: Business Value Creation and Performance Perspectives. In A. Turuk, B. Sahoo, & S. Addya (Eds.), *Resource Management and Efficiency in Cloud Computing Environments* (pp. 105–135). Hershey, PA: IGI Global. doi:10.4018/978-1-5225-1721-4.ch005

Zaibi, G., Peyrard, F., Kachouri, A., Fournier-Prunaret, D., & Samet, M. (2014). A New Encryption Algorithm based on Chaotic Map for Wireless Sensor Network. In A. Ruiz-Martinez, R. Marin-Lopez, & F. Pereniguez-Garcia (Eds.), *Architectures and Protocols for Secure Information Technology Infrastructures* (pp. 103–123). Hershey, PA: IGI Global. doi:10.4018/978-1-4666-4514-1.ch004

Zhang, J. (2015). A Dynamic Subspace Anomaly Detection Method Using Generic Algorithm for Streaming Network Data. In M. Gupta (Ed.), *Handbook of Research on Emerging Developments in Data Privacy* (pp. 403–425). Hershey, PA: IGI Global. doi:10.4018/978-1-4666-7381-6.ch018

Zou, Q., & Park, E. G. (2015). Trust and Trust Building of Virtual Communities in the Networked Age. In M. Gupta (Ed.), *Handbook of Research on Emerging Developments in Data Privacy* (pp. 300–328). Hershey, PA: IGI Global. doi:10.4018/978-1-4666-7381-6.ch014

Index

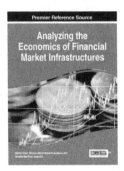

Stay Current on the Latest Emerging Research Developments

Become an IGI Global Reviewer for Authored Book Projects

Premier Reference Source

Emerging GIS Applications for Emergency and Disaster Management

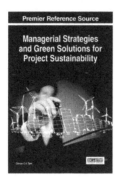

Premier Reference Source

Managerial Strategies and Green Solutions for Project Sustainability

Premier Reference Source

Comparative Approaches to Using R and Python for Statistical Data Analysis

Premier Reference Source

Solutions for High-Touch Communications in a High-Tech World

The overall success of an authored book project is dependent on quality and timely reviews.

In this competitive age of scholarly publishing, constructive and timely feedback significantly decreases the turnaround time of manuscripts from submission to acceptance, allowing the publication and discovery of progressive research at a much more expeditious rate. Several IGI Global authored book projects are currently seeking highly qualified experts in the field to fill vacancies on their respective editorial review boards:

Applications may be sent to:
development@igi-global.com

Applicants must have a doctorate (or an equivalent degree) as well as publishing and reviewing experience. Reviewers are asked to write reviews in a timely, collegial, and constructive manner. All reviewers will begin their role on an ad-hoc basis for a period of one year, and upon successful completion of this term can be considered for full editorial review board status, with the potential for a subsequent promotion to Associate Editor.

If you have a colleague that may be interested in this opportunity, we encourage you to share this information with them.

Printed in the United States
By Bookmasters